POLITICS AND RHETORIC
IN THE
CORINTHIAN EPISTLES

POLITICS AND RHETORIC IN THE CORINTHIAN EPISTLES

by
L. L. Welborn

MERCER UNIVERSITY PRESS

ISBN 0-86554-463-8 BS 2675.6 .L3 W45 1997 MUP/H437

Politics and Rhetoric in the Corinthian Epistles
Copyright ©1997
Mercer University Press, Macon, Georgia USA
All rights reserved
Printed in the United States of America

Library of Congress Cataloging-in-Publication Data

Welborn, L. L., 1953–   .
Politics and rhetoric in the Corinthian Epistles / L. L. Welborn.
x+238pp. 6x9" (15x23cm.).
Includes bibliographical references and indexes.
ISBN 0-86554-463-8 (alk. paper).
1. Bible. N.T. Corinthians—Language, style.
2. Rhetoric in the Bible.
3. Rhetoric, ancient.
I. Title.
BS2675.6.L3W45   1997
227'.206—dc21   97-41427
                                                CIP

TABLE OF CONTENTS

for Diane

PREFACE

Paul's relationship to ancient rhetoric has been the subject of renewed interest in recent decades. As is well known, several of the forms of rhetoric had their origin in the political sphere—in the assembly, in political trials, and in political pamphlets. The essays in this volume explore the influence of ancient politics upon the rhetoric of Paul's Corinthian correspondence. As it turns out, Paul was thoroughly familiar with the conventions of ancient political life, and used them to dissuade his converts from faction (chapter 1), to exhort to concord (chapter 2), to affect reconciliation (chapters 3 and 4), and to defend his character (chapter 5). Paul could count on the Corinthians' familiarity with the traditions of Greco-Roman politics. He did not need to discuss politics overtly. He could make use of political ideas and tactics to shape the Christian community.

The essays in this volume do not pretend to be comprehensive. They are preliminary investigations of a large and complex subject, which I hope to continue at a later time. Nor do these essays form a coherent entity; each explores an aspect of Paul's rhetoric in relationship to ancient theory and practice. Earlier, and in most cases shorter, versions of these essays appeared in the *Journal of Biblical Literature*, *New Testament Studies*, *Novum Testamentum*, and the *Zeitschrift für die neutestamentliche Wissenschaft*. I thank the editors and publishers for permission to reprint the essays, which in some cases I have retitled. I am grateful for the reception these essays have been given by a number of scholars.

Chapters 1 and 2 of this book were originally parts of a doctoral dissertation at Vanderbilt University under the direction of Daniel Patte, who guided my research with wisdom and grace. Gerd Luedemann introduced me to the subject of the factions in the church at Corinth. That my understanding of the Corinthian parties is no longer determined by the debate within German scholarship is owing to Robert Grant who undertook my education in the realities of Roman politics and who alerted me to the presence of political ideas in Paul. I became interested in the literary and rhetorical problems of Second Corinthians while working as a translator for Hans Dieter Betz. If any of the paths in this book lead to knowledge, it is thanks to Arnaldo Momigliano who told me what to read and why it was important. I am grateful to Barbara Levick and Geoffrey de Ste. Croix for reading and commenting upon several of the essays.

Several friendships have sustained me through the years of research and writing. Lloyd Spencer awakened an interest in ideology on long walks through the forest outside Tübingen. Paul Malcolm Puckett has encouraged my interest in Roman politics, especially as it is known from coins. Frank Thomas has been and is my confidant and counselor in life, as well as in letters. David Daniels and Steve Berry have been constant partners in dialogue about Christian communities in the city, ancient and modern. Three former students, Craig Wansink, Nancy Weatherwax, and Nicole Wilkinson, have shared in the development of my ideas at various stages. The lively correspondence of such friends is the reward for scholarly labor.

I am grateful to my assistant, Martha Anderson, for the care with which she prepared the text for publication. Suzanne Smailes, research librarian at United Theological Seminary, sought out and obtained numerous works which were difficult of access. I thank Vaughn CroweTipton, my editor at Mercer University Press, for his suggestions and cooperation.

My parents, Clary and Ann Welborn, and my aunts, Lillian and Mary Crenshaw, have provided encouragement and support over the years; they were my first teachers.

I dedicate this book to my wife Diane, who through the storms of academic life has been my rock, my joy, and my salvation.

ABBREVIATIONS

Abbreviations of biblical, intertestamental, and early Christian writings, and related periodicals and series, usually follow those listed in the *Journal of Biblical Literature* "Instructions for Contributors" (*Society of Biblical Literature Membership Directory and Handbook* [1994]: 223-40; the latest edition may be found at http://scholar.cc.emory.edu). References to classical texts, periodicals, and series follow the abbreviations listed in the *Oxford Classical Dictionary*. Abbreviations for authors, texts, periodicals, and series not found in the *OCD* follow Liddell-Scott-Jones, *A Greek English Lexicon*, and Glare, *Oxford Latin Dictionary*. Citations of patristic texts follow the abbreviations in Lampe, *A Patristic Greek Lexicon*.

ACKNOWLEDGMENTS

I am grateful to the original publishers for permission to publish revised versions of the following essays.

"On the Discord in Corinth: 1 Corinthians 1–4 and Ancient Politics," *Journal of Biblical Literature* 106 (1987): 85-111.

"A Conciliatory Principle in 1 Cor. 4:6," *Novum Testamentum* 29 (1987): 320-46.

"The Identification of 2 Corinthians 10–13 with the Letter of Tears," *Novum Testamentum* 37 (1995): 138-53.

"Like Broken Pieces of a Ring: 2 Cor. 1:1–2:13; 7:5-16 and Ancient Theories of Literary Unity," *New Testament Studies* 42 (1996): 559-83.

"The Dangerous Double Affirmation: Character and Truth in 2 Cor. 1:17," *Zeitschrift für die neutestamentliche Wissenschaft* 86 (1995): 34-52.

DISCORD IN CORINTH:
FIRST CORINTHIANS 1–4 AND ANCIENT POLITICS

ἔσονται σχίσματα καὶ αἱρέσεις
Agraphon of Jesus
Justin *Dialogue with Trypho* 35.3

The young Jewish gentleman whom Justin met one morning along the tree-shaded walks of Corinth[1] found grounds for the rejection of Christianity in the existence of factions and sects in the church. The Christian philosopher countered with a saying, which he attributes to Jesus, intended to show that even these things were foreknown and predetermined: ἔσονται σχίσματα καὶ αἱρέσεις.[2] The context makes it likely that this *unbekanntes Jesuswort*[3] is, in fact, a saying of Paul, for Trypho's examples of Christian schismatics are those who eat meat offered to idols (*Dial* 35.1). This reference naturally recalls the σχίσματα in the church of Paul's day, which appeared in connection with the assembly for the communal meal (1 Cor 11:18). The apostle responded bravely: δεῖ γὰρ καὶ αἱρέσεις ἐν ὑμῖν εἶναι (1 Cor 11:19). Justin, it seems, has made providence of Paul's necessity. But whether Paul alludes to an unknown saying of Jesus, or Justin derives the statement from Paul, their intention is the same: to shield the idea of the church from the nihilistic consequences of factional strife. Paul subjects the phenomenon of factions to an eschatological interpretation,[4] whereas

---

[1]Eusebius *Hist eccl* 4.18 reports that the ξυστός was in Ephesus, but Trypho's remarks seem to place the dialogue in Corinth (*Dial* 1.3).

[2]E. J. Goodspeed, *Die ältesten Apologeten* (Göttingen: Vandenhoeck & Ruprecht, 1914) 130. See the parallels in E. Hennecke and W. Schneemelcher, *New Testament Apocrypha* (Philadelphia: Westminster, 1963) 1:88.

[3]J. Jeremias, *Unbekannte Jesusworte* (Göttingen: Vandenheock & Ruprecht, 1948) 53-54.

[4]δεῖ with the appended ἵνα-clause seems to reflect an eschatological understanding. W. A. Meeks speaks of "apocalyptic determinism" (*The First*

Justin uses prophecy to show that divisions were foreknown by God. In both cases, the failure of the redeemed community refers us to a realm in which unity is attained: the will of God.

One suspects that the tendency to look away from political aspects of life in the church has exercised a subterranean influence on modern interpreters of the factions in Corinth as well. F. C. Baur's reduction of the parties involved in the strife from the four attested by the slogans echoed in 1 Cor 1:12 to two, the adherents of Paul and those of Peter, allows him to assert that early Christian history was not a meaningless rivalry between factions, but a rational, dialectical process, the realization of the spirit in the synthesis of Hellenistic and Judaistic Christianity.[5] Part of the perennial attraction of the theory that the opponents of Paul (again reduced to a single group, the "Christ party") are to be identified as spiritual enthusiasts or gnostics must be that it allows for the explanation of the controversy in religious terms, without reference to politics.[6] The strife between the Corinthian parties is thus transposed into the realm of Hellenistic mystery religions and syncretistic gnosis.[7] In the period since World War II, it has proven necessary for some to deny the existence of

---

Urban Christians [New Haven: Yale University Press, 1983] 67). Matt 24:10 seems to form the background of Paul's thought; see W. Grundmann, *TDNT*, 2.21-25; J. Munck, *Paul and the Salvation of Mankind* (Richmond: John Knox Press, 1959) 135-36.

[5]F. C. Baur, "Die Christuspartei in der korinthischen Gemeinde, der Gegensatz des paulinischen und petrinischen Christentums in der ältesten Kirche, der Apostel Petrus in Rom," *Tübinger Zeitschrift für Theologie* 4 (1831): 61-206; idem, *Paul* (London: Williams & Norgate, 1875).

[6]For the opponents of Paul as spiritual enthusiasts, see W. Lütgert, *Freiheitspredigt und Schwarmgeister in Korinth*, BFCT 12/3 (Gütersloh: Bertelsmann, 1908); A. Schlatter, *Die korinthische Theologie*, BFCT 18/2 (Gütersloh: Bertelsmann, 1914). For the opponents of Paul as gnostics, see W. Schmithals, *Gnosticism in Corinth* (Nashville: Abingdon, 1971); U. Wilckens, *Weisheit und Torheit: Eine exegetisch-religionsgeschichtliche Untersuchung zu 1. Kor. 1 und 2*, BHT 26 (Tübingen: Mohr-Siebeck, 1959); most recently, G. Sellin, "Das 'Geheimnis' der Weisheit und das Rätsel der 'Christuspartei' (zu 1 Kor 1-4)," *ZNW* 73 (1982): 69-96.

[7]Richard Reitzenstein, *Hellenistic Mystery Religions* (Pittsburgh: Pickwick, 1978) 426-500.

factions in the Corinthian church.[8]

Yet, however strong the aversion may be to the presence of political elements in the Corinthian epistles, it is impossible to resist the impression that Paul describes the situation in the church in terms like those used to characterize conflicts within city-states by Greco-Roman historians. Paul speaks first of σχίσματα (1:10). A σχίσμα is a rift, a tear, as in a garment; it is used metaphorically of a cleft in political consciousness (e.g., Herodotus 7.219; *PLond* 2710.13).[9] The verb from which the abstract noun derives is used by Diodorus to describe the civil strife at Megara: "the multitude was divided (σχιζόμενος) according to party" (12.66.2). The clearest indication of the meaning of σχίσμα in 1 Cor 1:10 is provided by the author of 1 Clement. Applying the example of Paul and the parties to the "abominable and unholy στάσις" in the church of his own day, he asks, "Why are there quarrels and anger and dissension and divisions (σχίσματα) and war among you?" (46:5). The terms with which σχίσμα is associated make it clear that it is neither a religious heresy nor a harmless clique that the author has in mind, but factions engaged in a struggle for power.[10]

Chloe's people bring news of ἔριδες in the Corinthian church (1:11). Ἔρις is hot dispute, the emotional flame that ignites whenever rivalry becomes intolerable. It invariably appears in accounts of ancient political life the moment the pressure of circumstances, that is, the approach of an enemy army or the election of mutually hostile consuls, draws the citizens into confused knots.[11] A single example will suffice. Plutarch

---

[8] J. Munck, "Menigheden uden Partier," *Dansk teologisk Tidsskrift* 15 (1952): 251-53, incorporated as the fifth chapter of *Paul and the Salvation of Mankind* (Richmond: John Knox, 1959) 135-67.

[9] Herodotus (7.219) uses σχίζω to describe the "division" in the Greek army before Thermopulae. At dawn the watchers came running from the mountains with news of the Persians' approach. Thereupon the Greeks held a council, Herodotus tells us, καὶ σφέων ἐσχίζοντο αἱ γνῶμαι. On the prohibition of the creation of σχίσματα in the νόμος of the gild of Zeus Hypsistos, see below.

[10] Cf. *Catalogus Codicum Astrologorum Graecorum* 11.2, ed. H. Lambertin (Brussels, 1898) 122.24: πολέμους, φόνους, μάχας, σχίσματα.

[11] Of the many examples that could be given: Thucydides 6.35: τῶν δὲ Συρακοσίων ὁ δῆμος ἐν πολλῇ πρὸς ἀλλήλους ἔριδι ἦσαν, 2.21:

(*Caes* 33) describes the state into which Rome was thrown by the news that Caesar had crossed the Rubicon. The tempest swept the inhabitants of the country into the city, while the senators, seizing whatever possessions came to hand, abandoned Rome. Conflicting emotions prevailed everywhere, and throughout the city violent disturbances erupted. As was inevitable in such a large city, those who were pleased at Caesar's coming encountered those who were in fear and distress, and both giving voice to their opinions, "they began to quarrel with one another" (δι' ἐρίδων ἦν).

In 1 Cor 3:3 Paul combines ἔρις with ζῆλος to describe the source of the Corinthians' divisive behavior. This ζῆλος is the gnawing, unquiet root of civil strife—the real, psychological cause of war, according to Lysias (2.48), not the minor infractions both parties allege. The Alexandrian mob that began the civil war against their Jewish fellow residents was driven by "jealousy" in Philo's judgment; enraged at the sight of the Jewish prince Agrippa, they seized a poor lunatic named "Carabas," dressed him in the robes of a king, and hailed him as "Marin" (Philo *In Flacc* 41).[12]

In 1 Cor 1:13 Paul asks rhetorically, μεμέρισται ὁ Χριστός, alluding by synecdoche to the notion of the church as the σῶμα Χριστοῦ. The translations fail to capture the political connotation that the verb undoubtedly had for its first readers. The customary term for "party" in Greek is μερίς, corresponding to Latin *pars*. In the proem to his account of the civil wars, Appian relates that the senate and the plebs "were split into parties" (ἐμερίζετο, *Bell Civ* 1.1; cf. Polybius 8.21.9) over the appointment of magistrates, the former supporting the consuls, the latter the tribune of the plebs, each seeking to prevail over the other

---

while the Peloponnesian army ravages the countryside, the Athenian people κατὰ ξυστάσεις τε γιγνόμενοι ἐν πολλῇ ἔριδι ἦσαν οἱ μέν κελεύοντες ἐπεξιέναι, οἱ δὲ τινες οὐκ ἐῶτες, Appian *Bell Civ* 2.2.6: the Senate elects Bibulus as Caesar's colleague in the consulship in order to hold him in check, καὶ εὐθὺς αὐτῶν ἦσαν ἔριδές τε καὶ ὅπλων ἐπ' ἀλλήλους ἰδίᾳ παρασκευαί. See also Appian *Bell Civ* 3.86.357; Josephus *Ant* 14.16.1 §470.

[12]See also Plutarch *Lycur* 4.2-3; 1 Macc. 8:16; Cicero *Tusc Disp* 4.8.17. In 2 Cor 12:20 and Gal 5:20 Paul again combines ζῆλος with ἔρις in the sense of "rivalry" or "jealous strife."

by increasing the power of its own magistrate. We may gain in clarity if we translate Paul's question: "Has the body of Christ been split into parties?"[13]

Another explicitly political term, διχοστασία, appears in the earliest witness to the Pauline epistles, P[46] (ca. 200 C.E.), a number of important uncial manuscripts, and the majority text as characteristic of the situation in the church at Corinth (3:3).[14] It was such "hardened difference of opinion," "bitter irresolve," that, according to Dionysius of Halicarnassus, paralyzed the Roman assembly (*Ant Rom* 8.72. 1, 4).[15] It is this "dissension" that Paul now identifies as the bane of the Corinthian church. What threatened the survival of the community of chosen people was not seductive gnostic theology or infectious Judaistic propaganda, but the possibility that its adherents might "behave like ordinary men" (3:3).

There is one last phrase that Paul uses to describe the demeanor of the Corinthian Christians: each is "puffed up on behalf of one against another" (4:6). It is symptomatic that this vivid image should prove so "difficult to fathom."[16] It is all too familiar to the student of political history as the caricature of the political windbag, the orator inflated at his

---

[13]G. Heinrici rightly designates 1 Clem. 46:7 a "commentary" on μεμέρισται (*Der erste Brief an die Korinther* [Göttingen: Vandenhoeck & Ruprecht, 1896] 61).

[14]P[46] D F G M a b it sy; Marcion, Cyp., Ir[gr], Thdrt., cf. C. Tischendorf, *Novum Testamentum Graece* 2 (Leipzig: Giesecke & Devrient, 1872) on 1 Cor 3:3. There is much to suggest that the word was originally present in the text, contra B. Metzger (*A Textual Commentary on the Greek New Testament* [New York: United Bible Societies, 1975] 548), who suspects the intrusion of a "Western gloss," though P[46] is closer to the Alexandrian type of text. The term is an established part of Paul's vocabulary: Gal 5:20; Rom. 16:17 (in a warning that immediately precedes mention of his friends and supporters in Corinth). Its appearance in 1 Clem 46:5 along with ἔρις and σχίσματα, in a passage that refers to "the epistle of the blessed Paul," is also suggestive.

[15]Cf. Diodorus 35.25.1: When Gracchus forms parties in support of his plan to abolish aristocratic rule, he is accused of securing power for himself διὰ τῆς πάντων διχοστασίας. See further, Herodotus 5.75; 1 Macc. 3:29; Plutarch *Mor* 478e-479a; Solon *Elg Fr* 3.37-38; Dionysius of Halicarnassus *Ant Rom* 5.66.4.

[16]H. Conzelmann, *1 Corinthians*, Hermeneia (Philadelphia: Fortress, 1975) 86.

own success (Ps-Plato *Alcibiades* 2.145e; Plutarch *Cicero* 887b; Epictetus *Diss* 2.16.10), the young aristocrat, the aspiring tyrant, filled with a sense of his own power (Alcibiades and Critias in Xenophon *Mem* 1.2.25; Gaius in Philo *Leg ad Gaium* 86.154; Pausanias in Demosthenes 59.97; see also Thucydides 1.132.1-3; Dio Chrysostom 30.19; 58.5), the supercilious office holder (Demosthenes 19.314; Philo *Leg ad Gaium* 69.255). With savage irony Paul imprints the familiar image of self-conceit which gives rise to partisanship upon the surface of the text, the way a flash transfixes an image on film.

It is no longer necessary to argue against the position that the conflict that evoked 1 Corinthians was essentially theological in character. The attempt to identify the parties with views and practices condemned elsewhere in the epistle, as if the parties represented different positions in a dogmatic controversy, has collapsed under its own weight. Johannes Weiss already saw the flaw in this approach: Paul's strategy in dealing with the parties makes it impossible to differentiate between them.[17] Paul refuses to analyze the opinions of the various factions, but speaks to the community as a whole, as though all the parties had coalesced in his mind into "one perverse, insubordinate, arrogant, and hostile group."[18] No one doubts that doctrinal differences existed, or that the claim to possess divine wisdom and knowledge played an important role in the controversy. But a number of scholars are now returning to the view of John

---

[17]J. Weiss, *Der erste Korintherbrief* (Göttingen: Vandenhoeck & Ruprecht, 1910) xxx-xxxi. Even the sophistical conceit customarily associated with the adherents of Apollos, owing to his Alexandrian background and reputed eloquence (Acts 18:24), is rebuked in connection with the Cephas party in 3:18-23! Some have seen in 3:10-17 veiled polemic against the Cephas party: P. Vielhauer, "Paulus und die Kephaspartei in Korinth," *NTS* 21 (1975): 341-52. G. Lüdemann (*Paulus, der Heidenapostel II: Antipaulinismus im frühen Christentum* [Göttingen: Vandenhoeck & Ruprecht, 1983] 118-23) argues from the literary structure of 3:6-17; this is a possibility, though θεμέλιος need not refer to Cephas specifically, since the building metaphor occurs frequently in writings on concord, e.g., Plutarch *Mor* 807c; Dio Chrysostom *Or* 38.15; Aelius Aristides *Or* 23.31; 24.8; 24.32-33.

[18]J. Weiss, *The History of Primitive Christianity* (New York: Scribner's, 1937) 1:339; similarly, D. Patte, *Paul's Faith and the Power of the Gospel* (Philadelphia: Fortress, 1983) 302.

Calvin: that the real problem being addressed in 1 Cor 1-4 is one of partisanship.[19] As Calvin observed, Paul deals in a different manner with false teaching in Galatians and Philippians. There he engages in polemic; but 1 Corinthians 1-4 is deliberative in character.[20] Paul does not seek to refute a "different gospel" (as in 2 Cor 11:4), but exhorts the quarreling Corinthians "to agree completely, . . . to be united in the same mind and the same judgment" (1:10).

It is a power struggle, not a theological controversy, that motivates the writing of 1 Corinthians 1-4. So much Weiss and Lietzmann were ready to accept.[21] But interpreters have been slow to grasp the implications of this insight. It has not yet been realized how closely the situation in the church at Corinth resembles the conflicts within city-states described by Greek and Roman historians.[22] Nor has it been recognized how much Paul's advice in 1 Corinthians 1-4 has in common with speeches on concord (περὶ ὁμονοίας) by ancient politicians and rhetoricians, such as Dio Chrysostom and Aelius Aristides.[23] It is our contention that Paul's goal in 1 Corinthians 1-4 is not the refutation of heresy, but what Plutarch (*Mor* 824C-E) describes as the object of the art of politics—the

---

[19]See, e.g., J. Hering, *The First Epistle of Saint Paul to the Corinthians* (London: Epworth, 1962) 44; H. Koester, *Introduction to the New Testament II: History and Literature of Early Christianity* (Philadelphia: Fortress, 1982) 121; D. A. Horrell, *The Social Ethos of Corinthian Correspondence: Interests and Ideology from 1 Corinthians to 1 Clement* (Edinburgh: T & T Clark, 1996).

[20]John Calvin, *The First Epistle of Paul the Apostle to the Corinthians* (repr.: Grand Rapids: Eerdmans, 1959) 8. On 1 Corinthians as deliberative rhetoric, see H. D. Betz, "The Problem of Rhetoric and Theology according to the Apostle Paul" in *L'Apôtre Paul: Personalité, Style, et Conception du ministère*, ed. A. Vanhoye, BETL 73 (Leuven: Peeters, 1986) 16-48.

[21]See also A. A. T. Ehrhardt, *Politische Metaphysik von Solon bis Augustin*, vol. 2 (Tübingen: Mohr-Siebeck, 1959) 10-12.

[22]J. Weiss (*Der erste Korintherbrief*, on 1:10) and H. Lietzmann (*Die Briefe des Paulus: An die Korinther I*, HNT [Tübingen: Mohr-Siebeck, 1910] on 1:10) provided parallels to Paul's exhortation from Greek historians, Thucydides, Polybius, and Dionysius of Halicarnassus; but their insights were not pursued.

[23]See Thrasymachus περὶ πολιτείας; Antiphon περὶ ὁμονοίας; Isocrates *Or* 4; *Ep* 3, 8, 9; Plato *Ep* 7; Socratic *Ep* 30; Ps.-Sallust *Ep* 2; Dio Chrysostom *Or* 38-41; Aelius Aristides *Or* 23-24; (Herodes Atticus) περὶ πολιτείας, among others.

prevention of στάσις.[24] If this is so, then much light should be thrown upon Paul's admonitions by an investigation of these chapters in the context of ancient politics.

I. THE SLOGANS IN 1 CORINTHIANS 1:12

Much energy has been expended on the interpretation of these slogans. Most scholars have worked under the assumption that the dispute was theological in character.[25] But despite all the attempts to arrive at the origin of these party cries, their form has never been investigated.[26] In seeking the formal derivation of these expressions, one is always led back to the realm of politics. For the form of the slogans clearly reflects the principle at work in the creation of ancient political parties: throughout antiquity personal adherence is the basic relationship from which party identification developed, as personal enmity is the social reality behind the concept of the opposing faction.[27] The most convincing evidence of

---

[24]There is no satisfactory treatment of στάσις, although the subject is treated briefly by D. Loenen, *Stasis* (Amsterdam: Noord-Hollandische Uitg. Mij., 1953) and A. Lintott, *Violence, Civil Strife and Revolution in the Classical City* (Baltimore: Johns Hopkins University, 1982).

[25]See notes 5-8 above and the overview in J. Hurd, *The Origin of 1 Corinthians*, new and corr. ed. (Macon GA: Mercer University Press, 1983) 96-107; N. A. Dahl, "Paul and the Church at Corinth in 1 Cor 1:10-4:21" in *Christian History and Interpretation: Studies Presented to John Knox*, ed. W. R. Farmer et al. (Cambridge: Cambridge University Press, 1967) 313-35. Note Reitzenstein's influential variant of the theological interpretation of the controversy in his *Hellenistic Mystery Religions*, 426. Reitzenstein holds that the Corinthians have divided themselves into θίασοι and named themselves after their respective mystagogues, like initiates in the mystery religions. This hypothesis, although attractive, leaves too many features of 1 Cor 1-4 unexplained.

[26]G. Lüdemann, *Paulus*, 119 n.51: "Eine Untersuchung der Form des Slogans von 1 Kor 1,12 steht noch aus."

[27]A fact which, in modern times, first seems to have been grasped by Fustel de Coulanges, "Le Patronat et la 'commendatio' dans la société romaine" in *Les Origines du systeme feodal* (Paris, 1890) 205-47; see now H. Hutter, *Politics as Friendship: The Origins of Classical Notions of Politics in the Theory and Practice of Friendship* (Waterloo, Ont.: Wilfrid Laurier University Press, 1978); D. F. Epstein, *Personal Enmity in Roman Politics 218–43 BC* (London: Helm, 1987).

this phenomenon is the fact that there are no generally accepted names, such as "Socialist" or "Christian-Democratic," for political parties in antiquity; rather, they are named after the *individuals* whose interests they served. Thus, one speaks of the "faction of Marius" or the "party of Pompey," employing terms such as στάσις and μερίς (Latin *factio*, *pars*) with the genitive of the proper name.[28] Or one speaks, still more succinctly and conveniently, of "those about Ismenias."[29] A declaration of allegiance to a party so personal in organization could take no form other than that which it is given in 1 Cor 1:12—"I am of Paul!" "But I, of Apollos!"[30]

---

[28]E.g., Plutarch *Ser* 4.3-4; 7.1; *Pompey* 65.1; Xenophon *Hell* 5.2.25; *Hellenica Oxyrhynchia* 17.1-2, ed. V. Bartoletti (Leipzig: Teubner, 1959). H. Strasburger, "Optimates," *RE* 18.1 (1939) col. 790: "Die Faktionen der Einzelpersönlichkeiten bzw. Bürger-kriegsparteien heissen στάσις mit dem Genitiv des Eigennamens, die Gegenpartei im gleichen Sinne ἐναντίη oder ἕτερα στάσις." For examples of the latter, see Plutarch *Sulla* 20.1; 23.6; 28.8; 32.2. For Greek usage in general, see L. Whibley, *Political Parties in Athens* (Cambridge: Cambridge University, 1889) 84; for Latin usage see M. Gelzer, *Die Nobilität der römischen Republik* (Leipzig: Teubner, 1912) 102ff.; J. Hellegouarc'h, *Le vocabulaire Latin des relations et des partis politiques sous la Republique* (Paris: Société d'Edition les Belles Lettres, 1963) 100-15; note esp. "The *factio* of Pompey and the nobles" in Ps.-Sallust *Ep* 2, 2.4; 4.2; 8.6; 9.4; 10.8; 11.6; Cicero speaks of the *partes* of Marius, Sulla, and, repeatedly, of Caesar: *Quinct.* 69; *Rosc* 16, 137; *Verr* 2.1.35; *Catil* 4.13; *Manil* 10; *Phil* 5.32; 13.39; *Fam* 10.33.1; *M. Brut* 2.4.5.

[29]οἱ περὶ τίνα, οἱ μετά, e.g., Thucydides 2.2.2; Aristotle *Ath Pol* 14.3; *Hellenica Oxyrhynchia* 17.1; 6.2; 7.2; 18.1; Xenophon *Hell* 3.5.4; 5.2.31; 5.3.13; 5.4.5; Demosthenes 37.39; 21.20; Plutarch *Per* 16; *Nic* 11; *Pelop* 6.2. In general, see G. M. Calhoun, *Athenian Clubs in Politics and Litigation* (Austin: University of Texas Press, 1913) 7, 13. Note esp. Josephus's description of the factions in Jerusalem politics in *Ant* 20.6.2 §131, οἱ περὶ 'Ανανίαν; *BJ* 2.12.5 §236, οἱ περὶ τὸν 'Ελεάζαρον (b. Dinai); *BJ* 2.17.9. §443, 445, 453, οἱ περὶ τὸν 'Ελεάζαρον (b. Ananias); *BJ* 2.19.5 §534, οἱ περὶ τὸν "Ανανον. See also Josephus's description of the faction leaders in Jerusalem politics in 62-64 A.D. in *BJ* 2.14.1 §275: "Each ruffian, with his own band of followers grouped around him (ἕκαστος δὲ τῶν πονηρῶν ἴδιον στῖφος ὑπεζωσμένος αὑτός), towered above his company like a brigand chief or tyrant."

[30]On the use of the genitive to express adherence, see C. Roberts, T. C.

For political history this is a fundamental insight, for which we have Matthias Gelzer and Ronald Syme to thank.[31] That it was arrived at so late is the result of the idealization of political history as the perpetual struggle of the "best men" against the "commons."[32] Freed of this misconception, Gelzer, Syme, and others developed a picture of ancient politics as a dynamic world of personal alliances, a cosmos of blood relations, clients, and friends, constellated around a few men of noble houses who contended for power against the background of the class struggle. There was, indeed, a broad material and conceptual divergence between popular and aristocratic programs running through the fabric of affairs, like a seam in a piece of iron.[33] But the principle at work in the formation of parties Sallust saw clearly:

> Some maintained that they were defending the rights of the commons, others that they were upholding the prestige of the senate; but under pretense of the

---

Skeat, and A. D. Nock, "The Guild of Zeus Hypsistos," *HTR* 29 (1936): 40-41. Note also the use of the genitive to describe rival sects devoted to rhetoricians in Quintilian 2.11.1-2.

[31]M. Gelzer, *Die Nobilität der römischen Republik* (Leipzig: Teubner, 1912), supplemented by F. Münzer, *Römische Adelsparteien und Adelsfamilien* (Stuttgart: J. B. Metzler, 1920). R. Syme, *The Roman Revolution* (Oxford: Clarendon Press, 1939), followed by L. R. Taylor, *Party Politics in the Age of Caesar* (Berkeley: University of California Press, 1949). On political parties in classical Greece, see Calhoun, *Athenian Clubs*; more recently, F. Sartori, *Le eterie nella vita Politica ateniese del VI e V secolo a.c.* (Rome: Bretschneider, 1957); O. Aurenche, *Les groupes d'Alcibiades, de Leogoras et de Teucros* (Paris: Belles Lettres, 1974). On the factors involved in the formation of factions in Jerusalem politics 62–66 A.D., see M. Goodman, *The Ruling Class of Judaea: The Origins of the Jewish Revolt against Rome A.D. 66–70* (Cambridge: Cambridge University Press, 1987) 198-212.

[32]E.g., Ps.-Xenophon *Constitution of the Athenians*; Plutarch *Per* 11; Cicero *Pro Sestio* 96-97. The great majority of scholars from the eighteenth century on, epitomized by Theodor Mommsen (*History of Rome* [New York: Scribner's, 1900]), believed in this conceptual antithesis, seeing in the antagonism between the optimate and the popular party an image of the strife of their own day.

[33]E.g., Sallust *Iug* 41.5; *Hist* 1.6-13; Cicero *Rep* 1.31; Caesar *BC* 1.35; Ps-Sallust *Ep* 2.5.1; Plutarch *Per* 11.

public welfare, each in reality was working for his own advancement (*Catil* 38).[34]

Political parties thus took the form of groups of clients and personal adherents pledged to particular leaders. *Amicitia* (i.e., shared interests, generally economic) held such associations together.[35] In the handbook of electioneering attributed to Quintus Cicero, the candidate is advised to make friends among the upper classes, but to avoid taking a stand on public issues (*Comm Pet* 53).[36] One notices how large a role the news of friendships, enmities, and, reconciliations plays in Cicero's correspondence. The conception of politics that his letters reflect also comes to expression in the slogans of 1 Cor 1:12.

The ephemeral nature of all the products of political life make it unlikely that actual examples of party slogans would survive. But nearly fifteen hundred specimens were unexpectedly brought to light by excavations at Pompeii, painted on the stucco of house walls in large letters.[37]

---

[34]*Sallust*, ed. and trans. J. C. Rolfe, LCL (Cambridge MA: Harvard University Press, 1970). The term ἕκαστος, used by Paul in 1:12 to designate the authors of the party cries, frequently appears in accounts of faction, sometimes describing the leaders, sometimes the followers, e.g., ἠγωνίζετο οὖν εἷς ἕκαστος αὐτὸς πρῶτος προστάτης τοῦ δήμου γενέσθαι, Thucydides 8.89.3; ἐχωριζόμεθα κατὰ τὰς αἱρέσεις, ἃς ἕκαστος ἡμῶν ἐδοκίμαζεν, Socratic *Ep* 32.2-3; Josephus *BJ* 2.14.1. Like the slogans which Paul parodies, the term ἕκαστος reflects the personal character of ancient politics.

[35]Too much was made by Syme and his students of ties of kinship, intermarriage, and *amicitia* in creating political factions. On the sense in which we may still use the term *amicitia* as the bond of political party, see P. A. Brunt, "'Amicitia' in the Late Roman Republic," *Proceedings of the Cambridge Philological Society* 11 (1965): 1-20.

[36]Note also the form of Caesar's commendation of his friends for office in Suetonius *Iul* 41.

[37]*CIL* 4. See the interesting sketch of local political life by F. Abbott, "Municipal Politics in Pompeii" in idem, *Society and Politics In Ancient Rome* (New York: Scribner's, 1916) 3-21; and more recently, J. L. Franklin, *Pompeii: The Electoral Programmata, Campaigns and Politics 71-79* (University Park: Pennsylvania State University Press, 1980) and H. Mouritsen, *Elections, Magistrates and Municipal Elite. Studies in Pompeian Epigraphy* (Rome, 1988).

These notices are sponsored not by the candidates themselves but by private citizens. They point to a large measure of popular participation in the election of magistrates, something that was also true of political life at Corinth.[38] The Pompeian posters are mainly the work of the candidates' friends and neighbors. But groups such as the dyers, the fullers, the goldsmiths, and the Isiacs also sponsor notices. Remarkably, the slogans make no mention of issues; no promises are made on behalf of a candidate, that he will watch over the markets with care or award public contracts fairly, though such matters clearly came under the control of local officials and were topics of lively interest.[39] The form of the notices accords with the personal character of ancient politics as we have come to know it. The slogans typically consist of the name of the candidate and his office, the sponsoring individual or group, and a verb of adherence or support. Thus, for example, *"Vatiam aed(ilem) Verus Innoces facit"* (*CIL* 4 no. 1080) or *"Vatiam aed(ilem) vicini"* (*CIL* 4 no. 443). How such party cries were used in voting assemblies can be seen from the papyri and legal texts. The procedure consisted in the proposal of names, then in a vote between them by formal acclamation.[40] Amid much wrangling, the candidates' supporters shouted, "Upright, loyal

---

[38]Republican electoral practices were evidently retained in many municipalities under the empire: see J. H. Kent, *Corinth VIII/3 The Inscriptions 1926-1950* (Princeton: American School of Classical Studies at Athens, 1966) 23: "the government of Corinth was in effect a miniature replica of the civic government of Republican Rome." For evidence of nominally democratic constitutions in a number of Greek cities, see J. Touloumakos, "Der Einfluss Roms auf die Staatform der griechischen Stadtstaaten des Festlandes und der Inseln im ersten und zweiten Jhdt. v. Chr." (diss., Göttingen, 1967) 11-15. For Pompeii, see P. Castrén, *Ordo Populusque Pompeianus. Polity and Society in Roman Pompeii* (Rome, 1975).

[39]Abbott, "Municipal Politics," 12. On the recommendation of a candidate by the *vicini*, see Mouritsen, *Elections, Magistrates, and Municipal Elite*, 19, 146-47, 176.

[40]On voting procedures in cities under the empire, see A. H. M. Jones, *The Greek City from Alexander to Justinian* (Oxford: Clarendon, 1940) 170-91; J. A. O. Larsen, *Representative Government in Greek and Roman History* (Berkeley and Los Angeles: University of California Press, 1966) 106-25.

Ptolemy!" and "Let Achilleus be crowned!" (*POxy* 1415).[41]
The positive counterpart of the factious behavior that Paul parodies in 1 Cor 1:12 is supplied by the orator Aelius Aristides in his speech to the Rhodians:

> When we visited you, we saw you even in the assembly using not only a single voice, but if I may say so, for the most part even a single word. For often it was enough for you to exclaim, "Well said!" and "Crown him!" and such like, with the name of the speaker (*Or* 24.56).

But it is Dio Chrysostom's pained account of the conduct of his fellow Prusans at their common gatherings that most recalls Paul's ironic report of the discordant voices in the Christian assembly. The orator describes

> the shouts of the partisans, uttered in hatred and abuse, . . . outbursts which are not for reasonable men or temperate cities, but rather for those who, . . . as Homer says, "In rage to mid-assembly go, and quarrel with one another as their anger bids" (*Or* 40.28-29; see also 39.4: οἱ στασιάζοντες οὐδ᾽ αὐτῶν ἀκούουσιν).

Analogous appropriations of the language of politics by voluntary associations and rhetorical schools cast light upon the form of the slogans in 1 Cor 1:12.[42] The law of the gild of Zeus Hypsistos, dated on palaeo-

---

[41]A. H. M. Jones, "The Election of the Metropolitan Magistrates in Egypt," *JEA* 24 (1938): 65-66. These examples are taken from the minutes of the councils of Oxyrhynchus and Hermopolis respectively, where elections had virtually ceased to be a reality and where flagging interest in local politics made compulsion necessary to secure candidates for the magistracies. But a century earlier in Greece there was no lack of spontaneous candidatures for local office; see Jones's conclusion on politics in the Greek cities of the empire in his *The Greek City*, 184: "On the whole it would seem that there was a sufficient supply of voluntary candidates till the latter part of the first century."

[42]The relevance of the evidence of the collegia was already demonstrated by Georg Heinrici, "Zur Geschichte der Anfänge paulinischer Gemeinden," *ZwTh* 1 (1877): 119ff.; idem, *Das zweite Sendschreiben des Apostel Paulus an die Korinther* (Berlin: Hertz, 1887) esp. 552-604. The texts discussed below are cited in connection with 1 Cor 1:12 by S. Pogoloff, *Logos and Sophia: The Rhetorical Situation of 1 Corinthians*, SBLDS 134 (Atlanta: Scholars Press, 1992) 251n.50.

graphical grounds to the reign of Ptolemy Auletes (69-58 B.C.),[43] instructs members: "It shall not be permissible for any of them . . . to make factions or to leave the brotherhood of the president for another brotherhood" (μ[η]ι[δ]ενὶ αὐτῶν ἐξέστωι . . . σχίματα συνίστασ[θαι] μηιδ' ἀπ[ο]χωρήισε[ιν ἐκ] τῆς τοῦ ἡγ[ου]μένου φράτρας εἰς ἑτέραν φράτραν).[44] The use of the genitive of the noun ἡγούμενος to identify the association to which members belong reflects the nature of group formation in the Greco-Roman world. The president of the association, elected for one year, is named in the document as "Petesouchos son of Teephbennis," and is described as "a learned man, worthy of the place and of the company," terms that echo the language of acclamation.[45] Members of the gild of Zeus Hypsistos (οἱ ἐκ τῆς τοῦ Διὸς Ὑψίστου συνόδου) might identify themselves as being "of the brotherhood of Petesouchos" (τῆς τοῦ Πετεσούχου φράτρας), in contrast to the members of another brotherhood or rival faction.[46]

A closer parallel to the form of the slogans in 1 Cor 1:12 is found in Quintilian's account of a choice between leaders of rival schools of rhetoric (2.11.1-2). Asked whether "he was a follower of Theodorus or Apollodorus (Theodoreus an Apollodoreus esset?), a certain teacher of rhetoric replied: "I am a partisan of the Thracians" (Ego parmularius

---

[43]C. Roberts, T. C. Skeat, and A. D. Nock, "The Gild of Zeus Hypsistos," HTR 29 (1936): 39, 42.

[44]Text and translation in Roberts, Skeat, and Nock, "The Gild of Zeus Hypsistos," 40-42. On σχίματα as an error for σχίσματα, see commentary, 51, where Nock refers to Aristotle 499a27 and 1 Cor.

[45]Roberts, Skeat, and Nock, "The Gild of Zeus Hypsistos," 40, ll.6-7: ἡγούμενον Πετεσοῦ[χον] Τεεφβέννιος, ἄνδρα λόγιον, τοῦ τόπου καὶ τῶν ἀνδρῶν ἄξιον, and the commentary, 45-47. Compare P. Mich. 2710, the νόμος of a guild of the freedmen of Claudius resident at Tebtunis, providing for the election of a ἡγούμενος for a year.

[46]On the use of the term φράτρα, rather than σύνοδος, see Roberts, Skeat, and Nock, "The Gild of Zeus Hypsistos," 52. On the tendency to create subunits and factions, which the νόμος seeks to limit, see the concluding comment of Nock, p. 87: "The prohibitions in this as in other texts relating to ancient clubs indicate the perils which threatened table-fellowship and illustrate the disorders of the Corinthian Eucharist."

sum).[47] The cleverness of the reply consists not only in the successful evasion of the question, but also in the appropriation of a battle-cry from the contests of the amphitheater,[48] where partisans of a star or a team of gladiators identified themselves, expressed their enthusiasms, and occasionally reflected their political views by calling themselves after various champions.[49] Assumed in both the question and the reply is a

---

[47]The translation modifies H. E. Butler, *The Institutio Oratoria of Quintilian*, vol. 1, LCL (Cambridge MA: Harvard University Press, 1980) 281. The *parmularius* is a partisan of the gladiators known as Thraces, who were armed with a little round shield or buckler, called the *parmula*; P. G. W. Glare, *Oxford Latin Dictionary* (Oxford: Clarendon, 1982) s.v. *parmularius*. The point of the retort is to ridicule the rivalry between teachers of rhetoric by comparing their debates with the contests between gladiators in the amphitheater.

[48]On the importance of theaters in Roman politics, see F. Abbott, "The Theater as a Factor in Roman Politics," *Transactions of the American Philological Association* 38 (1907): 49-56 and R. MacMullen, *Enemies of the Roman Order: Treason, Unrest, and Alienation in the Empire* (Cambridge MA: Harvard University Press, 1966) 168-70. Groups came to the amphitheater organized as guilds, sat in compact armies under acknowledged leaders, called *capita factionum* or *duces* (Suetonius *Tib* 37; *Nero* 20.3), and engaged in unison cheering (Tertullian *De Spect.* 7); on unison cheering by guilds, see L. Robert, *Les Gladiateurs dans l'Orient grec*, Bibliothèque de l'Ecole des hautes études 278 (Paris, 1940) 41; on the leatherworkers in Philadelphia, A. Alföldi, "Die Ausgestaltung des monarchischen Zeremoniells am römischen Kaiserhofe," *Mitteilungen des deutschen archäologischen Instituts, Römische Abteilung* 49 (1934) 79-83.

[49]For example, the Paridiani at Pompeii and their idol, the *pantomimus* Paris, on whom see G. O. Onorato, ed., *Iscrizioni pompeiane: La Vita pubblica* (Florence, 1957) 92, 166. Note also the "Vedius fans" of gladiation at Ephesus in the Severan period, in Robert, *Les Gladiateurs dans l'Orient grec*, 27. Fans of horse racing were divided into factions at Rome as early as the reign of Caligula; on the Greens and the Blues, see A. Maricq, "Factions du cirque et partis populaires," *Bulletin de l'Académie royale de Belgique* 36 (1950) 396-421. For examples of riotous partisanship caused by actors, see Dio 57.14.10; Tacitus *An* 1.77; Suetonius *Tib* 37. On dancers and *pantomimi* as a cause of factions forming among the people, see Suetonius *Nero* 16.2; Tacitus *An* 13.25, 28; 14.21 Vettius Valens, *Anthol* 5.10. According to Philostratus (*Vit Apoll* 1.5), "many cities" in Pamphylia and Lycia were split into factions over dancers and horses. For evidence of the participation of such groups in politics, see, for example, *CIL* 4.7585: "the *spectaculi spectantes* demand X for *duovir*," written in an archway near the amphitheater; *CIL* 4.7919: "We urge you to make X aedile. (Sponsored

form of self-identification determined by the personal character of ancient politics.[50] A member of a faction, whether in the assembly, the theater, or the school, identified himself and expressed his adherence by means of a formula that consisted of a personal pronoun, the verb "to be" (expressed or implied), and the genitive of a proper name.[51]

II. THE ROLE OF SOCIAL AND ECONOMIC INEQUALITY

In what may be the earliest reference to schisms in the Corinthian correspondence, Paul speaks without dissimulation, and almost in passing, of the divisions that appeared when the Christians gathered to celebrate the Lord's Supper (11:17-34). The source of the problem is stated clearly in 1 Cor 11:21-22: it is the contempt of the rich for the poor, an attitude typically exhibited by wealthy Romans toward the lower classes.[52] Those

---

by) Porphyrius, with the Paridiani." The connection between the theater and politics was intrinsic: candidates paid for *ludi* to gain support from the citizenry, thus mobilizing the theater factions. Rivalry between amphitheatric factions occasionally broke forth into violence, as in the riot at Pompeii in 59 A.D., known from a passage in Tacitus (*An* 14.17) and made famous by a painting on the wall of a house, which depicts contests going on in the arena, while in the seats and in the streets outside the amphitheater, battles rage among partisans of the contestants; see A. Maiuri, "Pompei e Nocera," *Rendiconti della Accademia de archeologia, Napoli* 33 (1958) 35-40. The massacre that ensued was the cimax of partisan rivalry which began with taunts preserved in graffiti on the walls of Pompeii—"Bad cess to Nucerians!"; "Good luck to all Nucerians and the hook for Pompeians and Pithecusans!"; Maiuri, "Pompei e Nocera," 35 n.5. For additional examples of riots and disorders resulting from the rivalry of amphitheatric factions, see MacMullen, *Enemies of the Roman Order,* 168-71, 338-39n.8, 339-40n.11.

[50]On this principle in general, see M. I. Finley, *Politics in the Ancient World* (Cambridge: Cambridge University Press, 1983) 62-68, and esp. 118-19.

[51]Contra M. Mitchell, *Paul and the Rhetoric of Reconciliation: An Exegetical Investigation of the Language and Composition of 1 Corinthians,* HUNT 28 (Tübingen: Mohr-Siebeck, 1991) 83-85.

[52]Cicero's speeches, letters, and treatises are full of scorn for the lower classes: e.g., they are "the dregs (*faex*) of the city," *Pro Flac* 17-18; "dirt" (*sordes*), *Ad Att* 1.16.11; "the bilge-water of the city" (*sentina urbis*), *Ad Att* 1.19.4. Dionysius of Halicarnassus (*Ant Rom* 8.71.3) speaks of the lower classes as "the indigent and unwashed"; see Z. Yavetz, "Plebs sordida," *Athenaeum* 43 (1965) 295-311.

who have houses and plenty to eat despise and humiliate those who are hungry and have nothing (οἱ μὴ ἔχοντες). Later, when the report of Chloe's people compels Paul to treat the matter at length, he seeks to deflate the pride that, in his view, has given rise to faction by stressing the reversal of status brought about by divine election:

> For consider your calling, brothers; not many of you were learned by worldly standards, not many were powerful, not many were nobly born. But God has chosen the foolish of the world to humiliate the learned, . . . the weak of the world to humiliate the strong, . . . the lowly born . . . and the despised, things that are nothing, to nullify things that are, so that no human being might boast in the presence of God (1:26-29).

Paul's attempt to create a sense of community as the reflex of a theological premise recalls Cicero's effort to mold a political bloc that would transcend conflict by redefining the term optimates as "the upright and well-disposed of all classes" (*Pro Sestio* 97; *Ad Att* 1.14.5; 1.20.3; 2.1.1; 9.7.6). But such ideological stratagems cannot mask the reality of social and economic inequality: some *were* educated, influential, and of noble birth, though "not many." It is not my purpose to discuss the "social stratification" of the Christian community.[53] Paul's statements are so revealing that virtually no one doubts that tensions between rich and poor were present in the church at Corinth.[54] It is my task rather to investigate the bearing of inequality on the instance of faction in the church.

No Greek or Roman would have denied that conflicts between classes played a large role in party struggles and civil strife, however the matter may have been presented in political pamphlets and in public debate. Aristotle, the real expert on the social and political life of the ancient city, says unequivocally: "Party strife is everywhere due to inequality"

---

[53]This has already been done admirably by G. Theissen, *The Social Setting of Pauline Christianity: Essays on Corinth* (Philadelphia: Fortress, 1982) 69-120, 145-74; see also M. Hengel, *Eigentum und Reichtum in der frühen Kirche: Aspekte einer frühchristlichen Sozialgeschichte* (Stuttgart: Calwer, 1973) 44-45; H. J. Klauck, *Hausgemeinde und Hauskirche im frühen Christentum*, SBS 103 (Stuttgart: Katholisches Bibelwerk, 1981) 28, 32-34; Meeks, *The First Urban Christians*, 67-69, 157-58.

[54]Thus already J. Weiss, *Der erste Korintherbrief*, 293; G. Bornkamm, *Early Christian Experience* (New York: Harper & Row, 1969) 126-28.

(πανταχοῦ γὰρ διὰ τὸ ἄνισον ἡ στάσις, *Pol* 5.1.6 1301b27). This judgment represents not only the result of his profound analysis but also, as we shall see, what was generally believed. That modern political historians have ignored the statements of most Greeks and Romans on the centrality of class conflict bears witness to the extraordinary influence of those profoundly antidemocratic thinkers, Plato and Cicero, for whom στάσις was the result of moral degeneration and the unprincipled ambition of the "demagoues."[55] But it also attests the scholars' own sympathies and inclinations. Thus, we have had to wait until the last decades of this century for the first comprehensive analysis of the class struggle on the political plane.[56]

When we turn to accounts of στάσις in ancient literature, we find that tensions between rich and poor are a constant feature. Solon's poems express his view of what had brought the plague of civil strife upon Athens: the "degrading bondage" of the poor to the rich had "roused from their sleep war and civil strife" (*fr* 4; see also *fr* 1, 3, 5, 6, 8, 10, 23-25, 27). In Thucydides' moving account of the violent στάσις at Corcyra in 427, no attempt is made to conceal the element of class struggle. The people, under the leadership of Peithias, brought to trial the "wealthiest of the oligarchs": the charge against them was conspiring to overthrow the democracy, "but some were in fact put to death, because money was owing to them, by those who had borrowed it." Reflecting upon the period of civil strife to which the terrible events at Corcyra

---

[55]See Plato's well-known description of Pericles as a "pastry chef" who stuffed the common people with material goods in *Gorgias* 502e-519d; Cicero *Pro Sestio* 100-102 and his disingenuous treatment of Catiline, "that nefarious gladiator," in the four Catiline orations. If Catiline's letter, preserved in Sallust (*Cat* 35.3), is to be believed, Catiline sought to defend the interests of the poor throughout his public life.

[56]P. A. Brunt, *Social Conflicts In the Roman Republic* (London: Chatto & Windus, 1971); R. Macmullen, *Roman Social Relations 50 B.C. to A.D. 284* (New Haven: Yale University Press, 1974) chap. 4; G. E. M. de Ste. Croix, *The Class Struggle In the Ancient Greek World* (Ithaca: Cornell University, 1981); M. I. Finley, *Politics in the Ancient World* (Cambridge: Cambridge University Press, 1983); J. Ober, "Aristotle's Political Sociology: Class, Status, and Order in the *Politics*" in *Essays on the Foundations of Aristotelian Political Science*, ed. C. Lord and D. O'Connor (Berkeley: Univ. of California Press, 1991) 112-35.

were but the prelude, Thucydides concludes: "the cause of all these evils was the desire to rule which greed and ambition inspire, and springing from them, that party spirit which belongs to men once they have become involved in factious rivalry" (3.81.4; 3.82.8).[57]

Xenophon is our source for civil strife at Corinth in the fourth century: he makes it clear that enmity between rich and poor was at the root of στάσις. A massacre occurred in 393 when a group of men whom Xenophon tendentiously calls οἱ πλεῖστοι καὶ βέλτιστοι sought an alliance with Sparta. On the last day of the festival of Eukleia, the supporters of democracy assassinated the aristocrats as they sat in the theater and walked about the agora (*Hell* 4.4.1-5). Diodorus provides a summary account of the στάσις at neighboring Argos, where 1,200 of the wealthiest citizens were put to death and their property confiscated when an oligarchic coup was uncovered (15.57.3-58.4; Plutarch *Mor* 814b). Diodorus's calculated references to the madness of the δῆμος and the crimes of its leaders do not obscure the fact that the bloody σκυταλισμός of 370 was in essence a class conflict. Evidence of στάσις in Greek cities of the Roman period is scattered and fragmentary. But from the Achaean town of Dyme comes an inscription recording a letter of the proconsul Q. Fabius Maximus which complains of "disorder" described as συγχύσις and ταραχή.[58] That the revolt resulted in part from economic grievances is evident from the burning of the public archives and the cancellation of debts, as from the enactment of legislation "contrary to the πολιτεῖαι granted to the Achaeans by the Romans," a reference to the oligarchical governments imposed by L. Mummius after crushing the revolt of the Achaean League.[59]

All these writers show themselves well aware that beneath the party

---

[57]The translation is that of C. F. Smith, LCL (Cambridge: Harvard University Press, 1975). See G. E. M. de Ste. Croix, *The Origins of the Peloponnesian War* (Ithaca NY: Cornell University Press, 1972).

[58]*Sylloge Inscriptionum Graecarum*, ed. W. Dittenberger, 3rd ed. (Leipzig: Hirzel, 1915-24) 2.684; see the excellent article by A. Fuks, "Social Revolution in Dyme in 116–114 B.C.E." in *Studies In History*, ed. D. Asheri and I. Schatzman, Scripta Hierosolymitana 23 (Jerusalem: Magnes, 1972) 21-27.

[59]L. Mummius, the destroyer of Corinth, is said by Pausanias (*Des Gr* 8.16.9) to have granted constitutions which "established property qualifications for holding office."

struggles which menaced the πόλις lay social problems, the realities of exploitation and inequality upon which the ancient economy depended, however disingenuous their judgments on the character and motives of the leaders of the δῆμος.[60] It makes little difference whether the picture that later authors, such as Appian and Plutarch, present of the strife between the senate and the Gracchi, for example, is a mere "stereotype of στάσις,"[61] as some historians contend. What matters is that ancient writers assumed that where there was discord, opposition between rich and poor lay behind. It helps us understand Paul's train of thought in 1 Corinthians 1-4 and in 11:17-34, the transition from the condemnation of factions to a discussion of social and economic differences. Paul's official reaction is what we would expect, given the history of the Christian movement and the nature of his project: he denies that the Corinthians are distinguished in the true, spiritual sense and contends that "the condition of the community demonstrates the freedom of God's electing grace."[62] It is surprising only that New Testament scholars should share this transfigured view of the situation in Corinth so unreservedly. It is, at any rate, clear that whatever he says, Paul *knew* better. Like Aristotle he knew that feelings of inequality arising from distinctions of wealth, noble birth, and higher learning are the ἀρχαὶ καὶ πηγαὶ τῶν στασέων (*Pol* 5.1 1301b5).[63]

---

[60]Josephus is an interesting example: στάσις is a key interpretive concept in his work on the Jewish War; see the preface to *BJ* and 4.3.2 §§128-34, as well as *Ant* 18.1.1 §8. Occasionally he shows himself aware that conflicts between rich and poor play a part in civil strife, i.e., *Ant* 20.8.8 §§179-80 and *BJ* 2.17.6 §§426-27, though he generally presents the leaders of the revolt as indigents and criminals. See T. Rajak, *Josephus. The Historian and His Society* (Philadelphia: Fortress Press, 1984) 91-96, 118-19.

[61]E. Badian, "Tiberius Gracchus and the Beginning of the Roman Revolution" in *Aufstieg und Niedergang der römischen Welt* 1/1, ed. H. Temporini (Berlin: de Gruyter, 1972) 707. But compare Cicero's understanding of the intent of the agrarian law in *Pro Sestio* 103 and the very different account of this period in Ste. Croix, *Class Struggle*, 351-54, 359-60.

[62]Conzelmann, *1 Corinthians*, 49.

[63]See also Aristotle *Pol* 3.8 1279b6-40 and 1310a3-10. Such passages would seem to refute the argument of M. Wheeler, "Aristotle's Analysis of the Nature of Political Struggle," *American Journal of Philology* 72 (1951): 145-61.

There can be no more striking confirmation that Paul actually saw the situation in this light than the terms he uses to describe the social makeup of the Christian community in 1 Cor 1:26f. For they are the very terms employed by Greek writers from the time of Solon to designate the major class divisions involved in στάσις. The supporters of oligarchic government are referred to as the "wise" (σοφοί or φρόνιμοι), the "powerful" (δυνατοί), the "nobly born" (εὐγενεῖς, γενναῖοι, or γνώριμοι), all substitutes for "the rich"; while "the poor," the supporters of democracy, are styled in antithesis the "vulgar" (μωροί or βάναυσοι), the "weak" (ἀσθενεῖς), the "lowly-born" (ἀγενεῖς or δημοτικοί).[64] Examples abound: discussing the causes of στάσις, Aristotle says that those who are of "noble birth" (εὐγενεῖς) frequently stir up faction by claiming unequal rights (*Pol* 5.1.3 1301b3).[65] Thucydides recounts the dissension that erupted within Athens as the Peloponnesian armies ravaged the countryside. The "men of influence" (δυνατοί) became angry with Pericles because they had lost their beautiful estates and expensive furnishings. In their resentment, they charged him with embezzlement (Thucydides 2.65.2; Plato *Gorgias* 576a).[66] Ion in Euripides assumes that the "worthy gentlemen"

Aristotle (*Pol*. 2.4 266a37-39) reports that some held the right of property to be the cause of party strife. This is doubtless a reference to Plato (*Rep* 550cd, 551d) who realized that any constitution which is based on a property qualification will eventually create two cities, one of the rich and the other of the poor, "dwelling together, but always plotting against each other." See A.Fuks, "Plato and the Social Question: The Problem of Poverty and Riches in the *Republic*," *Ancient Society* 8 (1977) 49-83.

[64]For Greek usage, see W. L. Freese, *Der Parteikampf der Reichen und der Armen in Athen zur Zeit der Demokratie* (Stralsund: C. Löffler, 1848) 24-25; Loenen, *Stasis*, 7-10; R. A. Neil, *Aristophanes' Knights* (Cambridge: Cambridge University Press, 1901) appendix 2, "Political Use of Moral Terms"; J. Bohatec, "Inhalt und Reihenfolge der 'Schlagworte der Erlösungsreligion,' 1 Kor. 1:26-31," *TZ* 4 (1948): 252-71; for Latin usage in full, J. Hellegouarc'h, *Le vocabulaire Latin*, 223-541.

[65]On εὐγενεῖς, see Euripides *Ion* 1540; Plato *Polit* 375a; 2 Macc. 10:13; 4 Macc. 6:5; 9:13,27.

[66]Thucydides uses δυνατοί to designate the political group supporting an oligarchical government: 1.24.5; 1.39.3; 3.27.3; 3.47.3; 4.51; 5.4.3; 8.73.2; he

(χρηστοί) are "wise" (σοφοί) and fears that they will regard his attempt to penetrate the highest ranks of Athenian society as that of a "nobody" (ὃ μηδέν), who is "weak" (ἀσθενής) and "baseborn" (νοθαγενής), in a word, as "foolishness" (μωρία) (Euripides *Ion* 595-97).[67] Paul's categories in analyzing the divisions in the community are like those of Aristotle, who recognized that "inasmuch as oligarchy is defined by birth (γένος), wealth (πλοῦτος) and education (παιδεία), the democratic characteristics are thought to be the opposite of these, low birth (ἀγένεια), poverty (πενία), and vulgarity (βαναυσία)" (*Pol* 6.1.9 1317b39-41). Paul only apparently makes use of a different category when he speaks of the "powerful" rather than the "wealthy": the δυνατοί are the πλούσιοι throughout Greek literature.[68]

It is obvious whose view of society is reflected in these terms. The absolute dichotomy they express corresponds to the wide gulf between the rich and the poor in the ancient economy. Paul uses the established terminology ironically, an acoustic phenomenon for which only the elect have ears. But irony is indirect opposition, an indirection that has given rise to that curious circumlocution οὐ πολλοί (1:26) for the explicitly political term ὀλίγοι.[69] Sallust is sometimes capable of direct confron-

---

also speaks of δυνατώτατοι as the prime movers in oligarchlc factions: 1.115.4-5; 2.2.3; 8.21; 8.44.1; 8.47.2; 8.48.1; 8.63.3; 8.90.1; 8.73.2.

[67]See also Theognis 33. On σοφοί, see further G. Grossmann, *Politische Schlagwörter aus der Zeit des Peloponnesischen Krieges* (Zürich: Leemann, 1950) 150-54. On ἀσθενής, see Plato *Rep* 364a; on ἀγενής, see Plato *Gorgias* 465b; Aristotle *Pol* 4.10; Josephus *BJ* 4.3.6 §148; Epictetus *Diss* 4.1.10.

[68]E.g., Thucydides 2.65; 3.70; 3.81; Plato *Laches* 186c; Xenophon *Hipparch.* 1.9-10; Aristophanes *Peace* 639; Philo *Som* 1.155; *De virt* 162; Josephus *BJ* 1.17.2 §326; 2.14.1 §275; 2.14.4 §§287, 411; 7.8.1 §260.

[69]In Thucydides, for example, the term ὀλίγοι denotes the aristocratic, pro-Spartan faction: 3.70; 3.74.2; 3.82.1; 4.86.4; 4.110.1; 4.123; 5.82.2-3; 8.9.3; 8.14.2; 8.38.3. In general, see Loenen, *Stasis,* 7-10. On πολλοί and the related terms πλῆθος, δῆμος Latin *multitudo*, which denote the majority of the people, the "poor," as opposed to the δυνατοί, see R. von Pohlmann, *Geschichte der sozialen Frage und des Sozialismus ln der antiken Welt,* 2nd ed. (München: Beck, 1912) 1.427; Loenen, *Stasis* 7; J. Hellegouarc'h, *Le vocabulaire Latin,* 506-16; note, for example, the usage of Thucydides in 2.37.1; 3.27.2; 3.72.7; 4.104.4; 8.73.6; 8.21; 1.25.1; 5.82.1 and Aristotle *Ath Pol* 27.4.

tation, of dissolving rhetoric and ideology into political history, as when he says: "Whoever was most opulent and most capable of inflicting harm was regarded as a *bonus* because he defended the existing state of affairs" (*Hist* fr. 1.12, ed. B. Maurenbrecher). Paul is more subtle and evasive; he translates the existing value terms without penetrating and unmasking them.

Now the question is this: How are the tensions between rich and poor, so evident in the epistle, related to the formation of factions? The individual Corinthians who are mentioned by name are all people of wealth and status: Chloe, whose slaves are Paul's informants (1:11),[70] Crispus, the former ἀρχισυνάγωγος (Acts 18:8),[71] Gaius, whose house was large enough to accomodate the entire congregation (Rom 16:23),[72] and Stephanas, a householder who visited Paul in Ephesus with two companions, apparently bringing material support (16:15-18).[73] It is to the latter and to "such men" that Paul attempts to subject the community (16:16). Evidently the leaders of the factions were persons of substance, for the terms that Paul uses to characterize those who would examine his apostolic credentials in 1 Cor 4:10—"wise" (φρόνιμοι), "strong" (ἰσχυροί), and "held in repute" (ἔνδοξοι)—are, like the epithets in 1:26, euphemisms for "the rich."[74] In both passages, the context makes plain that Paul is addressing those whom he regards as the prime movers in faction, the social and political elite. None of the "authorities" to whom the factions appeal are present in Corinth at the outbreak of the

---

[70]On the expression οἱ Χλόης in 1:11, see G. Theissen, *The Social Setting*, 92-94 and Meeks, *The First Urban Christians*, 59.

[71]Cf. E. Judge, "The Early Christians as a Scholastic Community," *JRH* 1 (1960): 129-41; Theissen, *The Social Setting*, 73-75; Meeks, *The First Urban Christians*, 57.

[72]Theissen, *The Social Setting*, 55-56, 89; Meeks, *The First Urban Christians*, 57. The church at Corinth was a λαὸς πολύς according to Acts 18:10.

[73]Theissen, *The Social Setting*, 55, 83, 87; Meeks, *The First Urban Christians*, 58. According to 1 Cor 16:17, Stephanas made up the ὑστέρημα of the Corinthians. The same term is found in Phil. 2:30 of the material support brought to Paul by Epaphroditus, the λειτουργὸς τῆς χρείας (Phil. 2:25).

[74]Loenen, *Stasis*, 7-10; Plato *Soph* 223b; Xenophon *Mem* 1.2.56; Isocrates 1.37.

crisis.[75] The real party leaders are thus local Christians (Chloe, Crispus, Gaius, and Stephanas) who seek to legitimate their power by appealing to renowned figures in the church.[76] The answer that the evidence suggests is one that is disturbingly familiar to the student of ancient politics:[77] the bondage of the poor to the rich is the breeding ground of faction. Poverty creates dependence, a relationship that ambitious aristocrats readily exploit in their struggle for power (Solon *fr* 4.1-22; Aristotle *Ath Pol* 2.1-3). The process is graphically described in the *suasoria* falsely attributed to Sallust and written perhaps under Tiberius.[78] The author complains that poverty and idleness have gradually driven the common people from the fields, forcing them to live without a fixed abode, to covet the riches of others,

---

[75]Rightly pointed out by A. Schreiber, *Die Gemeinde in Korinth* (Münster: Aschendorff, 1977) 154-60.

[76]This is similar to the interpretation offered by John Chrysostom, *Hom III in I Cor*, Migne, *PG* 61.24: "'That each one of you says, I am of Paul, and I of Apollos, and I of Cephas.' . . . And yet they were not speaking about himself, nor about Peter, nor about Apollos; but he signifies that if these were not to be leaned on, much less others. For that they had not spoken about them, he says further on: 'And these things I have transferred in a figure unto myself and Apollos, that you may learn in us not to go beyond the things which are written.' For if it were not right for them to call themselves by the name of Paul, and of Apollos, and of Cephas, much less of any others. If under the Teacher and the first of the Apostles, and one that had instructed so much people, it were not right to enroll themselves, much less under those who were nothing. By way of hyperbole then, seeking to withdraw them from their disease, he sets down these names. Besides, he makes his argument less severe, not mentioning by name the rude dividers of the Church, but concealing them, as behind a sort of masks, with the names of the Apostles." The translation follows *The Nicene and Post-Nicene Fathers*, vol. 12, 11.

[77]L. R. Taylor, "Nobles, Clients and Personal Armies" in *Friends, Followers and Factions. A Reader in Political Clientelism*, ed. S. Schmidt, et al. (Berkeley: University of California Press, 1977) 179-91; J. C. Scott, "Patronage or Exploitation?" in *Patrons and Clients in Mediterranean Societies*, ed. E. Gellner and J. Waterbury (London: Duckworth, 1977) 21-39; M. I. Finley, "Authority and Patronage" in his *Politics in the Ancient World*, 24-49.

[78]R. Syme, *Sallust* (Berkeley and Los Angeles: University of California Press, 1964) 348. For a summary of debate on the authorship and date of the second *Epistula ad Caesarem senem,* see K. Vretska, *Sallust: Invective und Episteln* (Heidelberg: Winter, 1961) 1.38-51.

and to barter their liberty, their services, and their share in the common sovereignty for slavery to one man (Ps-Sallust *Ep* 2.5.1-6). He appeals to Caesar to intervene in the crisis and put an end to the grievous bondage of the commons to the faction of the nobles (Ps-Sallust *Ep* 2.2.4).

We may rely upon Aristotle for further insight into how patronage contributed to the creation of factions. In the well-known account of the rivalry between Pericles and Cimon, Aristotle explains that Pericles introduced a per diem allowance for jurors "as a counter-measure against the wealth of Cimon. For Cimon, who had an estate equal to that of a tyrant, not only discharged the public services munificently, but also supplied food to many of his fellow-demesmen. Since Pericles' property was insufficient for such a lavish expenditure, he took the advice of Damonides, . . . as he was being worsted with his private resources, to distribute to the multitude (οἱ πολλοί) what was theirs, and so he instituted payment for jury service" (*Ath Pol* 27.3-4). The dynamic at work in ancient politics could hardly be more clearly revealed: the poverty of a large portion of the citizen body, the subsistence level at which the majority were forced to live, made possible the deployment of wealth in the creation of factions.

Cicero's speeches and letters provide ample documentation of the way aristocrats used patronage to garner political support. In his defense of Murena against a charge of electoral corruption, Cicero states without compunction that "men of slender means have only one way of earning favors or of repaying benefits to men of our order, and that is by helping us and escorting us about when we are candidates for office" (*Pro Murena* 70; see also Quintus Cicero *Comm Pet* 34-38). Dionysius of Halicarnassus reports that it was considered impious and unlawful for a client to vote against his patron or to be found in the number of his enemies (*Ant Rom* 2.9-11).[79] Aristocrats could impose sanctions upon those who failed to provide political support. In an emotional speech to the Roman assembly in 167 B.C., Marcus Servilius, "a man of consular dignity," threatened: "when the people proceed to the vote, I will go down and follow along with them all and learn who are base and ungrateful and who would prefer to be persuaded (δημαγωγεῖσθαι) in

---

[79]On the *fides*-relationship, see Gelzer, *Nobilität*, 52-54; J. Hellegouarc'h, *Le vocabulaire Latin*, s.v. *fides*.

war rather than commanded!" (Plutarch *Aem Paul* 31).[80] An inscription from Corinth shows how a client was expected to express his gratitude and support. On the base of a monument found in the agora, a certain M. Antonius Promachus has written, "for his friend and patron NN, because of his fine character and trustworthiness."[81]

What was the power that enabled the protagonists of the Corinthian parties to create divisions in the community? All the evidence suggests that their power was based on material wealth and the dependence it induced. The "household" (οἶκος/οἰκία) of Stephanas (1:16; 16:15) and that of Crispus (Acts 18:8) no doubt included slaves and freedmen.[82] The latter's influence is attested by the author of Acts, and Stephanas is praised by Paul as the patron of the community (16:15).[83] Gaius, the rich proprietor, is not only "host" (ξένος) to Paul and the "entire church" (Rom 16:23), but is probably also the employer of Tertius, who writes an epistle to Ephesus from his house (Rom 16:22), and of how many other hired laborers.[84] As city treasurer, Erastus would have exercised still greater influence, not only through disbursement of his private fortune, but also by control of public expenditure for streets, public buildings, and the market place.[85] Chloe is probably also to be reckoned among the

---

[80]On patronage as a factor in political life and the influence of patronage on voting, see G. E. M. de Ste. Croix, "Suffragium: from vote to patronage," *British Journal of Sociology* 5 (1954) 33-48.

[81]Kent, *Corinth*, no. 265, 107.

[82]See Aristotle's definition of οἰκία in *Pol* 1.2.1: "the complete household consists of slaves and freedmen"; see also Cicero *De off* 1.17.58; Acts 10:2,7. See the discussion in E. A. Judge, *The Social Pattern of Christian Groups in the First Century* (London: Tyndale, 1960) 30-39; Theissen, *The Social Setting*, 83-87; Meeks, *The First Urban Christians*, 29-30, 75-77. A. Strobel's contention that οἶκος equals Latin *domus* and thus includes only family members is not convincing ("Der Begriff des Hauses im griechischen und römischen Privatrecht," *ZNW* 56 [1965]: 91-100).

[83]See Meeks, *The First Urban Christians*, 58, 78, 118, 123, 137.

[84]On hired labor in antiquity, see P. Garnsey and J. Skydsgaard, *Non-slave Labor in Graeco-Roman Antiquity* (Cambridge: Cambridge Univ. Press, 1980).

[85]Kent, *Corinth*, 27. On community patronage and politics, see P. Veyne, *Le pain et le cirque: Sociologie historique d'un pluralisme politique* (Paris: Seuil, 1976).

δυνατοί of the Corinthian community.[86] Her slaves or freedmen report to Paul in Ephesus (1:11). Slaves, freedmen, hired laborers, business associates—the whole *clientela*—furnished not only an army of political supporters for the wealthy Christian who sought to exert control over the new movement, but also, more importantly, the experience of social distance by virtue of which he felt himself to be a person of higher rank, worthy of ruling the community (4:8).

It is not impossible that the interests and objectives of the lower classes found expression in the strife of the factions in the Corinthian church.[87] But Paul's statements are elliptical; one cannot be sure. In antiquity in general, the aims of the lower classes come to expression wherever there is talk of the cancellation of debts and the redistribution of land (χρεῶν ἀποκοπή, γῆς ἀναδασμός).[88] But this revolutionary programme was seldom put into effect by the poor themselves. It was the ambitious aristocrat who typically took up the slogan and used it to make himself a tyrant. There were, of course, genuine democratic revolutions, such as that at Samos in 412 C.E., in which the common people as a whole rose up against the oligarchs (Thucydides 8.21).[89] But the fact that a year later the leaders of the revolutionary regime, now termed a group of δυνατώτατοι, turned against the δῆμος and attempted to establish an oligarchy (Thucydides 8.63.3-73.2) leads one to suspect that these "democrats" had been members of the aristocracy all along, and were only pursuing their own interests. Nor is there any reason to doubt that many poor Christians regarded men such as Stephanas and Gaius as their

---

[86]We cannot be certain that Chloe lived in Corinth, but the fact that Paul mentions her name without introduction indicates that she and her *familia* were known to the Christians there.

[87]As suggested by Theissen, *The Social Setting,* 57; followed by D. Georgi, *Theocracy in Paul's Praxis and Theology* (Minneapolis: Fortress, 1991) 55.

[88]R. Pöhlmann, *Geschichte der sozialen Frage und des Sozialismus in der antiken Welt,* 3rd ed. (Munich: Beck, 1925) 1:322-419; 2:437-63. The evidence is assembled and analyzed by D. Asheri, *Distribuzioni di terre nell' antica Grecia.* Memorie dell' Accademia delle Scienze di Torino, ser. 4, no. 10 (Turin: Accademia delle Scienze, 1966) and idem, "Leggi greche sul problema dei debiti," *Studi classici e orientali* 18 (1969): 5-122.

[89]See also Thucydides' account (5.4) of the distribution of property confiscated at Leontini in connection a political revolution.

leaders. Tiberius and Gaius Gracchus, Marius and Caesar, all aristocrats by birth, were nonetheless genuine *populares*, supported and revered.[90] The point is simply that neither in 1 Corinthians nor in ancient literature in general is there evidence of the poor creating factions of their own. Rather, the tensions between rich and poor always present in στάσις are exploited by rich aristocrats in their contest for control of the state. There may be a clue to the real attitude of poorer Christians toward the party strife in the fact that it is they, in the person of Chloe's slaves, who bring Paul word of the dissension (1:11), a matter which was apparently omitted from the official correspondence of the church (7:1; 8:1; 12:1; 16:1; 16:12). Like the *plebs urbana*, they probably viewed with disfavor the quarrels of the notables, and sought peace and reconciliation.[91]

If we would form a proper conception of Paul's position in the controversy, we must not regard the apostle's support for persons of status such as Stephanas in isolation from his seeming valorization of those who are without wealth, birth, or education.[92] Taken together, Paul's actions bear a remarkable resemblance to Cicero's attempt in the eleventh hour of the republic to capture the lower classes for his own faction by means of a political fiction—the idealization of class affiliation (*Pro Sestio* 96-98). By expressing solidarity with the despised and oppressed (1:26-28), Paul sought, like a Greek politician of old, to "bring the δῆμος into his faction" (Herodotus 5.66).

III. POLITICS AND WISDOM IN 1 CORINTHIANS 1:17–2:5

In a carefully constructed argument in 1:17-2:5, Paul contrasts the "speech" and "wisdom of the world" with the "word of the cross" and

---

[90]Plutarch *Ti. Gracchus* 8.10; *C. Gracchus* 12.1, 5-7; 18.2-3. On Caesar's popularity with the *plebs*, see Z. Yavetz, *Plebs and Princeps* (Oxford: Clarendon Press, 1969) 38-82. A strong case has been made that Clodius led a genuine movement of the urban poor by W. Nippel, "Die *plebs urbana* und die Rolle der Gewalt in der späten römischen Republik" in *Vom Elend der Handarbeit*, ed. H. Mommsen and W. Schulz (Stuttgart: Klett-Cotta, 1981) 70-92.

[91]On demonstrations by the *plebs* in favor of peace, see R. Syme, *The Roman Revolution* (Oxford: Oxford University Press, 1939) 221, 230.

[92]Paul cannot be said simply to "take the side of those members of the community who come from the lower strata," so Theissen, *The Social Setting*, 57.

the "wisdom of God." Scholars have found the transition to this section abrupt and the point at issue perplexing.[93] The role of this passage in Paul's advice on factions depends upon the content of "wisdom" (σοφία) against which Paul polemicizes. Ulrich Wilkens confidently asserts that σοφία is a gnostic concept, a title that the Corinthians have applied to the heavenly redeemer, the exalted Christ.[94] He supports this thesis by a wide-ranging investigation of the concept "wisdom" in the history of religions and, above all, in gnosis. But Wilckens ignores the clues that Paul provides to the nature of σοφία.[95] From the first, Paul speaks not of wisdom in general but of σοφία λόγου (1:17), an expression that Walter Bauer rightly translates "cleverness in speaking."[96] Moreover, the context of Paul's discussion of wisdom and foolishness is the account of his "preaching" (εὐαγγελίζεσθαι, 1:17) and "proclamation" (καταγγέλλειν, 2:1). The identity of "wisdom" is thus established in relation to his own "discourse" (λόγος, 2:4): Paul denies that he came to the Corinthians "with excess of speech or of wisdom" (καθ᾽ ὑπεροχὴν λόγου ἢ σοφίας, 2:1) or that his message was delivered "in persuasive words of wisdom" (ἐν πειθοῖς σοφίας λόγοις, 2:4).[97] Ὑπεροχή is Plato's term for "prolix discourse" in the Politicus (283c), and πειθώ is defined as the product of rhetorical art in the Gorgias (453a: πειθοῦς δημιουργός ἐστιν ἡ ῥητορική). Most telling are the terms Paul uses to characterize wisdom's adepts in

---

[93]Wilckens, *Weisheit und Torheit*, 6; Conzelmann, *1 Corinthians*, 37; E. Peterson even suggests that 1 Cor 1:16-31 is a homily that Paul delivered in a synagogue in Ephesus or Corinth and later incorporated into the text of his epistle! ("1 Korinther 1, 18f. und die Thematik des jüdischen Busstages," *Bib* 32 [1951]: 97-103).

[94]Wilckens, *Weisheit und Torheit*, 68; G. Sellin attributes the wisdom theology to the influence of Apollos, whose party he believes Paul is combating throughout chaps. 1-4 ("Das 'Geheimnis' der Weisheit und das Rätsel der 'Christuspartei' [zu 1 Kor 1-4]," *ZNW* 73 [1982]: 69-96).

[95]Wilckens denies that Paul has anythlng to say about the content of σοφία! (*Weisheit und Torheit*, 68). He contends that the term is taken over from the Corinthians for whom its meaning was already well established in a gnostic sense.

[96]W. Bauer, *A Greek-English Lexicon of the New Testament and Other Early Christian Literature* (Chicago: University of Chicago Press, 1979) 759.

[97]On variants in the manuscript tradition, see Conzelmann, *1 Corinthians*, 55.

1:20. In a three-fold anaphora Paul asks, "Where is the wise man (σοφός)? Where is the scribe (γραμματεύς)? Where is the debater (συζητητής) of this age?" The first two questions recall passages from Isaiah (19:12 LXX: ποῦ εἰσιν νῦν οἱ σοφοί σου; 33:18: ποῦ εἰσιν οἱ γραμματικοί), but the third clause, the climax of the series by virtue of its length, contains a term that is *hapax legomenon* in the New Testament and the key to Paul's thought.[98] It is the "disputer," the "debater," whose cleverness God has brought to naught. The σοφία that Paul fears will undermine the community is nothing other than rhetoric.

This interpretation was the view of an older generation of scholars, more familiar with Greek and Latin authors.[99] But they did not fully comprehend the point of Paul's contrast between rhetorical skill and the word of the cross. In their reflections upon civil strife, ancient authors show themselves aware of the dominant role of rhetoric. It is regularly discussed whenever the forces that exacerbate conflict are sought. In his excursus on στάσις, a passage that exercised a profound influence on the political thinking of antiquity,[100] Thucydides discusses at length the role of language and rhetoric in creating discord. Throughout the Hellenic world, the conflict escalated as factions in one city learned deviousness and equivocation from the strife in another (3.82.3). Thucydides shows himself deeply concerned for the corruption of moral vocabulary through the cynical misuse of language:

> The customary understanding of words in relation to things was changed as one thought fit. Reckless daring came to be considered courageous loyalty to comrades, thoughtful hesitation became specious cowardice, moderation a cloak for unmanliness. (3.82.4)

The party leaders on each side adopted "fair-sounding slogans," using "political equality for the masses" instead of the forthright δημοκρατία, and "moderate aristocracy" rather than ὀλιγαρχία (3.82.8). "Fair

---

[98]Bauer, *A Greek-English Lexicon*, 775.

[99]E.g., Heinrici, *Der erste Brief*, 65-66; Weiss, *Der erste Korintherbrief*, xxxiii.

[100]On the influence of the excursus in general, see the appendix to M. Cogan, "The Role of the Speeches in Thucydides' History" (diss., University of Chicago, 1974). Note, e.g., the influence of Thucydides upon Josephus's understanding of the causes of the Jewish War, cf. Rajak, *Josephus*, 91-93.

words" were proffered by opponents, who then violated their "oaths of reconciliation" (3.82.7). Like Paul, Thucydides believed that addiction to a false kind of σοφία, or "cleverness," lay at the root of discord. Opponents in factional strife "are more willing to be called clever villains than good simpletons, for they are ashamed of the one but glory in the other" (3.82.7). Those engaged in civil strife cannot be reconciled because "they fear the intelligence (συνετός) of their opponents, . . . lest they be worsted in words or by their opponents' intellectual ingenuity" (3.83.3).

In the extant fragment of Thrasymachus's discourse on concord, great stress is laid upon the function of rhetoric in faction. Those who are engaged in party strife suffer from lack of understanding: "For thinking that they are speaking things contrary to one another, they do not perceive that they are doing the same thing, nor that the speech of their opponents lies within their own."[101] In the pseudo-Sallustian *Epistula ad Caesarum senem*, the author appeals for action that will put an end to party strife. It is noteworthy how large a part eloquence plays in the rise of faction. The author ostensibly warns Julius Caesar to beware the rhetorical skill of Cato, eloquent pupil of the Greeks (Ps-Sallust *Ep* 2.9.3). The "cleverness" (*calliditas*) and "caprice" (*libido*) of the leaders of faction threaten to overthrow the true "wisdom" (*consilium*) upon which the ancestors established the Roman state (Ps-Sallust *Ep* 2.10.6; 11.1). In his analysis of στάσις, Aristotle concludes that as a means of preventing factional strife "one ought not to put faith in sophistical arguments strung together for the sake of deceiving the multitude" (*Pol* 5.7.2 1308a1).

Thucydides' paradigmatic description of στάσις makes it clear that there was sufficient reason for concern about the power of words. The clever animal, the ζῷον πολιτικόν, misuses language, reverses the names, to make the unreal appear as real. Objectified, language is an uncanny force, drawing the speaker on until simulation devours value.

---

[101]*Die Fragmente der Vorsokratiker*, 3 vols., ed. H. Diels; 12th ed., rev. W. Kranz (Dublin: Weidmann, 1966–1967) 85 A 1. The speech, of which only the opening is preserved, is sometimes called περὶ πολιτείας. But the concern of the speech seems to be not with the πολιτεία as such, but with ὁμόνοια; cf. A. Fuks, *The Ancestral Constitution* (London: Routledge & Kegan Paul, 1953) 103.

Like these authors, Paul warns and reflects; he wishes to curb the misuse of language in the Christian ἐκκλησία. Paul's opponents in Corinth, who sought to lead the new movement by "persuasive words of wisdom," might have answered the apostle as the democratic rhetor, Diodotus, answered Cleon: it is the duty of the good citizen to be a good speaker, to employ fair argument, whatever eloquence, to advise the people responsibly. "As for words," he concludes, "whoever contends that they are not to be the guides of our actions is either dull of wit or has some private interest at stake" (Thucydides 3.42.2, LCL).

IV. KNOWLEDGE AND POLITICS IN 1 CORINTHIANS 2:6–3:3

In 1 Cor 2:6-3:3 Paul addresses himself to those who claim to possess higher religious knowledge, evidence of their superiority, as οἱ πνευματικοί, to the common lot of believers. The defensive tone of Paul's remarks suggests that some have questioned Paul's ability to impart such hidden wisdom. The interpretation of this passage has presented scholars with great difficulties, exegetical and theological. In particular, it is unclear how the apostle's claim to have penetrated the depths of the knowledge of God in 2:6-16 is related to the discussion of factions. The section seems to spring the bounds of its context: the emphatic, antithetical δέ (2:6) marks a contrast with what has gone before,[102] but in what respect? The vocabulary and conceptuality shift suddenly and unmistakably to the realm of the mystery religions.[103] Even the term σοφία, which furnishes the slender thread of linguistic continuity, undergoes a shift in meaning: no longer a catchword for rhetorical-philosophical training, it seems a cover for "gnosis."[104] But what has given greatest offense is the apparent contradiction between Paul's previous assertion that he knows and preaches nothing except the crucified Christ and his current claim to communicate hidden wisdom to the spiritually perfect.[105]

---

[102]Conzelmann, 1 Corinthians, 60.

[103]Reitzenstein, Hellenistic Mystery Religions, 431-36.

[104]Wilckens, Weisheit und Torheit, 52-89; Schmithals, Gnosticism in Corinth, 138-41, 151-55; D. Lührmann, Das Offenbarungsverständnis bei Paulus und in den paulinischen Gemeinden, WMANT 16 (Neukirchen-Vluyn: Neukirchener Verlag, 1965) 113-17.

[105]R. Bultmann, Faith and Understanding (New York: Harper & Row, 1969)

Thus, scholars have referred to the section as a "digression," an "interlude,"[106] an "abridgment," even a "counter"[107] to the preceding argument. Some have attempted to explain the shift in subject matter by pointing to the polemical tone of the passage. Thus it is maintained that Paul takes up the terms and concepts of the Corinthians, either because he shares certain elements of their understanding of the spirit and of revelation and wishes to refine and correct them,[108] or because he desires to demonstrate to the gnostic elite, in their own terms, that they are νήπιοι and σάρκινοι.[109] It has even been suggested that 2:6-16 is not the work of Paul, but an interpolation from the hand of a Corinthian gnostic![110] There is undoubtedly something "gnostic" about the passage, whether the views represented are Paul's own or those of the Corinthians. It is enough to note the frequency of the verb γινώσκειν in this passage—2:8 (twice), 11, 14, 16—without recalling the Corinthian slogan, πάντες γνῶσιν ἔχομεν from 1 Cor 8:1. It is unclear how one would determine whether the γνῶσις discussed here was the kind known to the church fathers Hippolytus (5.6.4) and Clement of Alexandria (in *Exc ex Theod* 78), or "mysteries" such as Paul reveals in 1 Cor 15:51 and Rom. 11:25, or merely a matter of greater insight into things spiritual, the product of education and culture. To present these possibilities as alternatives is, perhaps, to fail to comprehend that the situation is over-determined. It is not our task, at any rate, to define the content of γνῶσις in 2:6-16, but to indicate why such a topic belongs

---

1.71-74; Schmithals, *Gnosticism in Corinth*, 151.

[106]J. Weiss, "Beiträge zur paulinischen Rhetorik" in *Theologische Studien: B. Weiss zu seinem 70. Geburtstag dargebracht* (Göttingen: Vandenhoeck & Ruprecht, 1897) 204; idem, *Der erste Korintherbrief*, 52.

[107]Conzelmann, *1 Corinthians*, 57.

[108]Wilckens, *Weisheit und Torheit*, 52-60; Lührmann, *Das Offenbarungsverständnis*, 113-17; M. Winter, *Pneumatiker und Psychiker in Korinth: Zum religionsgeschichtlichen Hintergrund von 1. Kor. 2,6-3,4* (Marburger theologische Studien 12; Marburg: Elwert, 1975) 230.

[109]Bultmann, *Faith and Understanding*, 1.71-73; E. Käsemann, "1 Korinther 2,6-16" in *Exegetische Versuche und Besinnungen* (Göttingen: Vandenhoeck & Ruprecht, 1970) 1.276.

[110]M. Widmann, "1 Kor. 2,6-16: Ein Einspruch gegen Paulus," *ZNW* 70 (1979): 44-53, esp. 46.

to a discussion of factions.

Whoever has studied the history of civil strife at Rome knows that religious knowledge was constantly manipulated by the ruling elite, in whose hands control of the priestly colleges lay, for the benefit of one faction in rivalry with another.[111] As Caesar's colleague in the consulship in 59 B.C., Bibulus sought to prevent Caesar's proposed legislation by announcing that he intended "to watch the heavens" for bad omens (Dio Cassius 38.6; Suetonius *Iul* 20). Similarly, recourse was had to the Sybilline oracles in 56 by a tribune in the pay of Crassus to prevent Pompey from leading an army to Egypt (Dio Cassius 39.15). The letters of Cicero repeatedly show how Roman nobles used religion in their faction struggles: by presenting themselves to the people as those upon whom the gods had conferred the proper interpretation of the divine will (see esp. *Ad Quin Fr* 2.4.4-5; *Ad Fam* 1.4.2; 1.7.4-5; *Leg* 2.31; 3.27).

There are unmistakable clues in 1 Cor 2:6-3:3 that those who claim to be "spiritual" and to possess knowledge are to be identified with the protagonists of the Corinthian parties. The language used to distinguish those who are worthy to receive wisdom from those who pretend to knowledge is obviously drawn from the mystery cults; but there are clear political overtones. Paul imparts wisdom ἐν τοῖς τελείοις (2:6). In Greek literature the τέλειος is one who has "completed" his initiation into the mysteries and is thus "perfect."[112] In the philosophical tradition, the τέλειος is the true wise man.[113] But the term is also found in Plato's Laws and elsewhere as a description of the "perfect" citizen.[114] The phrase ἐν τοῖς τελείοις recalls the related expression, οἱ ἐν τέλει, found throughout Greek literature as a designation for "the

---

[111]L. R. Taylor, "Manipulating the State Religion" in *Party Politics*, 76-97; H. D. Jocelyn, "The Roman Nobility and the Religion of the Republican State," *JRH* 4 (1966/1967): 89-104; A. Wardman, *Religion and Statecraft among the Romans* (Baltimore: Johns Hopkins University Press, 1982) 42-52.

[112]Reitzenstein, *Hellenistic Mystery Reliqions*, 431-36; Wilckens, *Weisheit und Torheit*, 53-60; P. J. du Plessis, *TELEIOS: The Idea of Perfection in the New Testament* (Kampen: Kok, 1959).

[113]G. Delling, τέλειος, *TDNT* 8:69-72.

[114]Plato *Leg* 643d; 730d; see LSJ s.v. τέλειος, for other instances; Delling, τέλειος, *TDNT* 8:68.

influential," "those in office."[115] Thus Lucian speaks of the leaders of the Christian church in Palestine as οἱ ἐν τέλει (*Peregr* 12). The same ambiguity attaches to the term Paul uses to characterize those from whom God has hidden his wisdom: οἱ ἄρχοντες (2:6,8). We need not deny that the word has mythical connotations in this context,[116] amid talk of μυστήριον and σοφία ἀποκεκρυμμένη (2:7), to recognize that Paul refers to political powers.[117] The term seems to lie in the background when Paul later taunts his opponents: "Without us you have become rulers! And would that you did reign, so that we might share the sovereignty with you!" (4:8). Finally, the apologetic principle that Paul lays down in respect to the "spiritual man" (that is, himself) in 2:15—namely, that he is to be "judged" (ἀνακρίνεται) by no one—anticipates the verb used in reference to the examination of Paul's apostolic credentials in ch. 4. Thus, it is likely that throughout 2:6-3:3 Paul is speaking to the leaders of the rival factions. Like their counterparts in the πόλις, they sought to gain control of the ἐκκλησία by advancing claims to higher religious knowledge.

The force of their claim was not lost on the apostle Paul, despite his principled contention that he knows nothing except "Jesus Christ and him crucified" (2:2). The fact that Cicero was a theoretical skeptic did not prevent him from claiming to know the will of Jupiter when he wanted to destroy a political rival (*In Catil* 3.19-20). Polybius and Plutarch may look at religion with greater detachment when they explain how it served to strengthen the Roman social order, but not with more comprehension.[118] Paul understood that if he was to regain his position as the

---

[115]E.g., Sophocles *Aj* 1352; Ph. 385; Herodotus 3.18; 9.106; Thucydides 3.36; 1.10; Josephus *BJ* 1.12.5 §243; *Ant* 14.12.2 §302; 20.6.1 §121. Cf. Lucian *Deor conc* 15; *Iup trag* 18.

[116]Theodore of Mopsuestia in K. Staab, *Pauluskommentare aus der griechischen Kirche aus Katenenhandschriften*, NTAbh 15 (Münster: Aschendorff, 1933) 174; Wilckens, *Weisheit und Torheit*, 61-63.

[117]So already J. Schniewind, "Die Archonten dieses Äons, 1 Kor. 2,6-8" in *Nachgelassene Reden und Aufsätze*, ed. E. Kähler (Berlin: Töpelmann, 1952) 104-109: A. Feuillet, *Le Christ Saqesse de Dieu d'apres les Epitres pauliniennes* (Paris: Gabalda, 1966) 25-36.

[118]Polybius 6.56; 16.12.9-10; Plutarch *Mor* 822b; as well as Diodorus 1.2.2; Cicero *Rep* 2.2.4; *Leg* 2.7.15-16; Pliny *N H* 2.26.

teacher and guide of the community, he must persuade the Corinthians that he possessed σοφία ἐν μυστηρίῳ (2:7). He could call for an end to faction and exhort his rivals to become his imitators (4:16) only if he could convince them that he had "the mind of Christ" (2:16).

V. PAUL AS BRINGER OF CONCORD IN 1 CORINTHIANS 4:1-21

Paul concludes his appeal for concord in 4:1-21 with a demand for recognition of his qualifications as a conciliator of the factions. What begins as a firm refusal of an attempt to examine (ἀνακρίνειν) his apostolic credentials (4:1-3) is subtly transformed into a powerful assertion of his immunity from prosecution (4:3-5). He then attempts to undermine the confidence of the Corinthians by reminding them of their spiritual dependence (4:7) and by contrasting their complacency with his own sufferings as an apostle (4:8-13).

The reluctance of scholars to consider the political dimension of Paul's thought has ensured that the relation of this passage to the rest of the epistle has remained obscure. Thus, one is generally content to refer to the chapter as a "demonstration," an "application,"[119] or a "consequence"[120] of the preceding argument. But 4:1-13 is not merely an appendix to Paul's advice on factions; as a defense of his conduct as peacemaker and apostle, it is an integral part. In the ancient world, parties engaged in strife regularly made use of the courts as a means of attacking their political opponents.[121] To comprehend the connection between litigation and party strife one only has to recall that in Greece and Rome trials were held before a large section of the assembly or in the open forum where crowds were free to come and listen. Publicity, the partisan character of the juries, and the latitude in pleading and the introduction of evidence made the courts an efficient medium of political attack. The condemnation of Pericles, for example, was the result of a well-timed indictment by his political rivals; his apology is preserved in Thucydides (2.60-64; 2.65.2). The account of the στάσις at Corcyra illustrates the

---

[119]Conzelmann, *1 Corinthians*, 82.

[120]Wilckens, *Weisheit und Torheit*, 10.

[121]See Calhoun, *Athenian Clubs*, 97-106; more recently, D. Cohen, *Law, Violence and Community in Classical Athens* (Cambridge: Cambridge University Press, 1995) 87-118.

way the courts were used in the initial stages of party strife: the leaders of the oligarchic faction brought Peithias, the head of the popular party, to trial; when he was acquitted, he in turn brought suit against the five wealthiest men of the oligarchs for plundering the sacred precinct of Zeus (Thucydides 3.7.4). Demosthenes claims that for a time he was himself put on trial every day on various charges preferred by members of the opposing faction (18.249). Cicero's speeches provide detailed evidence of the importance of the courts in his political career. Through mastery of judicial oratory, he was able to eliminate numerous political rivals.[122]

Paul's language in 4:1-5 leaves little doubt that his opponents sought to "examine" his credentials in quasi-judicial proceedings.[123] The apostle attempted to silence their criticism by demonstrating its irrelevence: "It does not matter to me in the least that I should be judged by you or by any human court" (4:3). The verb used repeatedly to characterize the action of his opponents, ἀνακρίνειν (4:3,4; 2:14,15), has a broad judicial usage: it means "to examine closely," "to interrogate."[124] Thus it denotes the examination of witnesses or of the parties to a dispute, so as to prepare a matter for trial.[125] Of particular importance in this context is the use of the term to designate the examination of magistrates and other political leaders to establish their qualifications (Demosthenes 57.66, 70). We must think of a kind of ecclesiastical court, where the legitimacy of Paul's apostleship is to be tested. His initial response is to use eschatology to make his position seem unassailable: "It is the Lord who judges me. So do not pass judgment before the time, until the Lord comes, who will bring to light the hidden things of darkness, and disclose the purposes of the heart. Then each will receive such praise from God as he deserves" (4:4b-5). But threats were of no avail, judging from the course of events reflected in 2 Corinthians. Only after the anguished apology of 2 Corinthians 10-13, more savage in its irony than 1 Corinthians 4, could the apostle reassert his authority over the community.

---

[122]See Taylor, *Party Politics*, 98-118.
[123]J. Weiss, *Der erste Korintherbrief,* ad. loc. on legal terminology in this passage.
[124]Thucydides 1.95; Plato *Symp* 201e; C. Michel, *Recueil d'inscriptions grecques* (Paris, 1900) 409.9; Luke 23:14; Acts 24:8.
[125]Andocides 1.101; Isaeus 5.32; Demosthenes 48.31; Aristotle *Ath Pol* 56.6; *Sylloge Inscriptionum Graecarum* 953.46; Josephus *Ant* 17.5.7 §131.

By the time Paul concludes his advice on factions, it is clear that his early and hyperbolic praise of the Corinthians as "in every way enriched . . . in all speech and in all knowledge" (1:5) was also meant ironically. For it is the seeming growth of the community, their sense of greatness, which the apostle regards as the *cause* of faction.[126] Paul derides, "Already you are filled! Already you are rich!" (4:8). We are no longer surprised to find that it is to such a cause that Thucydides attributes the Peloponnesian War: "The truest explanation," he concludes, "I believe to have been the growth of the Athenians to greatness, which brought fear to the Lacedaemonians and forced them to war" (1.23.6). This conviction is an interpretive tool which Thucydides employs repeatedly in seeking to understand the origin of στάσις in the cities: civil strife ensued in Epidamnus after it had "become great" (1.24.3-4); the Corcyreans raised a rebellion against their mother city, Corinth, "in the insolence of power and wealth" (ὕβρει δὲ καὶ ἐξουσίᾳ πλούτου, 1.38.6). The principle cause of strife among equals, Aristotle concludes, is the desire to become greater (*Pol.* 5.2.1-2 1302a22-32).[127]

It may be dissimulation when the apostle claims, "I am not writing this to make you ashamed" (4:14). But it is the ostensible purpose of his admonition that the Corinthians "may learn . . . not to go beyond what is written" (4:6a). The phrase has occasioned the greatest consternation: some wish to delete it as a gloss, others find it "unintelligible."[128] But such advice is commonly offered by theorists and politicians who seek to prevent faction. As a safeguard against στάσις, Aristotle recommends that the greatest "care be taken to prevent people from committing

---

[126]So O. Bauernfeind, "Wachsen in allen Stücken," *ZST* 14 (1937): 483.

[127]Aristotle provides a more detailed list of αἰτίαι from an unknown source in *Pol* 5.2.3 1302a35-1302b3: κέρδος, τιμή, ὕβρις, φόβος, ὑπερο‑ χή, καταφρόνησις, αὔξησις παρὰ τὸ ἀνάλογον. Paul mentions several by name in 1 Corinthians.

[128]In addition to the commentaries, see O. Linton, "'Nicht über das hinaus was geschrieben steht' (1 Kor 4,6)," *TSK* 102 (1930): 425-37; P. Wallis, "Ein neuer Auslegungsversuch der Stelle 1. Kor. 4,6," *TLZ* 75 (1950) 506-508; M. D. Hooker, "Beyond the Things Which are Written: An Examination of 1 Cor IV.6," *NTS* 10 (1964): 127-32. Schmithals thinks that the phrase should be deleted as a gloss (*Gnosticism In Corinth*, 122n.11) and Conzelmann finds it "unintelligible" (*1 Corinthians*, 86).

any breach of the law . . . for transgression of the law (παρανομία) creeps in unawares" (*Pol* 5.7.1 1307b32-33). Plato's *Seventh Epistle* purports to be a message of "counsel" to Dion's friends who are beset by στάσις. The literary fiction of a συμβουλευτικὸς λόγος is carried through up to a point: Plato warns the ἑταῖροι that the evils of faction will not cease until they enact "common laws" by which all can abide (*Ep* 7. 336d-337b). In the speech entitled περὶ πολιτείας, sometimes attributed to Herodes Atticus, the citizens are urged to put an end to factional strife by living "in accordance with the law" (κατὰ νόμον) instead of destroying one another "lawlessly" (παρανόμως, 17-18, 29).[129] It may be objected that Paul does not speak of "the law" but of "what is written" (ἃ γέγραπται). But precisely this language is found in inscriptions that record the willingness of parties to a dispute to live within the terms of an agreement. Thus, *OGIS* 229 records the reconciliation between Magnesia and Smyrna after a period of hostility; the inhabitants of both cities are to swear the following oath:

> I will not transgress the agreement nor will I change for the worse the things which are written in it . . . and I will live in concord and without faction (καὶ οὐθὲν παραβήσομαι κατὰ τὴν ὁμολογίαν οὐδὲ μεταθήσω ἐπὶ τὸ χεῖρον τὰ γεγραμμένα ἐν αὐτῇ . . . καὶ πολιτεύσομαι μεθ᾽ ὁμονοίας ἀστασιάτως).[130]

Paul clarifies his own expression in a second ἵνα-clause: what he means is that they "should not be puffed up (φυσιοῦσθε) on behalf of one against another" (4:6b). The two motifs are sometimes combined in portraits of factious behavior: thus Philo describes the disastrous overreaching of Macro, who, disregarding the Delphic γράμμα, γνῶθι σαυτόν, "became puffed up beyond measure" (πλέον ἐφυσήθη τοῦ μετρίου) and sought to transcend his proper place as the emperor's subject (*Leg ad Gaium* 69).[131]

We may conclude. It is Paul's intention in 1 Corinthians 1-4 not merely to put an end to dissension but to transform the Corinthians'

---

[129][Erode Attico] *Peri Politeias*, ed. U. Albini (Florence: Monnier, 1968).
[130]*Orientis Graeci Inscriptiones Selectae*, ed. W. Dittenberger (Leipzig: Hirzel, 1903–1905).
[131]See also Demosthenes 59.97; Thucydides 1.132.1-3.

understanding of the conflict. In Paul's view, the strife of the factions is no petty quarrel, no *Cliquenstreit*, but a mirror of the cosmic conflict between the rulers of this age and the power of God. The theological interpretation that the apostle gives to the struggle is obviously designed to turn the Corinthian Christians away from politics. The fate of the community does not rest upon the precepts of statecraft, but upon the word of the cross. Thus, its members need not look to political leaders, but can await redemption from God.

Whether Paul succeeded in dissolving the immediate instance of faction is not apparent; surely the parties of 1 Corinthians 1-4 are somehow involved in the earnest opposition to Paul evidenced by 2 Corinthians. What is certain is that his attempt to avoid any complicity in the affairs of this world, to separate religion as far as possible from practical politics, proved to be of historic significance. Its repercussion can be heard in Augustine's negative valuation of the *civitas terrena* and in the political naturalism of Machiavelli and Rousseau. With Paul, the goddess *Dike*, who had struggled so long to free herself from the snares in which the sophists and politicians had entrapped her, soars aloft to a place no eye has seen, leaving the apostle as her only mediator. The unwelcome drives that found expression in the strife of the parties could not be abolished, so they were transfigured.

Fortunately, even this eschatological gesture does not mask entirely the reality of political conflict. Our investigation has discovered at many points correspondence between the situation of the church at Corinth and what historians, philosophers, and rhetoricians call στάσις. We can still recognize the phenomenon, though the apostle withholds the name. That the name could not be uttered is owing less to the possibility that some unwelcome eye might conceive something really seditious about Christianity than to the reluctance to acknowledge that within the movement which claimed to have accomplished the renunciation of enmity in word and deed there might still linger the antithetical instinct.

The image that emerges from this reading of 1 Corinthians 1-4 has the advantage of agreeing with the picture that a near contemporary, the author of 1 Clement, developed of these events. Whatever issues complicated the controversy, the problem that occasioned "the epistle of the blessed Paul" was essentially one of "partisanship," πρόσκλισις (47:1-4). The conflict differed from "the abominable and unholy στάσις (1:1) in the church of Clement's day only in that the Corinthians acquired less guilt by having made themselves "partisans of renowned apostles" (47:4). Alluding repeatedly to 1 Corinthians, the author writes: "Your σχίσμα has turned many aside, has cast many into despondency, many into despair, all of us into grief. And your στάσις continues!" (46:9). Corinth had a history of faction: from the bloody revolution of Cypselus (Herodotus 5.92) to their role in initiating the Peloponnesian War,[132] to the contemptuous act that sparked the revolt of the Achaean League (Strabo *Geogr* 8.6.23).[133] Politics remained a concern of the Corinthians under the empire, though the game was played for lesser stakes. The names of her ambitious citizens, their rivalries, and election promises are known to us from inscriptions recording their donations.[134] We deceive ourselves if we imagine that the Corinthian Christians were innocent of all this. It is more than probable that the Erastus who laid the limestone pavement adjacent to the theater *pro aedilitate sua pecunia*[135] is none other than the Corinthian οἰκονόμος mentioned by Paul in Rom. 16:23 and, thus, a Christian.[136]

It is useless to object that as a religious institution the Christian church enjoyed an immunity from internal struggles. The ἡγούμενος of the gild of Zeus Hypsistos also found it necessary to include in the rules of the organization an injunction which forbade action that would create σχίσματα: "No one is permitted to make himself the leader of a party, or cause divisions (σχίσματα συνίστασθαι), or to depart from the fraternity of the leader to another fraternity."[137] Like Paul's

---

[132]See H. M. Tierney, "Corinthian Power Politics" (diss., University of Chicago, 1968).

[133]According to Strabo, when a Roman delegation came to Corinth to announce that the League should be dissolved, the Corinthians rained filth on the ambassadors as they passed through the streets. See J. Wiseman, "Corinth and Rome I: 228 B.C.–A.D. 267" in *ANRW* 7.1, ed. H. Temporini (Berlin: de Gruyter, 1979) 459-61.

[134]Kent, *Corinth*, 22-26, 119-21.

[135]Kent, *Corinth*, 27, 99-100.

[136]See the discussion in H. J. Cadbury, "Erastus of Corinth," *JBL* 50 (1931): 42-58. On the title οἰκονόμος, see P. Landvogt, "Epigraphische Untersuchungen über den οἰκονόμος. Ein Beitrag zum hellenistischen Beamtenwesen" (diss. Strasbourg, 1908).

[137]*PLond* 2710.13 = F. Preisigke, *Sammelbuch griechischer Urkunden aus*

advice in 1 Corinthians 1-4, this statement illustrates what must have been one of the most important functions of such associations under the empire: they provided scope for the exercise of the political instinct at a time when, as Plutarch reports, "the affairs of the cities no longer include leadership in wars, or the overthrow of tyrannies, or the conclusion of alliances," or any of the other deeds appropriate to a public career (*Mor* 805a). In the church, Greek converts may have hoped to experience some of the δύναμις and ἐλευθερία of which they heard the apostle speak.

The author of 1 Corinthians 1-4 had higher aims. His life was devoted to the great politics: the proclamation of the word of the cross. Dissension and party spirit belonged to the life he had left behind (Gal. 5:20). Then came the discord at Corinth. 1 Corinthians 1-4 embodies the shock with which Paul discovered that in the supposedly peaceful assemblies of the Christians there had appeared "billowing forms and patterns like waves of the sea."[138] The apostle struggled against this moving chaos, like the steersman in Alcaeus's poem, caught in the storm and "bewildered by the στάσις of the winds."[139]

---

gypten (Wiesbaden: Harrassowitz, 1950) 5.7835.13. The translation follows the reading συνταγματαρχήσειν suggested by Dihle in *TDNT* 7:963n.2, rather than συντευματαρχήσειν proposed by C. H. Roberts, T. C. Skeat, and A. D. Nock, "The Guild of Zeus Hypsistos," *HTR* 29 (1936): 39.

[138]From Posidonius's description of the party strife caused by the Gracchi in F. Jacoby, *Die Fragmente der griechischen Historiker* 2 A (Leiden: Brill, 1957) 295.

[139]Alcaeus in D. L. Page, *Lyrica Graeca Selecta* (Oxford: Oxford University Press, 1968) 123-24.

A CONCILIATORY PRINCIPLE
IN 1 CORINTHIANS 4:6

I. AN EXEGETICAL CRUX

How many scholars have suspected that the words τὸ μὴ ὑπὲρ ἃ γέγραπται in 1 Cor 4:6 were what the author of 2 Peter had in mind when he warned his readers about δυσνόητά τινα in Paul's epistles? A number of otherwise stalwart interpreters have returned from the fray convinced that the text is hopelessly corrupt and resigned to their lack of understanding.[1] Other, more ingenious, critics have suggested that the phrase was originally a marginal gloss and have argued for conjectural emendation.[2] The majority persist in seeing the words as a reference to

---

[1]C. Holsten, *Das Evangelium des Paulus*. Vol. 1. *Der Brief an die Gemein-den Galatiens und der erste Brief an die Gemeinde in Korinth* (Berlin: Reimer, 1880) ad loc; Johannes Weiss, *Der erste Korintherbrief*, KEK 5 (Göttingen: Van-denhoeck & Ruprecht, 1910) 103; O. Linton, "'Nicht über das hinaus, was ge-schrieben ist' (1 Kor. 4,6)," *ThStKr* 102 (1930): 425-37; James Moffat, *The First Epistle of Paul to the Corinthians* (London: Hodder and Stoughton, 1938) ad loc.

[2]J. M. S. Baljon, *De Tekst der Brieven van Paulus aan de Romeinen, de Corinthiërs en de Galatiërs als voorwerp van de conjecturalkritiek beschouwd* (Utrecht: J. van Boekhoven, 1884) 49-51; Paul Schmiedel, *Die Briefe an die Thessalonicher und an die Korinther*, HCNT 2,1 (Tübingen: Mohr-Siebeck, [2]1892) 112-13; Carl Clemen, *Die Einheitlichkeit der paulinischen Briefe, an Hand der bisher mit bezug auf sie aufgestellten Interpolations und Compilations-hypothesen geprüft* (Göttingen: Vandenhoeck & Ruprecht, 1894); Wilhelm Bousset, *Der erste Brief an die Korinther. Die Schriften des Neuen Testaments*, ed. W. Bousset and W. Heitmüller, vol. 2 (Göttingen: Vandenhoeck & Ruprecht, [3]1917); W. F. Howard, *ExpT* 33 (1922): 479-80; Jean Héring, *La première épître de Saint Paul aux Corinthiens*, CNT 7 (Neuchâtel: Delachaux et Niestlé, [2]1959); Walter Schmithals, *Die Gnosis in Korinth*, FRLANT 66 (Göttingen: Vanden-hoeck & Ruprecht, [3]1969) 115n.1; John Strugnell, "A Plea for Conjectural Emendation in the New Testament, with a Coda on 1 Cor 4:6," *CBQ* 36 (1974): 543-58; cf. G. D. Kilpatrick, "Conjectural Emendation in the New Testament" in *New Testament Textual Criticism. Essays in Honor of Bruce M. Metzger* (Oxford: Clarendon, 1981) 349-60, esp. 351-52.

the Old Testament Scriptures,[3] though the point of such a reference is unclear. The author of the most recent critical commentary simply refuses the struggle, conceding at the outset that, "the phrase τὸ μὴ ὑπὲρ ἃ γέγραπται is unintelligible."[4] At least it is not impossible to state the causes of our difficulty. The elliptical form of the sentence is often felt to be the principal obstacle.[5] Part of the manuscript tradition, 01ᶜ C Dᶜ E² L P vg sy and the Byzantine text, undertakes to supply what is lacking, adding φρονεῖν at the end of the phrase.[6] But it is not only the absence of a verb which creates problems; the τό makes it clear that the following words are a kind of slogan.[7] Thus F and G omit the article, seeking to overcome the ellipsis by lessening its formulaic quality.

A second source of confusion is the relationship of the words τὸ μὴ ὑπὲρ ἃ γέγραπται to the clause that follows, ἵνα μὴ εἷς ὑπὲρ τοῦ ἑνὸς φυσιοῦσθε κατὰ τοῦ ἑτέρου. It seems impos-

---

[3]The list would almost coincide with the scholars who have written on 1 Corinthians; to mention only a few: H. A. W. Meyer, *Der erste Brief an die Korinther*, KEK 1 (Göttingen: Vandenhoeck & Ruprecht, 1839); J. G. Reiche, *Commentarius criticus in N.T.* (Göttingen: Vandenhoeck & Ruprecht, 1853); G. H. Ewald, *Die Sendschreiben des Apostels Paulus übersetzt und erklärt* (Göttingen: Dieterich, 1857); C. Holsten, *Das Evangelium des Paulus*; C. F. Georg Heinrici, *Der erste Brief an die Korinther*, KEK 5 (Göttingen: Vandenhoeck & Ruprecht, 1896) 148-49; Hans Lietzmann, *An die Korinther*, rev. W. G. Kümmel, HNT 9 (Tübingen: Mohr-Siebeck, 1949) ad loc; Lyder Brun, "Noch einmal die Schriftnorm I Kor. 4:6," *ThStKr* 103 (1931): 453-56; Morna D. Hooker, "'Beyond the Things Which are Written': An Examination of 1 Cor IV.6," *NTS* 10 (1963–1964): 127-32; C. K. Barrett, *The First Epistle to the Corinthians*, HNTC (New York: Harper & Row, 1968) ad loc; Hans Conzelmann, *1 Corinthians. A Commentary on the First Epistle to the Corinthians*, Hermeneia (Philadelphia: Fortress, 1975) 86.

[4]Conzelmann, *1 Corinthians*, 86.

[5]See the discussion in Heinrici, *Der erste Brief an die Korinther*, 147; Weiss, *Der erste Korintherbrief*, 102-103.

[6]*Novum Testamentum Graece*, ed. Constantinus Tischendorf, vol. 2 (Lipsiae: Giesecke & Devrient, 1872) 475, with the full list of witnesses.

[7]See Heinrici, *Der erste Brief an die Korinther*, 147; for Paul's use of τό to introduce quotations, see Gal. 5:14; 6:9; Rom. 13:9; C. F. D. Moule, *An Idiom Book of New Testament Greek* (Cambridge: Cambridge University, 1959) 110-11.

sible to construe the latter as a final (purpose) clause dependent upon τὸ μὴ ὑπὲρ κτλ.[8] Thus most scholars have chosen to take τὸ μὴ ὑπὲρ κτλ. and ἵνα μὴ εἰς κτλ. as the double object of μάθητε, so that the ἵνα-clause is understood to state the content of γέγραπται: what the Scripture demands is that you not be puffed up, each one on behalf of one against another.[9] Such an interpretation may lie behind the change of φυσιοῦσθε to φυσιοῦσθαι in codex Sinaiticus,[10] a change which Fritzsche makes grammatically consistent by striking εἰς and replacing ἵνα with ἕνα.[11] A similar construction is found in the Latin versions, which refuse to translate ἵνα μή: *ut in nobis (vobis) discatis ne supra quam scriptum est unus adversus alterum infletur pro alio.*[12] It is not difficult to understand why so much energy has been expended on the analysis of these clauses, for the latter (ἵνα μὴ εἰς κτλ.) is not only clear, but also consistent with Paul's purpose throughout 1 Cor 1–4 in giving counsel against faction. But even when the phrases are correctly construed, the stumbling block remains: the opacity of the words τὸ μὴ ὑπὲρ ἃ γέγραπται.

Interpreters have traditionally sought to penetrate this enigmatic phrase by identifying the referent of ἃ γέγραπται. Chrysostom[13] sug-

---

[8]Though Hooker attempts to do so in "'Beyond the Things Which are Written': An Examination of 1 Cor IV.6," *NTS* 10 (1963–1964): 128; see the discussion of syntax in Heinrici, *Der erste Brief an die Korinther*, 149-50, and Weiss, *Der erste Korintherbrief*, 103-104.

[9]So, e.g., Schmiedel, *Die Briefe an die Thessalonicher und an die Korinther*, ad loc; Philipp Bachmann, *Der erste Brief des Paulus an die Korinther*, KNT 7 (Leipzig: Deichert, 1936) ad loc; Lietzmann, *An die Korinther*, ad loc; E.-B. Allo, *Première épître aux Corinthiens*, EB (Paris: Gabalda, 1934) ad loc.

[10]*Novum Testamentum Graece*, ed. Tischendorf, 2,475; Weiss, *Der erste Korintherbrief*, 103.

[11]Karl Friedrich August Fritzsche, *De nonnullis posterioris Pauli ad Corinthios epistolae locis dissertationes duae* (Leipzig: Reclam, 1824) ad loc.

[12]*Novum Testamentum Graece*, ed. Tischendorf, 2,476, with citations from Aug. and Ambrst. Straatman's suggestion (*Kritische studiën over den 1en brief van Paulus aan de Korinthiërs*, vol. 2 [Leiden, 1865] 50-51) follows the tendency of the Latin versions.

[13]Johannes Chrysostomus, *Homiliae in Epistulam I ad Corinthios* in J. P. Migne, *Patrologia Graece*, vol. 61 (Paris, 1859) ad loc; the same interpretation

gested that the words allude to a saying of the Lord, such as Mk 10:44 or Matt. 7:1, something that, we may be sure, never occurred to Paul or his readers. Following Erasmus, Luther and other interpreters[14] have held that ἃ (ὃ) γέγραπται refers to that which Paul himself had written in the preceding chapters, where the principles of Christian conduct are laid down. But as Heinrici observed,[15] Paul would surely have written ἃ (πρὸ) ἔγραψα had he intended to call attention to his own teaching.

The majority of interpreters have always held that what Paul intended by ἃ γέγραπται was the Old Testament Scriptures. This conception is already embodied in the change from ἃ to ὃ in a broad stream of the manuscript tradition (D F G L, the majority of minuscules, syr arm go Chrys.).[16] The copyists evidently believed that Paul was thinking of a particular scripture, beyond which one should not go. The Latin versions (d e vg) reflect the same view when they translate *supra quam*.[17] The assumption that underlies this interpretation was clearly articulated by Hugo Grotius: "γέγραπται *in his libris semper ad libros V. T. refertur*."[18] But the passage that Grotius adduces already illustrates the difficulty of taking Paul's words as a reference to Scripture; for while Deut 17:20 may epitomize Paul's advice to the Corinthians, which of his readers could have guessed that it was this verse that he intended? Consequently, scholars have turned to the immediate context, to the passages cited in the course of Paul's argument.[19] But the quotations from Isaiah

---

is found in Theodoret, *Interpretatio Epistulae Primae ad Corinthios* in J. P. Migne, *Patrologia Graece*, vol. 82 (Paris, 1859) ad loc.

[14]See Georg Heinrici, *Der erste Brief an die Korinther*, 148.

[15]Heinrici, *Der erste Brief an die Korinther*; F. Godet (*Commentaire sur la première épître aux Corinthiens*, vol. 1 [Neuchatêl: Delachaux et Niestlé, 1886] ad loc) suggests ὃ προεγράφη.

[16]*Novum Testamentum Graece*, ed. Tischendorf, 2:475; Weiss, *Der erste Korintherbrief*, 102.

[17]*Novum Testamentum Graece*, ed. Tischendorf, 2:476.

[18]Hugo Grotius, *Annotationes in Novum Testamentum*, vol. 2 (Parisiis: Sumtibus autoris, 1646) ad loc.

[19]Morna D. Hooker, "'Beyond the Things Which are Written': An Examination of I Cor IV.6," *NTS* 10 (1963/1964): 127-32, anticipated by J. B. Lightfoot, *Notes on the Epistles of St. Paul from Unpublished Commentaries* (London: Macmillan, 1895) 199.

(29:14 in 1:19), Job (5:13 in 3:19), and the Psalms (94:11 in 3:20) describe the divine reversal of worldly wisdom, not a general rule of human conduct. No amount of exegetical artistry[20] is capable of making these verses what the context requires: a commandment enjoining humility and concord. Only Jer 9:23, ὁ καυχώμενος ἐν κυρίῳ καυχάσθω, cited by Paul in 1:31, would seem apposite to Paul's warning against factions. But Schmiedel, who holds that it is to 1:31 that Paul is recurring, acknowledges that a reference to such a remote citation in such general terms as Paul employs in 4:6 would be *unvorsichtig* and *ungenau*.[21]

If it has proven impossible for scholars to discover a particular scripture behind Paul's admonition, one might still interpret ἃ γέγραπται as an allusion to an ethical norm taught in the Scripture, such as humility or brotherly love. This explanation is favored by those commentators for whom the general sense is always plain, though the concrete expression is not.[22] It might have more to recommend it were

---

[20]Hooker (*NTS* 10 [1963/1964]: 127-32) simply assumes that Paul refers to Scripture, then goes on to seek the passages to which he refers. But the scriptures Paul cites in 1 Cor 1-3 require interpretation before they will fit the context of 4:6. Thus she construes the citations in 3:19-20 about the foolishness of human wisdom in God's eyes as references to the false teaching of some in Corinth which has resulted in rivalry. Then the citations in chs 1-2 are said to demonstrate that Paul's preaching of the "word of the cross" is the fulfillment of scripture (129-30). W. Wuellner ("Haggadic Homily Genre in 1 Corinthians 1-3," *JBL* 89 [1970]: 199-204, and E. Earle Ellis ("Exegetical Patterns in 1 Corinthians and Romans" in *Prophecy and Hermeneutic in Early Christianity* [Tübingen: Mohr-Siebeck, 1978] 214-20) have discovered pre-Pauline midrashim in 1 Cor 1:18-31 and 2:6-16; but it remains unclear how Paul's exhortation not to go beyond what is written relates to these expositions on human and divine wisdom.

[21]Schmiedel, *Die Briefe an die Korinther*, 112. To be sure, 3:21 points back to 1:31; but the phrase ἃ γέγραπται is not Paul's usual way of referring to Scripture. If Paul intended a reference to Jer 9:23 in 1 Cor 4:6, why did he not simply quote the scripture, as he cites Lev. 19:18 in Gal 5:14 and Deut 5:17-21 in Rom 13:9?

[22]E.g., Meyer, *Der erste Brief an die Korinther*, ad loc.; F. W. Grosheide, *The First Epistle to the Corinthians*, NIC (Grand Rapids: Eerdmans, 1953) 104; Conzelmann, *1 Corinthians*, 86; W. F. Orr and J. A. Walther, *I Corinthians*, AB 32 (Garden City NY: Doubleday, 1976) 178, 181; William Baird, *1 Corinthians* (Atlanta: John Knox, 1980) 20.

the scriptural citations in 1 Cor 1–4 concerned with humility, or a like virtue; but, as we have seen, the passages are chosen to support Paul's claim that "wisdom of this world is folly with God" (3:19).

If one is bound to think of ἃ γέγραπται as the Old Testament Scriptures, only one course remains: the words must be interpreted as an allusion to the Scripture as such, as the revealed limit of human knowledge. This view is essentially the interpretation of Origen in the Catenae,[23] and it has never lacked for supporters. Thus Holsten explains:

> Hier, wo es sich um den Gegensatz menschlicher und göttlicher Weisheit handelt, kann die Schrift auch nur als die Schranke gedacht sein, innerhalb welcher jede menschliche Erkenntnis und Weisheit sich zu bewegen hat . . . Lernt die Gemeinde . . . die Schranke der Gottes-Offenbarung in der Schrift innehalten, so wird dadurch . . . auch weiter abgewehrt, . . . dass nicht Einer zu Gunsten des Andern sich aufblähe.[24]

It is this understanding that the RSV reflects in its paraphrase: "that you may learn by us to live according to Scripture."[25] It underlies Heinrici's suggestion[26] that Paul's formula bears comparison with the expression καθὼς εἶπεν ἡ γραφή in John 7:38 and Conzelmann's assertion[27] that Paul's words amount, more or less, to the principle, μήτε προσ- θεῖναι μήτε ἀφελεῖν (Rev 22:19).

---

[23]Origen in *Catenae graecorum patrum*, vol. 5, J. A. Cramer (Oxford, 1844) 77, 11. 21-25: ἐάν τις ἕξιν ἔχων ὑποδεεστέραν πρὶν πληρῶσαι τὰ γεγραμμένα θέλῃ ἀναβῆναι εἰς τὰ ὑπὲρ ἃ γέγραπται, οὐδὲ νοήσει ἃ γέγραπται· ὥσπερ γὰρ κλίμακα οὐχ οἱόντε ἐστιν ἀνα- βῆναί τινα, μὴ ὁδῷ ἀναβαίνοντα ἀπὸ τῶν κατωτέρω κατὰ τὸ δυνατόν, τὸν αὐτὸν τρόπον ἐπὶ τῶν μαθημάτων τῶν θείων.

[24]Holsten, *Das Evangelium des Paulus*, 1:205.

[25]Similarly, the translations of Lietzmann, *An die Korinther, ad loc*; Grosheide, *Commentary on the First Epistle to the Corinthians, ad loc*; H. D. Wendland, *Die Briefe an die Korinther*, NTD 7 (Göttingen: Vandenhoeck & Ruprecht, 1968) ad loc.

[26]Heinrici, *Der erste Brief an die Korinther*, 148.

[27]Conzelmann, *1 Corinthians*, 86; see also W. C. van Unnik, "De la règle Μήτε προσθεῖναι μήτε ἀφελεῖν dans l'histoire du canon," *VigChr* 3 (1949): 1-36, also in W. C. van Unnik, *Sparsa collecta II*, NovTS 30 (Leiden: Brill, 1980) 123-56.

Proponents of this interpretation must of course acknowledge that Paul does not speak of the Scripture in this manner elsewhere in his epistles, but of ἡ γραφή,[28] or τὸ γράμμα.[29] But let us grant the exception: Paul intended to refer to the Scripture, as the limit of human wisdom. Yet nowhere in 1 Cor 1–4 does Paul seek to show that he and Apollos have lived according to the Scripture.[30] But that is precisely what the Corinthians are to "learn from us," if ἃ γέγραπται refers to the Scriptures! The real problem with every attempt to take ἃ γέγραπται as an allusion to the Scripture is not the impossibility of discovering the passage intended, nor the implausibility of the expression on the lips of Paul, but the fact that such a reference is irrelevant to Paul's argument.[31] Paul's concern throughout 1 Cor 1–4 is to dissuade from faction and to promote concord; thus Paul offers himself and Apollos as examples of harmonious conduct (3:5ff.) and urges the Corinthians "not to be puffed up, each one on behalf of one against another" (4:6b). What would be the point, in this context, of an exhortation to live according to Scripture?

One of the most significant aspects of the phrase, moreover, is almost completely ignored by those who seek to explain Paul's words as an appeal to Scripture, or as a reminder of his own teaching: the proverbial quality. The introductory τό and the elliptical style strongly suggest that Paul is quoting a saying that was known to his readers.[32] Ironically, the very elements that mark it as a commonplace make it difficult for subsequent generations to comprehend. Thus two uncial manuscripts omit the

---

[28]Gal 3:8; 3:22; 4:40; 1 Cor 15:3-4; Rom 1:2; 4:3; 9:17; 10:11; 11:2; 15:4; 16:26.

[29]2 Cor 3:6,7; Rom 2:27; 7:6. The closest approximation would be Rom 15:4, ὅσα γὰρ προεγράφη, εἰς τὴν ἡμετέραν διδασκαλίαν ἐγράφη, ἵνα διὰ τῆς ὑπομονῆς καὶ τῆς παρακλήσεως τῶν γραφῶν τὴν ἐλπίδα ἔχωμεν. But one cannot fail to notice the contrast in explicitness.

[30]So already Weiss, Der erste Korintherbrief, 103.

[31]A point rightly made by John Strugnell, "A Plea for Conjectural Emendation in the New Testament, with a Coda on 1 Cor 4:6," CBQ 36 (1974): 555.

[32]So already Weiss, Der erste Korintherbrief, 102: "Den gewöhnlichen Text aber kann man kaum anders verstehen als so, dass τὸ μὴ ὑπὲρ ἃ γέγραπται eine Art parole ist." Westcott-Hort prints τὸ Μὴ ὑπὲρ . . . , as do other editions, among them The Greek New Testament, 1966, ²1968, ³1975.

article, as we have noted, and few versions attempt to reflect it in translation.[33] Yet it is an important clue to the meaning of Paul's utterance.[34]

All that is needed, it would seem, is to locate the saying Paul has quoted. Ewald proposes an old Rabbinic maxim,[35] though Paul is not otherwise known to have adduced such authorities. Lightfoot mentions Terence, *Andr* 1.1.61: *id arbitror Adprime in vita esse utile ut ne quid nimis.*[36] Wallis arranges for Paul to express the same sentiment by repunctuating the sentence, separating τὸ μὴ ὑπέρ from ἃ γέγραπται. The former is taken to be a maxim equivalent to τὸ μηδὲν ἄγαν, while ἃ γέγραπται is rendered "ihr habt es hiermit schwarz auf weiss."[37] But the resulting proverb is too universal for the context, and the construction of ἃ γέγραπται is rather unlikely. The alternative is to suppose that the words are a slogan which originated in the church at Corinth. Thus Lütgert sees in the phrase Paul's counter to the claim of the gnostics, that they have received a revelation that goes "beyond the things which are written."[38] Morna Hooker suggests that "the saying is one which Paul himself coined and had already used in opposition to those who elaborated his teaching."[39] Any one of these hypotheses are,

---

[33]An exception is the NEB—"that you may learn to 'keep within the rules' as they say." C. K. Barrett (*A Commentary on the First Epistle to the Corinthians*, 104) and Conzelmann (*1 Corinthians*, 85) rightly print the words in quotation marks.

[34]Its importance was grasped by Heinrici (*Der erste Brief an die Korinther*, 147-48) and was fully appreciated by P. Wallis ("Ein neuer Auslegungsversuch der Stelle I Kor 4,6," *ThLZ* 75 (1950): 506-508).

[35]Ewald, *Die Sendschreiben des Apostels Paulus*, ad loc; followed by Godet, *Commentaire sur la première épître aux Corinthiens*, ad loc; Archibald Robertson and Alfred Plummer, *A Critical and Exegetical Commentary on the First Epistle of St. Paul to the Corinthians*, ICC (Edinburgh: T.&T. Clark, ²1914) ad loc.

[36]Lightfoot, *Notes on the Epistles of St. Paul*, 199.

[37]P. Wallis, "Ein neuer Auslegungsversuch der Stelle I. Kor. 4,6," *ThLZ* 75 (1950): 506-508.

[38]Wilhelm Lütgert, *Freiheitspredigt und Schwarmgeister in Korinth* (Gütersloh: Bertelsmann, 1908); Lietzmann (*An die Korinther*, ad loc) also postulates a Corinthian slogan, as does F. F. Bruce, *I and II Corinthians*, NCBC (Grand Rapids: Eerdmans, 1971) 48-49.

[39]Hooker, *NTS* 10 (1963/1964): 132.

of course, entirely possible; the problem is that, if the words contain an underlying allusion to a Corinthian slogan, their meaning is unlikely to be accessible to us.[40] The most plausible explanation of how the slogan might have originated in the Corinthian church remains that of Heinrici:

> so enthalten die wie in Anführungsstrichen angeführten Worte wahrschein-lich eine Reproduction des Schlagworts, mit dem die Verkündigung des Apostels und der ihm Gleichgesinnten missgünstig beleuchtet wurde.[41]

But it is hardly imaginable that Paul's Corinthian opponents would have dared to ridicule in this manner one so well-versed in Scripture.[42] Even had they sensed the sovereign freedom from the letter and the ironic attitude toward Moses which finally becomes apparent in 2 Cor 3, it is unlikely that they would have represented his teaching as lying "beyond what is written," still less likely that Paul would have used their mali-cious slogan to instruct the Corinthians.[43] We may conclude that the words μὴ ὑπὲρ ἃ γέγραπται are a saying or a proverb which Paul had reason to believe would be known to the Corinthians, whether from the surrounding culture or from their particular milieu. That the source of the slogan has not been located is owing to the casual and speculative manner in which scholars have gone about the search, taking no account of the rhetorical form or context of Paul's remarks.

Out of the failure of previous attempts to comprehend the received text has arisen the call for conjectural emendation, feeding upon these barren interpretations the way a fire devours dry logs. In 1884 Johannes Baljon suggested that τὸ μὴ ὑπὲρ ἃ γέγραπται should be re-moved from the text as a gloss by an early scribe, originally noted in the

---

[40]As Lietzmann has seen clearly, *An die Korinther*, ad loc.

[41]Heinrici, *Der erste Brief an die Korinther*, 148.

[42]Thus already Weiss, *Der erste Korintherbrief*, 102-103.

[43]Heinrici apparently felt the weakness of his own explanation, and so ventured a second proposal in a footnote: the words refer to a community rule, the rule of brotherly love, *Der erste Brief an die Korinther*, 149n.: "Lässt man bei ἃ γέγραπται die Beziehung auf das AT fallen, so liegt es nicht fern ab, an das Gemeindestatut der Christenbruderschaft zu denken, das als Hauptsatz die Gleichheit vor Gott und die Pflicht der Bruderliebe enthalten haben müss." But there is no evidence in Paul's epistles of the existence of such a rule; indeed, the problems addressed in 1 Cor speak against it.

margin.[44] What the copyist found in his archetype were the words ἵνα ἐν ἡμῖν μάθητε ἵνα εἶς ὑπὲρ τοῦ ἑνός κτλ.; but over the α of the second ἵνα was written the word μή. What was the scribe to do? He was reluctant simply to add the μή to his copy of the text, so he placed in the margin the observation τὸ μὴ ὑπὲρ ἃ γέγραπται, that is, "the μή was written above alpha." Later, when the manuscript was copied again, this note found its way into the text. This hypothesis is by no means the only conjecture that has been offered;[45] but it has attracted the greatest number of supporters, and has recently been improved by Strugnell,[46] so that it may be considered in place of the others. It is no argument against Baljon's hypothesis that it is ingenious, even humorous; there are, however, more substantial grounds for objection. As Strugnell notices, the gloss is rather implausible in content; observations of this sort are not found in Greek manuscripts of the period.[47] Moreover, had a scribe intended to make such a comment, he would probably have written τὸ μὴ ὑπὲρ τὸ α γέγραπται, as J. M. Ross suggests.[48] But Strugnell seeks to overcome these difficulties by reinterpreting the gloss:

---

[44]J. M. S. Baljon, *De Tekst der Brieven van Paulus aan de Romienen, de Corinthiërs en de Galatiërs als voorwerp van de conjecturaalkritiek beschouwd* (Utrecht: J. van Boekhoven, 1884) 49-51; see also *Novum Testamentum Graece*, ed. J. M. S. Baljon (Groningen: Wolters, 1898) ad loc. Baljon was preceded in this suggestion by Bornemann, as he himself indicated.

[45]For other conjectures (e.g., Fritzsche, Straatman), see Schmiedel, *Die Briefe an die Korinther, ad loc.* and C. Clemen, *Die Einheitlichkeit der paulinischen Briefe*, ad loc. For an earlier collection of conjectures, see W. Bowyer, *Critical Conjectures and Observations on the New Testament* (London, 1772, ²1782, ³1812) and the German edition of this work (Leipzig, 1774–1775).

[46]John Strugnell, "A Plea for Conjectural Emendation in the New Testament, with a Coda on 1 Cor 4:6," *CBQ* 36 (1974): 555-58; in addition to the works cited above in n.2, see Walter Schmithals, *Die Gnosis in Korinth*, FRLANT 66 (Göttingen: Vandenhoeck & Ruprecht, ³1969) 115, and A. Legault, *NTS* 18 (1971/1972): 227-31. It is simply false to claim, as Strugnell does (556n.32), that Weiss and Heinrici were "tempted" by Baljon's suggestion. Heinrici characterized it as "(ein) Beispiel findiger Selbstgenügsamkeit," *Der erste Brief an die Korinther*, 149n. Weiss concluded that "solche Versuche werden von der Kritik niemals ernst genommen werden," *Der erste Korintherbrief*, 104.

[47]Strugnell, "A Plea for Conjectural Emendation," 556.

[48]J. M. Ross, *ExpT* 82 (1970): 215-17.

what the scribe meant by the observation τὸ μὴ ὑπὲρ ἃ γέγραπ-ται was "the μή is beyond what was written." "In other words, the scribe in his gloss is saying that he added a μή to a text that didn't have one."[49] Strugnell's version undoubtedly makes better sense of the gloss; it is reasonable in content and unobjectionable in form. But even this revised interpretation is exposed to criticisms, most of which Strugnell anticipates. He acknowledges, for example, that τὸ Χ ὑπὲρ ἃ γέγραπται is not the form taken by marginal annotations in the papyri of the period.[50] Nor does the similar Jewish terminology of קרי and כתיב appear until later. If, on the one hand, the scribal gloss is deleted, Paul is made to express a strange and sarcastic sentiment. But if one accepts the conjecture, and deprives μάθητε of its object, one is left with an anacoluthon that many will find intolerable: ἵνα ἐν ἡμῖν μάθητε ἵνα μὴ εἷς ὑπὲρ τοῦ ἑνὸς φυσιοῦσθε κατὰ τοῦ ἑτέρου.[51]

It need hardly be said that the historical critic will not hesitate to emend the text of the New Testament whenever the evidence warrants; the same principles should apply here as obtain in the criticism of other ancient literature. Strugnell's version of Baljon's conjecture is eminently plausible, though it is not, perhaps, as convincing as Weiss's account of how the received text, which he also finds unintelligible, came to be in its present form.[52] Nevertheless, before we adopt one conjecture or

---

[49]Strugnell, "A Plea for Conjectural Emendation," 557.

[50]Strugnell, "A Plea for Conjectural Emendation," and see n.31, above; but see n.35 in Strugnell's article where questions are raised about the evidence for a regular form in the papyri of the period.

[51]Strugnell, "A Plea for Conjectural Emendation," and see n.31, above. Strugnell's final proposal is that the μή fell out in the phrase ἵνα ἐν ὑμῖν μὴ μάθητε ἵνα εἷς κτλ., rather than after the second ἵνα. He does not explain why he prefers the less well-attested ὑμῖν to ἡμῖν, but the effect of the substitution is to load Paul's remark with irony.

[52]Weiss (Der erste Korintherbrief, 102, 104) suggests, following the Latin versions, that ἵνα μή should be dropped as a "verdächtige Dublette." The original text would then have read ἵνα ἐν ἡμῖν μάθητε τὸ μὴ ὑπὲρ τοῦ ἑνὸς φυσιοῦσθαι, crediting Straatman's proposal. The lack of a subject was supplied by the addition of ἃ γέγραπται, and doubts over εἷς or ἕνα drew a second ἵνα into the text. But then, Weiss drew back from his own

another, we should thoroughly examine the ancient evidence, literary and epigraphic, for anything that might throw light on the language of Paul. Only then shall we know whether the text can be satisfactorily explained, or whether it requires emendation.

Before we enter upon such an examination, we may summarize the results of previous research. Despite the failure of prior attempts to arrive at a persuasive interpretation, several facts have been learned about Paul's elliptical statement of purpose in 1 Cor 4:6. Although readers of early Christian literature naturally take every mention of what is "written" as an allusion to the Old Testament scriptures, owing, no doubt, to the predominance of the citation formula καθὼς γέγραπται,[53] Paul's words in this instance probably do not contain a reference to the Scripture. Paul does not otherwise refer to the Scripture in this manner. And an allusion to Scripture at this point in his argument is strictly irrelevant. Secondly, the meaning of the difficult phrase τὸ μὴ ὑπὲρ ἃ γέγραπται is closely related to the clause that follows, ἵνα μὴ εἷς ὑπὲρ τοῦ ἑνὸς φυσιοῦσθε κατὰ τοῦ ἑτέρου. So much is implied by the parallel structure of the purpose clauses, as Wallis has seen.[54]

---

reconstruction: "Wie der Text gelautet hat und welche Unglücksfälle ihn entstellt haben, wird wohl nie ermittelt werden" (104).

[53]In Paul's authentic epistles alone, 1 Cor 1:31; 2:9; 2 Cor 8:15; 9:9; Rom 1:17; 2:24; 3:10; 4:17; 8:36; 9:33; 11:26; 15:3,9,21; note also γέγραπται γάρ in 1 Cor 1:19; 3:19; 9:9; 15:45; Gal. 3:10; 4:22,27; Rom 12:19; 14:11 and καθάπερ γέγραπται in Rom 3:4; 9:13; 10:15; 11:8. Heinrici makes the assumption explicit (Der erste Brief an die Korinther, 149): "Die wie ein Schlagwort angeführte Wendung: τὸ μὴ ὑπὲρ ἃ γέγραπται hält die Mitte zwischen der feierlichen Citationsformel καθὼς γέγραπται und dem einfachen ἔγραψα, mit dem Paulus auf seine Briefe verweist." But, in fact, this amounts to an admission that τὸ μὴ ὑπὲρ ἃ γέγραπται is neither Paul's way of referring to Scripture nor his typical allusion to his own teaching. It occupies a "middle position" only because Heinrici places it there, under the assumption that it refers to a "Gemeindestatut," that lies midway between the authority of Scripture and Paul's own dicta. There is, however, no evidence for the existence of such a statute in Paul's churches.

[54]P. Wallis, "Ein neuer Auslegungsversuch der Stelle 1 Kor. 4,6," ThLZ 75 (1950): 507. Weiss verges upon this insight, recognizing that the clauses are "völlig parallel" (Der erste Korintherbrief, 103), yet persists in regarding τὸ μὴ ὑπὲρ κτλ. and ἵνα μὴ εἷς κτλ. as the double object of μάθητε (103),

Paul explains his object in having exemplified, by reference to himself and Apollos, what he had to say to the Corinthians on the subject of factions:[55] it was in order that they might learn the meaning of the phrase, "not beyond the things which are written," in order that they might not be puffed up, each one on behalf of one against another. How the purpose clauses are related to each other remains to be determined—whether, that is, the first is seen as the means to the second as an end,[56] or whether the two stand in simple apposition. But that they are related is clear—and significant; for the second clause is as transparent and coherent as the first is, seemingly, opaque and unrelated. Paul's negation of the attitude of self-importance that arises from association with one person rather than another is a clear expression of the opposition to factiousness which is his theme throughout the first four chapters (1:10-12; 3:3-4; 3:21; 4:8-9). The verb φυσιοῦσθαι is found again at the end of the section (4:18-19), where it characterizes the arrogant and self-willed behavior of some in the Corinthian church. This verb, and its cognate φυσάω, are used frequently by orators and political historians to paint an image of the self-conceit that gives rise to partisanship. Thus Demosthenes depicts Aeschines, the author of so much discord in Athens, "as he strides through the marketplace, his long robe reaching to his ankles, equal in his going to Pythocles, his cheeks puffed out, as if to say, 'Here is one of Philip's most intimate friends!'"[57] Xenophon characterizes Alcibiades and Critias, leaders of the extremist faction, as "puffed up at their own power" (πεφυσημένω ἐπὶ δυνάμει).[58] Philo de-

---

though he sees "dass der eigentliche Anstoss in dem Neben einander des doppelten Objekts zu μάθητε liegt" (104). The solution proposed here is to regard the ἵνα-clauses as parallel but independent statements of purpose, giving reasons why Paul has applied the allusive discussion of certain matters to himself and Apollos for the sake of the Corinthians.

[55]Benjamin Fiore ("Covert Allusion in 1 Corinthians 1-4," *CBQ* 47 [1985]: 94) views the matter of factions as the primary object of 1 Cor 1-4. He observes that in relation to this subject, "Paul and Apollos become figures . . . to which the community is to look for their own improvement (4:6)."

[56]So Holsten, *Das Evangelium des Paulus*, vol. 1, 149.

[57]Demosthenes 19.314; see also 59.97.

[58]Xenophon *Mem.* 1.2.25; see also the characterization of political orators as "puffed up" in Ps-Plato *Alcibiades II*, 145E and Plutarch *Cicero* 887B.

scribes Macro as "puffed up beyond measure" (πλέον ἐφυσήθη τοῦ μετρίου),[59] and contrasts Gaius, who is "puffed up" (πεφύσησαι) with pride, with the Dioscuri, who exhibited brotherly love.[60] We shall not go wrong if we allow our interpretation of the first, enigmatic clause in 1 Cor 4:6 to be guided by the second, which is clear in itself and relevant to the context, rather than the other way around.

Finally, the words μὴ ὑπὲρ ἃ γέγραπται are evidently a proverb, or a principle in proverbial form. This is the only satisfactory explanation of the introductory article and the elliptical sentence structure. Further, it is more likely that the words were a well-known maxim, with broad cultural currency, than a local slogan, with its origins in the Corinthian church; for Paul includes the saying in a letter addressed to the entire congregation, in the expectation that it will be known and understood. It is this proverbial quality which accounts for our difficulty in understanding. For it is the ironic law of everything historical that the most familiar is changed by time into something strange, and the best known is lost irretrievably, because it never needed to be uttered.

II. PAUL'S COUNSEL OF CONCORD

In seeking to identify the source of the principle to which Paul alludes in 1 Cor 4:6, we shall do well to bear in mind what every ancient orator knew: there are arguments which are appropriate to particular situations, materials which are specific to rhetorical forms (Aristotle *Rhet* 1.4-8).[61] In other words, we shall usefully limit our search for the proverb which Paul is quoting, if we first determine the rhetorical category and context of his remarks. For the purpose of this investigation, we shall define the rhetorical unit as consisting of 1 Cor 1-4. It may be that these

---

[59]Philo *Leg ad Gai* 69.

[60]Philo *Leg ad Gai* 86; 154, Caesar was never "puffed up" by the honors shown him; 255, Petronius's successive offices have "puffed him up with pride"; see also Dio Chrysostom 30.19, tyrants are "puffed up in soul"; 58.5.

[61]These are the so-called "material" topics. Aristotle *Rhet* 1.4.7 says that the deliberative orator in a political context will discuss revenues, war and peace, protecting the country, imports and exports, and legislation; see the more detailed list in [Aristides] *Ars rhetorica*, ed. L. Spengel, *Rhet Gr* II.503-504.

chapters, with the paraenesis in 5:1-6:11, constitute a separate letter.[62] Johannes Weiss, whose commentary on 1 Corinthians remains unsurpassed, doubted the integrity of the canonical epistle, basing his conclusions upon breaks in the train of thought, discrepancies in reports of events, sudden changes of tone, and differences in outlook and judgment.[63] Wolfgang Schenk sought to strengthen Weiss's hypothesis with observations of a formal, linguistic sort;[64] he demonstrated, for example, how many of the elements of an epistolary conclusion are to be found in 1 Cor 4:14-21. But even if 1 Cor 1:1-6:11 is not an independent letter, it is manifestly a rhetorical unit enclosed within the canonical whole, its beginning and end clearly marked by hortatory periods in 1:10 and 4:16.[65]

It is not difficult to determine the rhetorical species of 1 Cor 1-4: it belongs to the συμβουλευτικὸν γένος. It is Paul's purpose in writing to dissuade the Corinthians from their quarrelsome conduct.[66] Thus he

---

[62]See the overview in John Hurd, *The Origin of 1 Corinthians*, new and corr. ed. (Macon GA: Mercer University Press, 1983) 43-47; more recently, Helmut Merklein, "Die Einheitlichkeit des ersten Korintherbriefes," *ZNW* 75 (1984): 153-83. After Weiss (see n.63 below) various division hypotheses have been proposed; see most recently Christoph Senft, *La première épître de Saint Paul aux Corinthiens*, CNT 2nd ser. 7 (Neuchâtel: Delachaux & Niestlé, 1979) 17-25.

[63]Weiss, *Der erste Korintherbrief*, xxxix-xliii, and the later summary in *Das Urchristentum* (Göttingen: Vandenhoeck & Ruprecht, 1917) 245-72; *The History of Primitive Christianity*, vol. 1 (New York: Wilson-Erickson, 1937) 323-41.

[64]Wolfgang Schenk, "Der 1. Korintherbrief als Briefsammlung," *ZNW* 60 (1969): 219-43.

[65]C. J. Bjerkelund, *Parakalo: Form, Funktion und Sinn der Parakalo-Sätze in den paulinischen Briefen* (Oslo: Universitetsforlaget, 1967) 141-42, 145-46; Nils A. Dahl, "Paul and the Church at Corinth according to 1 Corinthians 1:10-4:21" in *Studies in Paul* (Minneapolis: Augsburg, 1977) 43-46, 52.

[66]The whole of 1:1-4:21 is apotropaic, though this is most evident in 1:10-13 and 3:1-4:21; note the imperatives in 3:10, 18, 21; 4:5, 16. Paul characterizes his purpose in writing as "admonishing" (νουθετῶν) in 4:14. See the description of the purpose of deliberative rhetoric in Aristotle *Rhet* 1.3.3 1358b8: "The deliberative kind is either hortatory or dissuasive; for both those who give advice in private and those who speak in the assembly invariably either exhort or dissuade"; after Aristotle: *Rhet ad Her* 1.2.2; Quintilian 3.4.15; 3.8.6; 9.4.130. See the studies of the συμβουλευτικὸν γένος by J. Klek, *Symbuleutici qui dicitur*

urges them to consider that their actions are harmful and disgraceful, as writers on rhetoric recommend.[67] Narrative is kept to a minimum, since deliberative speech is concerned with the future and seeks to advise about things to come.[68] Like a good deliberative orator, Paul assigns blame where it is due,[69] and makes use of παραδείγματα.[70]

But we may go further than this in our attempt to identify the genre of Paul's remarks: careful reading of the chapters shows that Paul's advice is related to a particular type of deliberative discourse, that which is customarily entitled περὶ ὁμονοίας. A number of examples of this genre have fortunately survived, several in the form of epistles.[71] Their

---

sermonis historia critica (Kirchhain: Schmersow, 1919); Ingo Beck, *Untersuchungen zur Theorie des Genos Symbuleutikon* (Hamburg, 1970). See the definitions of the symbouleutic letter in Ps-Demetrius τύποι Ἐπιστολικοί 11 and Ps-Libanius Ἐπιστολιμαῖοι Χαρακτῆρες 5 in V. Weichert, *Demetrii et Libanii qui ferunt* Τύποι Ἐπιστολικοί et Ἐπιστολιμαῖοι Χαρακτῆρες (Leipzig: Teubner, 1910).

[67]Paul presents the dissension of the Corinthians as harmful in 1:10-16; 3:1-4; 3:16-23 and as shameful in 3:3; 4:8-13,18-21; see esp. 4:14 where Paul's denial οὐκ ἐντρέπων ὑμᾶς γράφω ταῦτα presupposes that their actions have been shameful. Needless to say, Paul does not pedantically employ the technical terms βλαβερόν and αἰσχρόν. See the discussion of the τέλοι of deliberative rhetoric in Aristotle *Rhet* 1.3.5-4.7 1358b-1359b; Quintilian 3.8.22; 3.8.33; 3.4.16; 3.8. 1-3; *Rhet ad Her* 3.2.3-4.8; for discussion of "ends" in later rhetoricians, see Alexander in L. Spengel, *Rhet Gr* III.1-2 and the more detailed analysis of various aspects of "the beneficial," "the just," etc. in [Aristides] *Ars rhetorica* in L. Spengel, *Rhet Gr* II.503-504.

[68]Narrative is limited to 1:11-16; see Aristotle *Rhet* 1.3.4 1358b13; Quintilian 3.8.6. The whole of 1:1-4:21 treats behavior which the Corinthians are to avoid in the future; in 4:18-21 Paul promises to come and inspect their conduct.

[69]Blame is cast upon the Corinthians in 1:12-13; 3:1-4; 4:8-13,18-19; see the discussion of blame in deliberative discourse in Aristotle *Rhet* 1.9.28 1367b-1.9.37 1368a; Quintilian 3.7.28.

[70]For the *exempla* used by Paul in chs. 1-4 see below; see the discussion in Aristotle *Rhet* 1.4.8-9.39, esp. 1368a26: "Speaking generally, of the topics common to all rhetorical arguments . . . examples (παραδείγματα) are the most suitable for deliberative speakers"; Quintilian 3.8.36: in the *inventio* of this *genus*, the emphasis lies upon the *exempla*.

[71]E.g., Thrasymachus περὶ πολιτείας; Antiphon περὶ ὁμονοίας

authors, generally statesmen or philosophers, seek to conciliate rival factions by dissuading from strife (στάσις) and exhorting to concord (ὁμόνοια).[72] Like Paul, they urge their hearers

> that you all say the same thing and that there be no divisions among you, but that you be united in the same mind and the same judgment (ἵνα τὸ αὐτὸ λέγητε πάντες, καὶ μὴ ᾖ ἐν ὑμῖν σχίσ- ματα, ἦτε δὲ κατηρτισμένοι ἐν τῷ αὐτῷ νοΐ καὶ ἐν τῇ αὐτῇ γνώμῃ, 1:10).

Following a period of civil strife in Nicaea, Dio Chrysostom delivered a speech in which he appealed to the citizens to maintain their attitude of peace, concord, and friendship toward one another.[73] After complementing the city upon its antiquity and renown, he observes: "I rejoice at the present moment to see you having one voice, and desiring the same things" (ἔγωγε ἥδομαι νῦν ὁρῶν ὑμᾶς ἓν μὲν σχῆμα ἔχον- τας, μίαν δὲ φωνὴν ἀφιέντας, ταὐτὰ δὲ βουλομένους, 39.3). This observation is elaborated by a series of rhetorical questions: "For what spectacle is more enchanting than a city with the same mind (ὁμοφρονούσῃ)? What sound is more awe-inspiring than its harmonious voice? What city is less liable to failure than that which deliberates

---

Isocrates *Or* 4; *Ep* 3, 8, 9; Ps-Plato *Ep* 7; Ps.-Demosthenes *Ep* 1; Socratic Epp. 30-32; Ps-Sallust *Ep* 2; Dio Chrysostom *Or* 38-41; Aelius Aristides *Or* 23-24; [Herodes Atticus] περὶ πολιτείας. Among early Christian writings, the so-called First Epistle of Clement is a clear example of the genre. Cf. W. C. van Unnik, *Studies over de zogenaamde eerste brief van Clemens. I. Het litteraire genre*, Mededelingen der Kon. Ned. Akademie van Wetenschappen, Afd. Letterkunde, NR 33:4 (Amsterdam: Noord-Hollandse Uitgevers Maatschappij, 1970).

[72]There is no satisfactory treatment of στάσις, though see the concise study of D. Loenen, *Stasis* (Amsterdam, 1953); A. Lintott, *Violence, Civil Strife and Revolution in the Classical City* (Baltimore: Johns Hopkins University Press, 1982); on ὁμόνοια see H. Kramer, *Quid valeat homonoia in litteris graecis* (Göttingen, 1915); Athanasios Moulakis, *Homonoia. Eintracht und die Entwicklung eines politischen Bewusstseins* (München: Paul List, 1973).

[73]Dio Chrysostom *Or* 39; the text is that of the LCL, ed. H. Crosby (Cambridge: Harvard University Press, 1946); see the discussion of this address in C. P. Jones, *The Roman World of Dio Chrysostom* (Cambridge: Harvard University Press, 1978) 89-91.

the same things? To whom are blessings sweeter than to those who are of one heart and mind (ὁμονοούντων)?" (39.3). He concludes with a prayer to the gods, that

> from this day forth they implant in this city a yearning for itself, a love, a single judgment (μία γνώμη), and that it desire and think the same thing (καὶ ταὐτὰ βούλεσθαι καὶ φρονεῖν); and, on the other hand, that it cast out discord and contentiousness and party spirit (39.8).

When a class struggle erupted at Rhodes, Aelius Aristides sent a written address on concord in which, like Paul, he asks his readers to consider that "if we engage in faction, it (ἡ πατρίς) is lost; but if we are of a single judgment (μιᾷ δὲ γνώμῃ χρησαμένων), it becomes both fairer and greater" (24.37).[74]

It is striking how many of the metaphors and images employed by political orators in depicting factious communities are found in Paul's exhortation in 1 Cor 1–4. First, there is Paul's parody of the Corinthians' slogans. Dio Chrysostom asks the Nicaeans, "Is it not manifest that . . . those who are caught up in dissension do not listen to one another?" (οὐ γὰρ δῆλον ὅτι . . . οἱ δὲ στασιάζοντες οὐδ᾽ αὐτῶν ἀκούουσιν; 39.4), and then goes on to compare a city at variance with itself with a chorus that does not keep together, and which, consequently, no one wishes to hear. Similarly, in a discourse delivered in his native Prusa counselling concord with the Apameians, Dio describes the uproar created by the factious, "cursing and abusing each other," and effects to hear

---

[74]Aelius Aristides *Or* 24 in *Aelii Aristidis Smyrnaei quae supersunt omnia*, ed. Bruno Keil, Vol. II (Berlin: Weidmanns, 1958) 65. For further parallels to Paul's expressions in 1:10, see the speech of Agelaus in Polybius 5.104.1: εἰ λέγοντες ἓν καὶ ταὐτὸ πάντες . . . δύναιντο . . . σώζειν σφᾶς αὐτούς καὶ τὰς πόλεις; Thucydides 4.17.1ff., the speech of the Lacedaemonian envoys to Athens offering peace: ἡμῶν γὰρ καὶ ὑμῶν ταὐτὰ λεγόντων . . . ; the description of political harmony in Lysias 25.21: ὅτε μὲν γὰρ ἀκούοιτε τοὺς ἐν ἄστει τὴν αὐτὴν γνώμην ἔχειν, and the contrasting characterization of those engaged in στάσις: τοὺς μὴ τὴν αὐτὴν γνώμην ἔχοντας; Dionysius of Halicarnassus *Ant Rom* 3.10: ἵνα καταρτισθῇ ἡ στασιάζουσα πόλις; Plutarch *Mor* 813B.

the shouts of the partisans . . . in the stadium and the theater . . . cries which are not for reasonable men, but rather for those who, as Homer puts it, "In rage to midassembly go, and quarrel with one another as their anger bids."[75]

All this recalls Paul's ironic portrait of the Corinthians, each with his own party cry: ἕκαστος ὑμῶν λέγει ἐγὼ μέν εἰμι Παύλου, ἐγὼ δὲ Ἀπολλῶ, ἐγὼ δὲ Κηφᾶ, ἐγὼ δὲ Χριστοῦ (1:12).

Paul's description of the quarrelsome Corinthians as "babies" (νήπιοι), fed with milk, rather than solid food (3:1-2) has its counterpart in this literature as well, where the factious are frequently characterized as immature. Dio Chrysostom informs the Nicomedians and the Nicaeans that in their contention over titles they are viewed by their Roman governors as "children" (παιδίοι):

for we often offer children the most trivial things in place of things of greatest worth; and those children, in their ignorance over what is truly valuable and in their pleasure over what is of least account, delight in what is a mere nothing (38.37).[76]

Similarly, Aelius Aristides tells the citizens of the κοινόν of Asia that in their strife over titles they are like children who fight with their own shadows (23.62).[77]

The architectural metaphor lent itself readily to the attempt to promote concord. In 1 Cor 3:9-15 Paul compares the Christian community to a building and its ministers to builders. Paul himself, the ἀρχι-τέκτων, has laid the foundation, now another is building upon it. But each should take care how he builds. Plutarch employs a similar image in his advice to a young man on the art of politics, whose noblest function, Plutarch asserts, is "to instill concord and friendship in those who dwell together and to remove strifes, discords, and all enmity."[78] The wise politician is compared to "an architect who chooses subordinates

---

[75]Dio Chrysostom *Or* 40.28; the translation is that of H. Crosby in the LCL; see the discussion of this speech in C. P. Jones, *The Roman World of Dio Chrysostom*, 91-93.

[76]Dio Chrysostom *Or* 38; the translation is that of H. Crosby in the LCL.

[77]Aelius Aristides *Or* 23 in *Aelii Aristidis*, ed. Keil, vol. 2, 32-54.

[78]Plutarch *Praecepta gerendae reipublicae* 824C-E.

and craftsmen who will not spoil his work but will cooperate to perfect it." But the bad statesman chooses colleagues whose convictions are not his own; he "will be found to be no better than a builder or carpenter who through ignorance and error makes use of such squares and rulers and levels as are sure to make his work crooked."[79]

In 3:16-17 Paul charges those who create strife and dissension with destroying the temple of God. Of course these verses contain an allusion to one of Paul's favorite metaphors, the Christian as the divine ναός (cf. 6:19); but one might suspect the existence of another, underlying analogy between the factious and temple-defilers. Thus one is not surprised to find in Aelius Aristides' discourse on concord a comparison of those who create discord with "temple-robbers" (ἱεροσύλοι, 24.50).[80]

Finally, Paul offers himself and Apollos, the guides of the community, as examples of harmonious conduct: they are "coworkers" (συνεργοί, 3:9), they are "one" (ἕν, 3:8). Paul explains: "These things, brothers, I have exemplified by reference (μετεσχημάτισα)[81] to myself and Apollos for your benefit (δι' ὑμᾶς), in order that you might learn from our example (ἐν ἡμῖν) etc." (4:6a). And he exhorts: "Become imitators of me!" (μιμηταί μου γίνεσθε, 4:16).[82] A similar strategy is adopted by the anonymous author of a fictitious exchange between

---

[79]Ibid., 807C-D; the translation is that of H. Fowler in the LCL (Cambridge: Harvard University Press, 1936) 205. To be sure, Plutarch applies the metaphor to a somewhat different point: the stateman's choice of friends. Note similar metaphors in Dio Chrysostom 38.15 where the city is compared with an οἶκος; 39.5 with its οἰκοδομήματα; in Aelius Aristides 24.8, 32-33 the οἶκος is a model.

[80]Aelius Aristides Or 24.50.

[81]Benjamin Fiore ("Covert Allusion in 1 Corinthians 1-4," CBQ 47 [1985]: 85-102) has explored the paradigmatic function of Paul's references to himself and Apollos throughout these chapters, without, however, discussing the role of παραδείγματα in deliberative discourse. On the speaker's use of himself as παράδειγμα in deliberative speeches, see Aristotle Rhet 1.2.5; 2.1; Quintilian 3.8.13; Isocrates 15.278.

[82]See H. D. Betz, Nachfolge und Nachahmung Jesu Christi im Neuen Testament, BHTh 37 (Tübingen: Mohr-Siebeck, 1967) 153-69; Willis P. de Boer, The Imitation of Paul (Kampen: Kok, 1962).

Speusippus and Xenocrates, found among the Socratic Epistles.[83] Xenocrates recalls how, after Plato's death, "we divided into those sects which each of us judged appropriate to himself" (ἐχωριζόμεθα κατὰ τὰς αἱρέσεις, ἃς ἕκαστος ἡμῶν ἐδοκίμαζεν, *Ep* 32.2). Speusippus responds out of concern for the good of the philosophical community left by Plato and the friendship between Xenocrates and himself (*Ep* 30.1). He pleads with Xenocrates to return to Athens and "keep the school together" (*Ep* 30.1). As his principal argument Speusippus offers the example of Plato himself, his constant "association" (συνου- σία) with his friends, how "he cared for some as a parent, for others as a benefactor" (*Ep* 30.2). Speusippus then drives home his exhortation: "I counsel you, then, considering it to be good and right, to show the greatest possible gratitude to Plato, and in the way most appropriate to him. And you would show such gratitude, if by returning to the Academy, you kept the school together" (*Ep* 30.3). Similarly, Aelius Aristides offers "a human example" (ἀνθρωπείων παράδειγμα) of the ὁμόνοια that he wishes to cultivate between the cities of Asia—namely, the concord between the rulers, Marcus and Verus.[84] The emperors' greatest possession is the "concord and zeal they display toward one another." The citizens of Asia should strive "to imitate" (μιμεῖσθαι) them as far as possible (23.78).[85]

---

[83]Socratic Epp. 30-32; Greek text in R. Hercher, *Epistolographi Graeci* (Paris, 1871) and *The Cynic Epistles*, ed. Abraham J. Malherbe (Missoula MT: Scholars Press, 1977) 296-301. The original order of the epistles is 31, 32, 30, not that found in the tradition. J. Sykutris (*Die Briefe des Sokrates und die Sokratiker* [GKA 18; Paderborn, 1933] 81-91, 113) discusses the *konziliatorische Bestreben* of these letters.

[84]Aelius Aristides *Or* 23.78.

[85]See also Aelius Aristides *Or* 24.32-33, where the Rhodians are counselled "to imitate" (μιμήσασθαι) the σχῆμα and τύπον of the well-run household, paying particular attention to how the rulers and fathers in the household administer affairs. All this is then applied to the Rhodian situation (34-35): the rulers should set an example of concord by voluntarily giving up some of their authority and refraining from harming their inferiors. See also Dionysius of Halicarnassus *Ant Rom* 7.66.4-5 and Ps-Plato *Ep* 7.336C: the ἑταῖροι are advised "to imitate" (μιμεῖσθαι) their leader, Dion.

Even the discussion of "wisdom" in 1 Cor 1:17-2:5, whose relation to the overarching theme of factions has puzzled interpreters,[86] is found to be a recurrent feature of literature on concord. For the σοφία which Paul fears will undermine the community is not wisdom in the abstract, but σοφία λόγου, "cleverness in speaking" (1:17).[87] In their attempts to dissuade from civil strife, ancient orators show themselves aware of the exacerbating role of rhetoric. In the pseudo-Sallustian *Epistula ad Caesarem senem*, the author appeals for action that will put an end to party strife.[88] He warns Julius Caesar: the "cleverness" (*calliditas*) and "caprice" (*libido*) of the leaders of faction threaten the true "wisdom" (*consilium*) upon which the ancestors founded the state.[89] In the extant fragment of Thrasymachus's discourse on concord,[90] stress is laid on the

---

[86]U. Wilckens, *Weisheit und Torheit. Eine exegetisch-religionsgeschichtliche Untersuchung zu 1. Kor. 1 und 2*, BHTh 26 (Tübingen: Siebeck-Mohr, 1959) 6; Conzelmann, *1 Corinthians*, 37; E. Peterson ("1 Korinther 1,18f. und die Thematik des jüdischen Busstages," *Bib* 32 [1951]: 97-103) even suggests that 1 Cor 1:16-31 was a homily which Paul delivered in a synagogue in Ephesus and later incorporated into the epistle.

[87]Rightly, Walter Bauer, *A Greek-English Lexicon of the New Testament and Other Early Christian Literature* (Chicago: University of Chicago, 1979) 759. The context of Paul's discussion of wisdom and foolishness is the account of his "preaching" (1:17) and "proclamation" (2:1). The identity of "wisdom" is thus established in relation to his "discourse" (2:4). Paul denies that he has come to the Corinthians with "excess of speech or wisdom" (2:1) or that his message was delivered in "persuasive words of wisdom" (2:4). Thus σοφία is not a gnostic concept, as Wilckens and others contend, but rhetoric. On the whole subject see H. D. Betz, "The Problem of Rhetoric and Theology according to the Apostle Paul" in *L'Apôtre Paul. Personalité, Style et Conception du Ministère*, ed. A. Vanhoye, *Bibliotheca Ephemeridum Theologicarum Loveniensium* (Leuven: Leuven University, 1986) 16-48.

[88]Ps.-Sallust *Ep* 2; for a summary of debate on the authorship and date of the epistle, see K. Vretska, *Sallust. Invective und Episteln*, vol. 1 (Heidelberg: Winter, 1961) 38-51.

[89]Ps-Sallust *Ep* 2.9.3; 2.10.6; 2.11.1.

[90]H. Diels, *Die Fragmente der Vorsokratiker* 85 A 1. The speech, of which only the opening is preserved, is sometimes called περὶ πολιτείας; but its concern is not with the πολιτεία as such, but with ὁμόνοια, as A. Fuks (*The Ancestral Constitution* [London: Routledge & Kegan Paul, 1953] 103) points out.

role of rhetoric in creating strife. Those engaged in factional struggles suffer from a lack of genuine understanding: their speech deludes them, for thinking that they are saying things contrary to one another, they do not see that the speech of their opponents lies within their own.[91]

It goes without saying that there are many things in 1 Cor 1-4 that have no counterpart in ancient political rhetoric; perhaps these are even more significant than the typical features we have examined, precisely because they are specifically Christian.[92] Yet enough parallels have been adduced that we may conclude that Paul's use of a particular rhetorical form was clear to his readers, who were familiar with the ancient forms of political discourse. We have also noted the importance of genre in guiding Paul's choice of language and images. We may hope, therefore, to find the key to Paul's perplexing phrase, τὸ μὴ ὑπὲρ ἃ γέγραπ- ται in the literature on concord.

III. A CONCILIATORY PRINCIPLE

We are not disappointed. Despite the consternation that the phrase has occasioned, the advice "not to go beyond what is written" is commonly applied by philosophers and statesmen to those who threaten to arouse discord. Sometimes the principle takes the form of an exhortation to abide by the established laws. As a safeguard against στάσις, Aristotle recommends that the greatest "care be taken to prevent people from committing any breach of the law . . . for transgression of the law (παρανομία) creeps in unawares."[93] Plato's Seventh Epistle purports to

---

[91]See the discussion of the role of rhetoric in creating στάσις in Thucydides 3.82.3-8; Aristotle Pol 5.7.2 1308a.

[92]Arnaldo Momigliano, "Biblical Studies and Classical Studies: Simple Reflections about Historical Method," Biblical Archaeologist (1982): 227: "To conclude, I may well ask myself where a classical scholar can help biblical scholars most usefully. My answer would be that in the field of political, social, and religious history, differences are more important than similarities—and therefore knowledge of Greco-Roman history can be useful only for differential comparison."

[93]Aristotle Pol. 5.7.1 1307b32-33. See also Plato's account of an oath to obey the laws in the Critias 120A: κατὰ τοῦ πυρὸς σπένδοντες ἐπώμνυσαν δικάσειν τε κατὰ τοὺς ἐν τῇ στήλῃ νόμους καὶ κολάσειν εἴ

be a message of "counsel" to Dion's friends who are beset by στάσις. The literary fiction of a συμβουλευτικὸς λόγος is carried through up to a point: Plato warns the ἑταῖροι that the evils of faction will not cease until they enact "common laws" by which all can abide.[94] In the speech entitled περὶ πολιτείας, sometimes attributed to Herodes Atticus, the citizens are urged to put an end to factional strife by living "according to law" (κατὰ νόμον), instead of destroying one another "lawlessly" (παρανομῶς).[95] The speaker concludes by contrasting his own discourse in favor of an alliance that would put an end to discord with that of his opponents, who dare to counsel the citizens "to have neither commonwealth, nor law, nor judgment" (μήτε πολιτείαν εἶναι μήτε νόμον μήτε δίκας, 36). "But these things are opposite to those which I speak" (ταῦτα γάρ ἐστιν ἐναντία τούτοις οἷς ἐγώ λεγώ, 37). In the second pseudo-Sallustian epistle, the harmony of the Roman state in earlier times is attributed to the fact that "no man's power was superior to the laws" (*nullius potentia super leges erat*).[96]

In a well-known passage in the *Memorabilia* (4.4.15-16), Xenophon has Socrates explain the connection between obedience to the laws and the pursuit of concord. Socrates praises Lycurgus for establishing obedience to the laws as the norm in Sparta. He asks:

> Among rulers in cities, are you not aware that those who do most to make the citizens obey the laws are the best, and that the city in which the citizens are most obedient to the laws has the best time in peace and is irresistible in war?

Socrates explains that the object of obedience to the laws is the attainment of concord: "And, indeed, agreement (ὁμόνοια) is deemed the greatest blessing for cities: their senates and their best men constantly exhort the citizens to agree." Socrates asserts:

τίς τι πρότερον παραβεβηκὼς εἴη, τό τε αὖ μετὰ τοῦτο μηδὲν τῶν γραμμάτων ἑκόντες παραβήσασθαι.

[94]Ps-Plato *Ep* 7.336D-337B.

[95][Herodes Atticus] περὶ πολιτείας 17-18, 29 in [Erode Attico] *Peri Politeias*, ed. Umberto Albini (Firenze: Monnier, 1968) 32, 34, 71-73, 87.

[96]Ps-Sallust *Ep* 2.5.3.

And everywhere in Greece there is a law that the citizens shall promise under oath to agree, and everywhere they take this oath (καὶ πανταχοῦ ἐν τῇ Ἑλλάδι νόμος κεῖται τοὺς πολίτας ὀμνύναι ὁμονο- ήσειν, καὶ πανταχοῦ ὀμνύουσι τὸν ὅρκον τοῦτον).

He concludes:

The object of this, in my opinion, is not that the citizens may vote for the same choirs, not that they may praise the same flute players, not that they may select the same poets, not that they may like the same things, but that they may obey the laws. For those cities whose citizens abide by them prove strongest and enjoy the most happiness; but without agreement (ὁμόνοια) no city can be made a good city, no house can be made a prosperous house.

The proposition that underlies Socrates' argument was repeatedly restated and almost universally believed by Greeks and Romans: the essential condition of a harmonius life in the πόλις was obedience to the laws. It suffices to recall the dictum of Euripides' *Suppliant Women* (312-13): "The power that keeps cities of men together is noble preserva- tion of the laws" (τὸ γάρ τοι συνέχον ἀνθρώπων πόλεις τοῦτ' ἐσθ', ὅταν τις τοὺς νόμους σῴζῃ καλῶς).

When the conflict lies between cities, or when the established laws do not apply, the factions are exhorted to submit to other written docu- ments, such as treaties of peace. In his discourse *On the Peace with Sparta*, Andocides speaks for the delegates who have returned to Athens with a draft of terms, and urges a vote for peace. He concludes the appeal by placing his hearers before the choice between peace and war; everything depends upon whether they are willing to abide by the things that have been written: πᾶσί τε τοῖς γεγραμμένοις χρωμένοις ἔστιν εἰρήνην ἄγειν. εἰ δὲ μηδὲν ἀρέσκει τούτων, πολε- μεῖν ἕτοιμον.[97]

When there are no written documents, but the conciliator nevertheless wishes to create a barrier against hostility, he appeals to the factions to take an oath or to make a solemn promise, and not to depart from the

---

[97]Andocides *On the Peace with Sparta* 40-41; the text is that of the LCL, *Minor Attic Orators*, vol. 1, ed. K. J. Maidment (Cambridge: Harvard University Press, 1941) 528-30.

words which have been spoken. The first epistle of Demosthenes is a speech in letter form urging the Athenians to bring about ὁμόνοια among themselves for the sake of the mutually beneficial (τὸ σύμ- φερον). The author concludes with the following exhortation:

> Let every man of you repeat to himself a solemn promise to perform whatever he in particular shall be able and shall elect to do. And see to it that he does not break this pledge or shirk his responsibility, saying that he was deceived or over-persuaded.[98]

Nowhere do we get a clearer glimpse of the role of oaths and agreements in providing assurance of concord than in the speech which Menenius Agrippa is said to have delivered during the great secessio of the plebs (Livy 2.32.7-12; Dionysius of Halicarnassus *Ant Rom* 6.83-86). The speech is a true λόγος προτρεπτικὸς εἰς ὁμόνοιαν (cf. Florus 1.17). In the account of Dionysius of Halicarnassus (*Ant Rom* 6.84.3-4), Menenius concludes:

> The last assurance we shall give you is that in use among all men, both Greeks and barbarians, which no lapse of time shall ever overthrow, namely the one which through oaths and treaties makes the gods sureties for the performance of agreements. Under this assurance many bitter enmities between private individuals and many wars that have arisen between states have been composed. Come now, accept this assurance also, whether you permit a few of the principal members of the senate to give you their oaths in the name of the whole body, or think fit that all senators who are named in the decree shall swear over the sacrificial victims to maintain the agreement inviolable.

Menenius appeals: "Do not traduce assurances given under the sanction of the gods and confirmed by the pledging of hands and by treaties, nor destroy the noblest of all human institutions!"

In Aelius Aristides' attempt to reconcile the Rhodians, he tells them that whenever anger assails, they should summon as its antagonist the following λογισμός:

---

[98]Demosthenes *Ep* 1.14-15; the translation is that of N. W. and N. J. DeWitt in the LCL, vol. 7 (Cambridge: Harvard University Press, 1949) 207. The authenticity of the work is doubted; see J. A. Goldstein, *The Letters of Demosthenes* (New York: Columbia University Press, 1968).

ἡ πατρὶς ἡμῖν σωτέα κοινῇ ἵν' ἔχωμεν ἐφ' ᾗ φρονοῦμεν·
οὐκοῦν στασιαζόντων μὲν ἀπόλλυται, μιᾷ δὲ γνώμῃ χρησαμένων ἅμα καλλίων καί μείζων γίγνεται. τί οὖν ἡμᾶς
αὐτοὺς καταλύομεν;[99]

If each one is willing to say these things to himself, Aristides concludes, and does not destroy them by deed (ἀλλ' ἔργῳ μὲν ἀπολλύειν), the country will not be given over to troubles.[100]

The most famous reconciliation agreement in antiquity was that which ended the Athenian civil war in 403 B.C.[101] The agreement was recorded for public consultation (Isocrates 18.20) and was often cited in antiquity as a model of political enlightenment.[102] Plutarch gives the exact date on which Thrasyboulos and his followers marched back into Athens and claims that the event was still being celebrated in his own day (*Mor.* 349F). The ancient authors agree that the adoption of the reconciliation agreement was in large measure attributable to the efforts of Pausanias (Aristotle *Ath Pol* 38.4; Diodorus Siculus 14.33.6). Xenophon (*Hell* 2.4.38) records that the reconciliation was adopted on these terms, that the two parties should be at peace with one another (οἱ δὲ διήλλαξαν ἐφ' ᾧτε εἰρήνην μὲν ἔχειν πρὸς ἀλλήλους). When the armies had been disbanded, an assembly was convened. Thrasyboulos addressed the aristocratic faction in a manner strikingly reminiscent of 1 Cor 1–4:

> I advise you, men of the city, to know yourselves. And you would best learn to know yourselves were you to consider what grounds you have for arrogance, that you should undertake to rule over us. Are you more just? But the commons, though poorer than you, never did you any wrong for the sake of money; while you, though richer than any of them, have done many disgraceful things for the sake of gain. . . . Well then, would you say that you

---

[99]Aelius Aristides *Or* 24.37.

[100]Aelius Aristides *Or* 24.38.

[101]Thomas Clark Loening, *The Reconciliation Agreement of 403/402 B.C. in Athens. Its Context and Application*, Hermes 53 (Stuttgart: Franz Steiner, 1987) esp. 13-52.

[102]E.g., Aristotle *Ath Pol* 39.6; Isocrates 18.3; Thucydides 3.82-85; Diodorus Siculus 14.33.6; Plutarch *Lysias* 21.3-4.

are superior in intelligence? . . . Nevertheless, my comrades, I am not the man to ask you to violate any one of the pledges to which you have sworn (ἀξιῶ ἐγὼ ὧν ὁμωμόκατε παραβῆναι οὐδέν), but I ask you rather to show this virtue also, in addition to your other virtues,—that you are true to your oaths and are god-fearing men (ὅτι καὶ εὔορκοι καὶ ὅσιοί ἐστε).[103]

Xenophon (*Hell* 2.4.42) observes,

When he had said this and more to the same effect, and had told them that there was no need of their being disturbed (ὅτι οὐδὲν δέοι ταράτ- τεσθαι), but that they only had to live under the laws that had previously been in force (ἀλλὰ τοῖς νόμοις τοῖς ἀρχαίοις χρῆσθαι), he dismissed the assembly.

Though the reconciliation was subsequently threatened by plots, concord prevailed, because the parties did not violate their pledges. Xenophon concludes his account thus:

And, pledged as they were under oath, that in very truth they would not remember past grievances, the two parties even to this day live together as fellow citizens and the commons abide by their oaths (καὶ ὁμόσαντες ὅρκους ἦ μὴν μὴ μνησικάκειν, ἔτι καὶ νῦν ὁμοῦ τε πολιτι- τεύονται καὶ τοῖς ὅρκοις ἐμμένει ὁ δῆμος, *Hell* 2.4.43).

We come closer to the actual wording of the principle as given by Paul if we explore more broadly the rhetorical situation.[104] Paul makes no secret of the particular exigence which has invited his response in 1 Cor 1–4: Chloe's people have arrived with news of ἔριδες in the Corinthian church (1:11). Paul finds himself cast in the role of conciliator. Paul accepts the role in an effort to position himself above the fray. As Aristotle observes (*Pol* 1297a6-7), "everywhere it is the arbitrator that is most trusted, and the man in the middle is an arbitrator" (πανταχοῦ δὲ

---

[103]Xenophon *Hellenica* 2.4.39-42; text and translation is that of C. L. Brownson in the LCL (Cambridge: Harvard University, 1968) 168-71.

[104]On the concept of rhetorical situation, see Lloyd F. Bitzer, "The Rhetorical Situation," *Philosophy and Rhetoric* 1 (1968) 1-14. Francis Cairns (*Generic Composition In Greek and Latin Poetry* [Edinburgh: University of Edinburgh, 1972] 6) discusses the relationship of social situation to genre in general.

πιστότατος ὁ διαιτητής, διαιτητής δ' ὁ μέσος). It is interesting to observe how skillfully Paul plays the part, being careful, as Plutarch advised, "to converse with both parties and to join neither."[105] A similar situation has occasioned most of the discourses on concord; a philosopher or rhetorician is asked to speak words that will reconcile rival factions. But there was an instance of conciliation which was far better known to the citizens of the ancient world: arbitration. The practice of submitting disputes to a neutral person or body was firmly established in Greece from a very early period.[106] Private διαιτηταί were regularly employed to settle claims on an equitable basis.[107] Arbitration was also widely used in the international field to compose differences between city-states[108] and to secure harmony among members of alliances.[109] The practice continued under the Empire, since Rome found it a useful instrument of policy.[110] The senate frequently adjudicated disputes between provincial cities until the third century A.D., often employing local agents.[111] An important part of the arbitrators function was the communication of a written statement of the judgment (ἐπιγραφή) to

---

[105]Plutarch *Praecepta gerendae reipublicae* 824B.

[106]See the article by T. Thalheim in *PW* 5.313ff.; A. Steinwenter, *Streitbeendigung durch Urteil, Schiedsspruch und Vergleich nach griechischen Recht* (Berlin, 1925).

[107]M. H. E. Meier, *Die Privatschiedsrichter und die öffentlichen Diäteten Athens* (Halle, 1846); B. Hubert, *De arbitris atticis et privatis et publicis* (Göttingen, 1885); for Roman history, see Karl Heinz Ziegler, *Das Private Schiedsgericht im antiken römischen Recht*, MBPAR 58 (München: Beck, 1971).

[108]A. Raeder, *L'Arbitrage international chez les Hellènes* (Christiana, 1912); M. N. Tod, *International Arbitration Amongst the Greeks* (Oxford: Clarendon, 1913).

[109]On this dimension of interstate arbitration, see L. Piccirilli, *Gli Arbitrati Interstali Greci* (Pisa, 1973).

[110]Livy bks. 30-45; E. de Ruggiero, *L'arbitrato pubblico presso i Romani* (Rome, 1893); E. Badian, *Foreign Clientelae* (Oxford: Oxford University, 1958).

[111]Texts and commentary in Robert K. Sherk, *Roman Documents from the Greek East. Senatus Consulta and Epistulae to the Age of Augustus* (Baltimore: Johns Hopkins University Press, 1969); F. F. Abbott and A. C. Johnson, *Municipal Administration In the Roman Empire* (Princeton: Princeton University Press, 1926).

the disputants.[112] To secure for the arbitral decision greater permanence and more publicity, measures were taken to have it inscribed upon stone or metal.[113] From these inscriptions we learn the details of the arbitral process—the appointment of the tribunal, the presentation of the evidence, the formulation of the award, the penalties and sanctions, etc. In connection with the arbitrator's attempt to encourage compliance with the terms, we find a formula which promises to throw light upon the language of Paul.

After a period of hostilities the cities of Magnesia and Smyrna were reconciled by a treaty of friendship.[114] The text of the agreement negotiated between them records an oath which the citizens of both sides are to swear:

> I shall abide by the agreements which I have concluded for all time . . . and I shall transgress nothing of what is in the agreement, nor shall I change for the worse the things written in it, in any way or on any pretext; and I shall live in concord and without faction (ἐμμενῶ ἐν ταῖς συνθήκαις αἷς συντέθειμαι εἰς ἅπαντα τὸν χρόνον . . . καὶ οὐθὲν παραβήσομαι κατὰ τὴν ὁμολογίαν οὐδὲ μεταθήσω ἐπὶ τὸ χεῖρον τὰ γεγραμμένα ἐν αὐτῇ οὔτε τρόπῳ οὔτε μηχανῇ οὐδεμιᾷ καὶ πολιτεύσομαι μεθ' ὁμονοίας ἀστασιάστως).[115]

An inscription found at Delos records a resolution passed by the citizens of Latos and Olus entrusting the arbitration of their existing differences to Cnossus.[116] The observance of the agreement is guaranteed by a pledge taken by the citizens of both sides in common: τὰ δὲ κριθέντα καὶ ἀγγραφέντα ὑπὸ τῶν Κνωσίων βέβαια καὶ κύρια ἦμεν ἐς τὸν πάντα χρόνον, καὶ μηκέτι ὑπολείπεσθαι αὐτοῖς περὶ μηθενὸς ἔνκλημα μηθὲν παρευρέσει μηδεμιᾷ.[117] Melitea and Perea submitted their differences over lands and boundaries to arbitration

---

[112]M. N. Tod, *International Arbitration Amongst the Greeks* (Oxford: Clarendon, 1913) 152ff.
[113]Ibid., 154.
[114]*OGIS* 229, ca. 242 B.C.E.
[115]Ibid., lines 61-65.
[116]Ditt. *Syll.*³ 712, ca. 102/101 B.C.E.
[117]Ibid., lines 28-30.

on the occasion of their political union (συμπολιτεία).[118] The arbitrators attempt to give their judgment binding force by imposing a fine upon anyone who withdraws from citizenship with respect to the things which are written (τοῖς γεγραμμένοις).[119]

The formula was not limited, however, to instances where outstanding differences needed to be resolved. It was also used in a positive sense by those who sought to effect political union (συμπολιτεία).[120] So, for example, when two small, neighboring cities, Stiris and Medeon, entered into συμπολιτεία, they drew up a ὁμολογία which concluded with the following provision:

> It shall not be permissible for the Medeonians to break away from the Stirians nor the Stirians from the Medeonians. Whichever of the two sides does not abide by the things which are written shall pay to those who do ten talents of silver (μὴ ἐξέστω δὲ ἀποπολιτεύσασθαι τοὺς Μεδεωνίους ἀπὸ τῶν Στιρίων μηδὲ τοὺς Στιρίους ἀπὸ τῶν Μεδεωνίων· ὁπότεροι δὲ κα μὴ ἐμμείνωντι ἐν τοῖς γεγραμμένοις, αποτεισαντων τοις εμμειναντοις αργυριου ταλαντα δέκα).[121]

Paul's use of the preposition ὑπέρ reflects the conventional language of the counsel of concord. The preposition ὑπέρ, either with an object, or in combination with another word, is used to describe the immoderate pride which gives rise to faction.[122] In the 'Αθηναίων πολιτεία, Aristotle relates how Solon exhorted the wealthy not to be covetous: "Restrain in your hearts those stubborn moods, plunged in a surfeit of abundant goods, and moderate your pride!" (5.3). Aristotle observes:

> And he always attaches the blame for civil strife (στάσις) wholly to the rich; this is why he says at the beginning of the poem that he fears "Both

---

[118]Ditt. *Syll.*³ 546, ca. 212 B.C.E.

[119]Ibid., lines 15-18.

[120]On συμπολιτεία see J. A. O. Larsen, *Greek Federal States* (Oxford: Oxford University Press, 1968).

[121]Ditt. *Syll*³ 647.55-57.

[122]Similarly, P. Marshall, *Enmity in Corinth: Social Conventions in Paul's Relations with the Corinthians*, WUNT 23 (Tübingen: Mohr-Siebeck, 1987) 197.

love of money and o'erweening pride (ὑπερηφανία)," implying that these were the causes of the prevailing enmity (5.3).[123]

Paul himself exhorts the Roman Christians: "I bid everyone among you not to think himself beyond what it is proper to think (μὴ ὑπερφρο- νεῖν παρ' ὃ δεῖ φρονεῖν), but to think with sober judgment, each according to the measure of faith which God has assigned him" (Rom. 12:3).[124] The term ὑπέρ denotes a self-conception which threatens to destroy community by placing itself beyond the measure of unanimity.

The injunction "not to go beyond the things which are written" has a specific function and a characteristic form in each of the contexts we have examined. In the arbitral agreements, in particular, it was a fixed part of the machinery, with a well-defined role. Paul abstracted the admonition from its context and gave it the character of a maxim.[125] But Paul had correctly recognized that wherever in ancient political life this principle was found, it served the same general purpose: negatively, it erected a barrier against faction; positively, it facilitated a reconciliation. These were Paul's own purposes in 1 Cor 1–4, to which the principle μὴ ὑπὲρ ἃ γέγραπται was admirably suited. Nor does Paul seem to have been the only one who recognized the existence of the general principle that dissension is a transgression of what is written. Philo explains the discord created by Macro as resulting from his disregard of

---

[123]See also οὐκ ὑπέρφευ φρονεῖν, Aeschylus *Pers* 820; ὑπερβασία, Sophocles *Sept* 734-39; ὑπερέχειν, Aristotle *Rhet* 2.2.6; ὑπερόπτης, Aristotle *EN* 4.3.21, 1124a29; ὑπερφίαλος, Homer *Od* 1.134, 227; ὑπὲρ τὸν ἀλαθῆ λόγον, Pindar *Od* 1.28; ὑπὲρ δύναμιν, Thucydides 6.16.2; ναύκληρον μεγέθει μὲν καὶ ῥώμῃ ὑπὲρ τοὺς ἐν τῇ νηὶ πάν- τας . . . τοὺς δὲ ναύτας στασιάζοντας πρὸς ἀλλήλους περὶ τῆς κυβερνήσως, ἕκαστον οἰόμενον δεῖν κυβερνᾶν, μήτε μαθόντα πώ- ποτε τὴν τέχνην μήτε ἔχοντα ἀποδεῖξαι διδάσκαλον ἑαυτοῦ μηδὲ χρόνον ἐν ᾧ ἐμάνθανεν, Plato *Rep* 488B; ὑπὲρ ἄνθρωπον εἶναι, Plato *Leg* 839D; ὑπὲρ ὅρκια, Homer *Il* 3.299.

[124]Compare the use of ὑπέρ as an adverb in 2 Cor 11:23, διάκονοι χρισ- τοῦ εἰσιν . . . ὑπὲρ ἐγώ. Cf. Euripides *Med* 627: ὑπὲρ μὲν ἄγαν.

[125]On the use of maxims in deliberative discourse, see Aristotle *Rhet* 2.21. Paul employs the kind of maxim which Aristotle terms "well-known"; it requires neither proof nor epilogue.

the Delphic γράμμα, γνῶθι σαυτόν.[126] Like Paul, he combines with this the observation that Macro "was puffed up beyond measure" (πλέον ἐφυσήθη τοῦ μετρίου).[127]

After having spoken figuratively of relations between the Corinthian factions, exemplifying what he had to say by reference to himself and Apollos, Paul wished to state plainly what he intended that the Corinthians should learn and the kind of conduct he hoped they would avoid. The result is the two purpose clauses which now stand in 1 Cor 4:6. Our investigation has shown that the former, with its appeal to the principle μὴ ὑπὲρ ἃ γέγραπται, is as coherent with Paul's purposes throughout 1 Cor 1–4 as the latter: both serve to dissuade from faction and to promote concord. We cannot know whether Paul's purposes were achieved. We hear no more of the parties in 2 Corinthians, though one or more of them may have coalesced into the more serious opposition to Paul evident, above all, in 2 Cor 10–13. But of one thing we may be sure: Paul would not have been misunderstood by anyone familiar with the conventions of ancient political life when he wrote the words τὸ μὴ ὑπὲρ ἃ γέγραπται.

---

[126]Philo Leg ad Gai 69.

[127]Ibid. Note also the well-known case of Pausanias of Sparta in Thucydides 1.132.1-3 and Demosthenes 59.97, who became "puffed up" (φυσηθείς) at his victories, so that his life departed from the "established customs" (νομίμοι), and it became clear that he did not want to remain an equal in the political order. He had a verse celebrating his victory over the Persians inscribed on the tripod at Delphi, as if the achievement had been his own, and not the common work of the allies. The Spartans felt that his act was a "transgression" (ἀδίκημα, παρανομία) and had the verses chiselled off, inscribing on the tripod instead the names of all the cities which had fought against the Persians.

A CONCILIATORY CONVENTION
AND PAUL'S REFERENCES TO THE "LETTER OF TEARS"

In 1897, the Irish scholar James Houghton Kennedy put forward the hypothesis that "the epistle referred to in 2 Cor 2:4 as written ἐκ πολλῆς θλίψεως καὶ συνοχῆς καρδίας was not our 1 Corinthians but an epistle whose closing portion we possess in chapters 10-13 of 2 Corinthians."[1] Kennedy's proofs consisted of inferences from internal evidence, a series of cross-references from 2 Cor 1–7 to 2 Cor 10–13. The references were of two kinds: the first consisted of general descriptions in chapters 1–2 and 7 of a previous letter of Paul to Corinth, to which the writing now preserved in 2 Cor 10–13 was seen to correspond; the second consisted of special allusions to the content of the severe epistle, which refer to specific words and phrases of 2 Cor 10–13.[2]

Kennedy's arguments proved convincing to many at the beginning of the century. Moffatt rearranged the text of 2 Corinthians in accordance with the hypothesis.[3] Gerald Rendall tested the theory to determine whether at any point it involved contradictions with the language or implications of the record; he concluded that the idea conferred reality on the circumstances and plausibility on the motives, to the extent that these could be reconstructed.[4] Kirsopp Lake provided a powerful summary,

---

[1] J. H. Kennedy, "Are There Two Epistles in 2 Corinthians?" *The Expositor* 6 (1897): 233; repr. in idem, *The Second and Third Epistles of St. Paul to the Corinthians* (London: Methuen, 1900) xiii.

[2] In his article in *The Expositor* (n. 1, above), Kennedy first presented the proofs derived from a comparison of specific passages (234-36), then examined the general marks of identification (294-300). In *The Second and Third Epistles* (63-68, 79-94), the order of presentation is reversed.

[3] J. Moffatt, *The Historical New Testament* (New York: Scribner's, 1901) 174-91. See also his statements in support of Kennedy's hypothesis in idem, *An Introduction to the Literature of the New Testament* (New York: Scribner's, ³1918) 119ff.

[4] G. Rendall, *The Epistles of St. Paul to the Corinthians* (London: Macmillan, 1909) passim, but esp. 4-6.

condensing and tightening Kennedy's arguments.[5] The theory underlies the commentaries of Alfred Plummer and R. H. Strachan,[6] and was the key to daring reconstructions of the history of Paul and Corinth by C. H. Dodd and T. W. Manson.[7] By the middle of the century, it seemed that Kennedy had triumphed.[8]

Yet Kennedy's work made little impression upon contemporary German scholars.[9] This was not because Germans were ignorant of Kennedy, as references in Windisch show,[10] but rather because, some decades before, objections had been raised against a similar hypothesis put forward by Adolf Hausrath.[11] To many, the objections seemed insuperable. Objections assumed a variety of forms, but amounted, essentially, to this: despite evidence for the priority of chs. 10-13, and the appearance of verbal cross-references, the correlation is less than perfect.

---

[5]K. Lake, *The Earlier Epistles of St. Paul: Their Motive and Origin* (London: Rivingtons, [2]1914) 151-60.

[6]A. Plummer, *A Critical and Exegetical Commentary on the Second Epistle of St. Paul to the Corinthians*, ICC (Edinburgh: T.&T. Clark, 1915) esp. xxii-xxvi; R. H. Strachan, *The Second Epistle of St. Paul to the Corinthians*, MNTC (New York: Harper, 1935) xivff.

[7]C. H. Dodd, "The Mind of Paul (I)," repr. in his *New Testament Studies* (Manchester: Manchester University, 1953) 80-81; T. W. Manson, "St. Paul in Ephesus (4): The Corinthian Correspondence," *BJRL* 26 (1941-1942): 327-41, repr. as "The Corinthian Correspondence (2)" in his *Studies in the Gospels and Epistles*, ed. M. Black (Manchester: Manchester University Press, 1962) 210-24.

[8]Of course, there were still those who maintained the unity of 2 Corinthians, such as A. Menzies, *The Second Epistle of the Apostle Paul to the Corinthians* (London: Macmillan, 1912) esp. xxxiv-xlii. But see the judgment of F. Watson, "2 Cor x-xiii and Paul's Painful Letter to the Corinthians," *JTS* 35/2 (1984): 328: "one can justifiably speak of a consensus among English speaking scholars of the first half of the century in favour of the identification hypothesis."

[9]Kennedy left no mark upon A. Jülicher, *Einleitung in das Neue Testament* (Tübingen: Mohr/Siebeck, 1906), nor upon H. Lietzmann, *An die Korinther I/II*, HNT (Tübingen: Mohr/Siebeck, 1909), nor even upon J. Weiss, *Das Urchristentum*, ed. R. Knopf (Göttingen: Vandenhoeck & Ruprecht, 1917).

[10]H. Windisch, *Der zweite Korintherbrief*, KEK 6 (Göttingen: Vandenhoeck & Ruprecht, 1924; repr. 1970) 13n.1.

[11]A. Hausrath. *Der Vier-Capitel-Brief des Paulus an die Korinther* (Heidelberg: Bassermann, 1870).

The "offence" that Paul mentions in 2:5 and 7:12 is not discussed in chs. 10-13; while the actual content of chs. 10-13, that is, Paul's defense of his apostleship against Judaistic opponents, is passed over in silence in what Paul says about the painful epistle in chs. 2 and 7. The discrepancy was already noted by Max Krenkel in his influential essay of 1890.[12] His arguments were repeated with emphasis by Richard Drescher a few years later.[13] The one thing which, on Hausrath's view, was certain to be found in the severe epistle is not contained in what is believed to be a fragment of this writing in chs. 10-13; while, what appears in the last four chapters fails to correspond to the apostle's account of the severe epistle in 2:4 and 7:8. The matter seemed to have reached an impasse.[14]

Critics who have sought to maintain, in the face of objections, the identification of 2 Cor 10–13 with the "letter of tears" have typically resorted to the explanation that what we possess in the last four chapters

---

[12]M. Krenkel, "Der persönliche und briefliche Verkehr des Apostels mit der Gemeinde zu Korinth" in his *Beiträge zur Aufhellung der Geschichte und der Briefe des Apostels Paulus* (Braunschweig: Schwetschke, 1895) 268-73.

[13]R. Drescher, "Der zweite Korintherbrief und die Vorgänge in Korinth seit Abfassung des ersten Korintherbriefes," *ThStKr* 70 (1897) 43-111, esp. 58ff.

[14]Windisch provides an instructive example of the ambivalence of the critics and the ambiguity of the evidence. He grasped the reasons that led Hausrath and Kennedy to equate chs. 10–13 with the "letter of tears," *Der zweite Korintherbrief*, 17ff., 81-82, 92-93, 425. But Krenkel's objections had made an impression which Windisch could not overcome, ibid., 14, 18, 93. Thus, Windisch judged that the "letter of tears" had been lost. He proposed that chs. 10–13 were the reaction of Paul to a fresh outbreak of the crisis reported to Paul after the dispatch of chs. 1–9, ibid., 17-18, 431. Windisch was aware of the speculative nature of his own hypothesis—that it required him to posit a series of events for which there was no support in the text: the return of one or more emissaries, another visit to the church, and in Corinth yet another attack by opponents of the apostle's work, ibid., 431-32. He knew how unlikely it was historically that the cycle of strife and reconciliation should repeat itself in so brief a scope. Yet Windisch felt driven to this solution by the less than perfect correlation between Paul's account of his severe epistle and the content of chs. 10-13. However implausible and speculative, Windisch's hypothesis avoided contradiction with any statement of the received epistle, ibid., 17-18; so already Krenkel, *Beiträge*, 306. For this reason, Windisch's theory has proven attractive to a number of scholars, among whom are Barrett, Bruce, and Furnish.

is not the whole of the severe epistle, but only its concluding part. In the earlier portion, now lost, the apostle apparently dealt in detail with the case of the ἀδικήσας. Thus Hausrath allowed that none of the extant fragments provide as much information about the wrongdoer as is presupposed by statements in chs. 2 and 7, so that we must still reckon with a lost epistle, or a portion thereof.[15] He conjectured that chs. 10-13 were a Pauline addendum to a letter of the Ephesian church which dealt with the offence against Paul and the collection for the Jerusalem saints.[16] Schmiedel, likewise, sought to address the incompleteness of chs. 10-13, the fact that, contrary to expectations, the ἀδικήσας is not mentioned. He found the wrongdoing hinted at in 10:6, in the παρακοή Paul was ready to avenge.[17] Yet he allowed that Paul should have been more explicit, if chs. 10-13 were the "letter of tears." Thus he proposed that the section had been lost in which Paul dealt with the ἀδικήσας; it was suppressed, he believed, by the Corinthian church in an effort to conceal its shame.[18] Kennedy argued that chs. 10–13 were the concluding section of an epistle of which the earlier portion had been lost, like the letter referred to in 1 Cor 5:9.[19] The intensive pronoun (αὐτός) and the copulative particle (δέ), which introduce the last four chapters (10:1), function to continue and to emphasize a discussion already begun. He found this hypothesis confirmed by the following verses, which allude to charges against the apostle, not as if they were now introduced, but as if they had already been mentioned.[20]

---

[15]Hausrath, *Der Vier-Capitel-Brief,* 28. Hausrath has been criticized for suggesting that the four chapters are the whole of the severe epistle, first by Lake, *The Earlier Epistles,* 162, then by H. D. Betz, *2 Corinthians 8 and 9: Two Administrative Letters of the Apostle Paul,* Hermeneia (Philadelphia: Fortress, 1985) 13. This misconception had its origin with Kennedy, *The Second and Third Epistles,* xiv; if Kennedy had direct access to Hausrath, he misunderstood him on this point.

[16]Hausrath, *Der Vier-Capitel-Brief,* 28.

[17]P. Schmiedel, *Hand-Commentar zum Neuen Testament,* vol. 2: *Die Briefe an die Korinther* (Freiburg: Mohr/Siebeck, ²1892) 61.

[18]Ibid., 62.

[19]J. Kennedy, "Are There Two Epistles in 2 Corinthians?" *The Expositor* 6 (1897): 288-90; idem, *The Second and Third Epistles,* xiv-xvi.

[20]Kennedy, *The Second and Third Epistles,* 96-98.

It is possible that chs. 10-13 are a fragment of a larger epistle whose initial section has been lost. The abruptness of 10:1f. might therein find its explanation. The intensive pronoun (αὐτός) might mark a contrast between Paul and whoever (the Ephesians, Timothy) had spoken previously. Perhaps it is not without significance that Paul employs the first person singular predominately in the last four chapters. The particle, δέ, is adversative and copulative, and could thus have served to distinguish what follows from a related discussion that went before.[21] Thus, certain characteristics of chs. 10-13, and in particular its opening words, αὐτὸς δὲ ἐγὼ Παῦλος, lend some support to the conjecture that these chapters are but the concluding portion of what was once a larger work.

But this is not the only conclusion that the evidence warrants. The phrase αὐτὸς δὲ ἐγὼ Παῦλος, may not be intended to mark a contrast between the apostle and others, or between these chapters and what preceded. Paul elsewhere uses related expressions to accentuate his own authority, e.g., ἴδε ἐγὼ Παῦλος in Gal 5:2, αὐτὸς ἐγώ in 2 Cor 12:13 and Rom 15:14, without implying such distinctions.[22] Nor do chs. 10-13 give the impression of incompleteness; the argument seems self-contained.[23] Only the prescript may be lacking. 2 Cor 10-13 would then be a work which, like Paul's letter to the Galatians, made its beginning in medias res, without the customary "thanksgiving" (cf. Gal 1:6).[24]

However one evaluates the evidence, the argument that chs. 10-13 are only part of the "letter of tears, "and that the name of the ἀδικήσας and the incident he provoked have been removed by a redactor, is

---

[21]H. W. Smyth, *Greek Grammar* (Cambridge MA: Harvard University Press, 1920) §§2834-36.

[22]So already J. Kennedy, "Are There Two Epistles in 2 Corinthians?" *The Expositor* 6 (1897): 288; Windisch, *Der zweite Korintherbrief,* 290-91, with parallels from Greek literature; R. Bultmann, *Der zweite Brief an die Korinther,* KEK 6 (Göttingen: Vandenhoeck & Ruprecht, 1976) 182.

[23]H. D. Betz, *Der Apostel Paulus und die sokratische Tradition: Eine exegetische Untersuchung zu seiner "Apologie" 2 Kor 10-13,* BHTh 45 (Tübingen: Mohr/Siebeck, 1972) 13-42; cf. the "Epilogue" to D. Georgi, *The Opponents of Paul in Second Corinthians* (Philadelphia: Fortress, 1986) 336-37.

[24]Windisch, *Der zweite Korintherbrief,* 291, who points to Phil 1:3 D* as a stylistic parallel.

ein reines argumentum e silentio, as Hans Dieter Betz correctly observed.[25] As such, it will never prove very convincing, even if it corresponds to the facts. Nor does this solution address the whole problem which critics of Hausrath and Kennedy have identified. Paul's failure to mention the object of dispute in 2 Cor 10–13, namely, the charges of certain missionary rivals, in references to the severe epistle in chs. 1-2 and 7, still remains to be explained. Few interpreters have been convinced by Bornkamm's argument that, since the opponents were *umherziehende Wanderapostel*, they had abandoned Corinth by the time that chs. 1–2 and 7 came to be written; thus Paul could devote his whole attention in the letter of reconciliation to the restoration of good relations with the community.[26] Other solutions must be discovered, if the identification of chs. 10–13 with the "letter of tears" is to be maintained.

Francis Watson has advanced the discussion by observing that the discrepancy between chs. 10-13 and the "letter of tears" is not as great as the critics allege.[27] In his comments on the severe epistle in chs. 1-2 and 7, Paul does not, in fact, pass over in silence the substance of chs. 10-13, that is, the challenge to his apostolic authority. It is clear from 2:5-11 and 7:12 that a member of the Corinthian church had committed an offence against Paul. But the way in which Paul speaks of the matter implicates the church in his act of defiance. For, prior to the severe epistle, the Corinthians had taken no action against the offender (2:5-9). It was the purpose of the severe epistle to evoke the loyalty which was not forthcoming, to reveal to the Corinthians their zeal for Paul (7:7,12). The reprimand was directed not just at an individual, but at the entire church, to test their earnestness and obedience (2:4,9; 7:11). That the Corinthians knew themselves to be its object is apparent from the nature of their response, which consisted in "godly grief" and "repentance" (7:7-10). All of this corresponds perfectly to the situation

---

[25]Betz, *Der Apostel Paulus*, 6.

[26]Bornkamm, *Vorgeschichte*, 19; criticized by Betz, *Der Apostel Paulus*, 7, and C. Machelet, "Paulus und seine Gegner. Eine Untersuchung zu den Korintherbriefen" in *Theokratia*, ed. W. Dietrich (Leiden: Brill, 1973) 187-88.

[27]F. Watson, "2 Cor x–xiii and Paul's Painful Letter to the Corinthians," *JTS* 35/2 (1984): 324-46. Watson's argument for the unity of chs. 1–9 is unconvincing; but his discussion of the identification of the painful epistle marks the only real advance in this area in almost a century.

of chs. 10-13, where the attacks of rival missionaries have moved the church to revolt against Paul.[28]

Watson found, moreover, a reference to the offence against Paul, and to the offender, in 2 Cor 10–13.[29] Each painful word of the last four chapters makes it clear that this work is the apostle's response to a denial of his authority. At issue is Paul's legitimacy, his status as a true apostle (11:5; 12:12).[30] Doubts have been raised by Paul's opponents: they have questioned the mode of his existence and the authenticity of his gospel (11:1-21).[31] But the Corinthians have let themselves be persuaded; the opponents have made prey of them (11:3-4, 19-20). They regard Paul as weak and ineffectual: by letter, he seems bold and strong; but he is humble and weak when face to face (10:1,10-11; 11:21). The Corinthians have concluded, it seems, that Paul is powerless to punish offenders (10:1-6; 12:19-21). They suspect that the reason for his incapacity is a lack of divine authorization (13:10). His ministry has a merely human basis (10:2); he does not live by the power of God (13:4). They will not submit to Paul's authority, unless he can provide proof of the claim that it is Christ who speaks in him (13:1-3). Thus, the offence which provoked the last four chapters is that, during Paul's second visit to Corinth, he was accused of being a false apostle by certain members of the congregation, because of his failure to manifest the authority characteristic of the apostolic office.[32]

The crucial question is whether this attack upon Paul's apostolic legitimacy can be identified with the grievous offence which lies at the base of the "letter of tears." In 10:2 Paul distinguishes between the congregation and "some (τινες) who consider that we are acting according to human standards." But a few verses later, in 10:7, the plural pronoun is replaced by the singular: "If anyone (τις) is confident that he belongs

---

[28]Ibid., 340-42.

[29]Ibid., 342-46.

[30]Watson calls attention to E. Käsemann's treatment of the topic in "Die Legitimat des Apostels. Eine Untersuchung zu II Korinther 10-13," *ZNW* 41 (1942): 33-71.

[31]Betz, *Der Apostel Paulus*, 100-37.

[32]F. Watson, "2 Cor x–xiii and Paul's Painful Letter to the Corinthians," *JTS* 35/2 (1984): 345. Watson views the charge of misappropriation of funds in 12:16-18 as derived and secondary.

to Christ, so also do we." Again, in 10:11, the apostle warns, "Let such a person (ὁ τοιοῦτος) understand that what we are in word through epistles when absent, such we are in deed when present." The unnamed person of whom Paul speaks is evidently the leader of a group which has challenged Paul's authority. This corresponds exactly to 2:5-6, where the one who caused pain, and must now be punished, is referred to as τις and ὁ τοιοῦτος. In 10:2 Paul pleads with the congregation to spare him the necessity of punishing those who challenge his authority; the church is asked, in other words, to take disciplinary measures against one of its members. In 2:5ff. one finds that the church has severely punished an offender in whose offence some have taken part. Thus 2 Cor 10–13 may be identified with the "letter of tears".[33]

There can be no doubt of the importance of Watson's insights. Chs. 10-13 make discreet reference to the Corinthian offender and his offence against Paul. Chs. 1-2 and 7 reflect the Corinthians' complicity in a revolt against Paul's authority. Watson follows unconsciously in the steps of Hausrath and Schmiedel.[34] The latter, one recalls, had glimpsed an allusion to the offence against Paul in the language of 10:6, in the παρακοή Paul was ready to avenge. Like Hausrath before him, Watson suggests that doubts about Paul's authority had their origin in the apostle's failure to inflict punishment upon an offender, though Watson avoids Hausrath's mistake of identifying the wrongdoer with the incestuous man.[35] Closer reading of chs. 10-13 might well discover additional passages in which Paul alludes to the wrong that was done, just as closer attention to chs. 1-2 and 7 might reveal further references to the opponents and their attack upon Paul.

But even with Watson's observations, the substance of the objection against the identification hypothesis remains. For what is alleged by the critics is not merely that there is no evidence of complicity by the Corinthians in a wrong that was done to Paul, but that the substance of the challenge to the legitimacy of Paul's apostleship is passed over in

---

[33]Ibid., 345-46.

[34]Watson, ibid., 325n.10, acknowledges that he was unable to obtain a copy of Hausrath's book; his knowledge of Hausrath rests upon Heinrici and Kennedy. Nor does he refer to Schmiedel's commentary. Thus he seems to be unaware of the degree to which he recapitulates their arguments.

[35]Ibid., 342-46.

silence in what Paul says about the severe epistle in chs. 1-2 and 7.[36] The lack must finally be acknowledged: there is no mention in the letter of reconciliation (2 Cor 1:1–2:13; 7:5-16; 13:11-13) of Paul's weakness (11:21), of his failure to produce the σημεῖα τοῦ ἀποστόλου (12:11-12), of his refusal to accept support from the community, interpreted as an admission of his inferiority to the other apostles (11:5ff.; 12:13), of the craft and deceit by which he aimed to defraud the Corinthians through the collection (12:16-18). These are the charges of chs. 10-13, on the basis of which the Corinthians and Paul's opponents question the legitimacy of his apostleship.[37] Of all these charges, there is not one word in what Paul says about the severe epistle in 2 Cor 2 and 7.

But perhaps it is the critics' assumption that is at fault, and not a discrepancy in the letters of Paul. It is assumed by critics of the identification hypothesis that Paul ought to have made explicit mention of the former object of dispute in the letter preserved in 2 Cor 1:1–2:13; 7:5-16; 13:11-13. It is this assumption which has given cogency to objections against Hausrath's hypothesis. But is the assumption warranted? Only investigation of the genre of a letter such as Paul has composed in 2 Cor 1:1–2:13; 7:5-16; 13:11-13 can provide an answer to this question.[38] Is reference to the cause of strife permitted by the rules of the genre? Does it lie within the constraints imposed? Such an investigation has not been undertaken, at least not with the present question in mind.[39]

---

[36]Thus, rightly, Bornkamm, *Vorgeschichte*, 16: "der eigentliche Inhalt des letzten Briefteiles, die Abschüttelung der Rivalen, in dem Versöhnungsbrief (2 Kor 2 und 7) mit Stillschweigen übergegangen wird."

[37]E. Käsemann, "Die Legitimität des Apostels. Eine Untersuchung zu II Korinther 10-13," *ZNW* 41 (1942): 34-36.

[38]The importance of genre in composition was recognized in antiquity: see esp. Plato *Phaedrus* 264C-D; *Gorgias* 503E-504A; 506D-E; Aristotle *Poetics* 50A-B; *Anonymous Seguerianus* 435.10-19; 436.4-12 (Spengel). It is fully appreciated by F. Cairns, *Generic Composition in Greek and Roman Poetry* (Edinburgh: University Press, 1972) and by M. Heath, *Unity in Greek Poetics* (Oxford: Clarendon Press, 1989) 37-38, 94-95, 150-54. Heath concludes that "the assessment of a text's appropriate construction always involves questions of content: are the functions of the genre fulfilled?" (154).

[39]To be sure, there have been discussions of the genre of 2 Cor 1–7, e.g., L. Belleville, "A Letter of Apologetic Self-Commendation: 2 Cor 1:8–7:16,"

The conciliatory aim of the letter preserved in 2 Cor 1:1–2:13; 7:5-16; 13:11-13 was recognized by scholars not long after it was determined by Johannes Weiss that these chapters once constituted an independent work.[40] Weiss was followed by A. Loisy, who referred to 2 Cor 1:1–2:13; 7: 5-16 as a "lettre de concilation".[41] It was Hans Windisch who first observed that 2 Cor 1:1-2:13; 7:5-16 fits the description of a "conciliatory epistle" in Ps-Libanius.[42] The aim of the ἐπιστολὴ θεραπευτική, according to Ps-Libanius (Ἐπιστολιμαῖοι χαρακτῆρεις 15), is to conciliate someone who has been caused grief; thus one avoids, insofar as possible, mention of the cause of strife.[43] The theorist directs that the author of a conciliatory letter write to the one who has been grieved:

> But if you were upset by what was said or done, be assured, most excellent sir, that I shall most certainly no longer make mention of what was said (εἰ δ᾽ ἐπὶ τοῖς λεχθεῖσιν ἢ πραχθεῖσιν ἠχθέσθης, ἴσθι, κράτιστε

NovT 31/2 (1989): 142-63. What has not been discussed is the relevance of genre to the phenomenon of reference.

[40]J. Weiss first suggested that 2 Cor 1:1–2:13; 7:5-16 was once an independent work in his review of Halmel in ThLZ 19 (1894): 513-14, then in idem, Das Urchristentum, 245ff. A growing number of scholars now regard 2 Cor 1:1–2:13; 7:5-16 as an independent work, though some append ch. 8, others ch. 9. The judgment of Georgi, Opponents, 335, is characteristic: "The seams in 2:13-14 and 7:4-5 are the best examples in the entire New Testament of one large fragment secondarily inserted into another text. The splits are so basic, and the connections so obvious, that the burden of proof now lies with those who defend the integrity of the canonical text."

[41]A. Loisy, "Les épîtres de Paul," Revue d'histoire et de littérature religieuses 7 (1921): 213. Bornkamm, Vorgeschichte, 19, referred to 2 Cor 1:1–2:13; 7:5-16 as the "Versöhnungsbrief"; he was presumably influenced in the choice of this term by Windisch. This designation of the genre of 2 Cor 1:1–2:13; 7:5-16 has been widely accepted in subsequent scholarship, though a thorough investigation is still wanting.

[42]Windisch, Der zweite Korintherbrief, 8.

[43]Text and translation in A. Malherbe, Ancient Epistolary Theorists (Atlanta: Scholars Press, 1988) 68-69. The author remarks: "Some also call this the apologetic style" (ταύτην δὲ καὶ ἀπολογητικήν τινες καλοῦσιν). On the authorship and date of this writing, see J. Sykutris, "Proclus, Περὶ Ἐπιστολιμαίου" Byzantinisch-Neugriechische Jahrbücher 7 (1928–1929): 108-18.

ἀνδρῶν, ὡς οὐκέτι τῶν ῥηθέντων λόγον ὅλως ποτὲ ποιή- σομαι).[44]

The reason for reticence is supplied by a concluding enthymeme: "For it is my aim always to heal my friends rather than to cause them grief" (σκοπὸς γὰρ μοι θεραπεύειν ἀεὶ τοὺς φίλους ἐστὶν ἤπερ λυπεῖν).[45]

Examination of extant conciliatory epistles demonstrates that the handbook of Ps-Libanius does not merely formulate theory, but describes the actual practise of letter-writers over the years.[46] From the shrine of Poseidon in Calauria, where the orator Demosthenes found asylum, he gazed across the sea to his native Athens and composed an appeal for his restoration (Ep 2).[47] Nowhere in the course of his conciliatory apology does Demosthenes mention the exact nature of the accusations against him. He argues, instead, for the probity of his conduct throughout the course of his career (Ep 2.1-12). When he finally treats of the Harpalus affair, it is after he has convinced the reader of his innocence, and in a context that is strongly evocative of pity.[48] Even then, the actual charge (of bribe taking) is not mentioned; he represents himself as the victim of

---

[44]Malherbe, *Epistolary Theorists*, 76-77.

[45]Ibid.

[46]On the relationship between the manuals and the actual practise of letter writing, see Malherbe, *Epistolary Theorists*, 5.

[47]Text in *Demosthenis orationes*, vol. 3, ed. F. Blass (Leipzig: Teubner, 1907); *Demosthenis orationes*, vol. 4, ed. S. Butcher and W. Rennie (Oxford: Clarendon, 1931). Translation in N. W. DeWitt and N. J. DeWitt, *Demosthenes VII: Funeral Speech, Erotic Essay, Exordia, and Letters*, LCL (Cambridge MA: Harvard University Press, 1949). Commentary in J Goldstein, *The Letters of Demosthenes* (New York: Columbia University, 1968) 195-200, 235-46. The authenticity of the letter has been questioned, but is defended by Goldstein. If authentic, the letter would fall in the years 324–322 B.C.E., the last two years of the orator's life.

[48]In the *commiseratio* at §14. From §13 to the end of the epistle, Demosthenes appears to discuss his grievous suffering; in fact, he continues to argue for his innocence. On appeals for pity and their placement, see Isocrates 16.48; Aristotle *Rhet* 3.14.11 1415b26-27. Demosthenes appeals for pity according to the commonplaces of "contrary to deserts" and "contrary to expectation"; see Aristotle *Rhet* 2.8.2 1385b13-14.

circumstance (*Ep* 2.14). He might have written more in exoneration, but refrains in order to conciliate his readers (*Ep* 2.25). Nor are his accusers (Dinarchus and Hyperides) mentioned by name; he speaks only of "certain members of the council" (τινες τῶν ἐν τῇ βουλῇ, *Ep* 2.2). When he speaks of himself as the object of mistreatment, he speaks not of "me," but of "such a person" (ὁ τοιοῦτος, *Ep* 2.8). Thus he avoids a defensive posture and mitigates the harshness of blame.[49] At every point, his reticence is dictated by his purpose, by the outcome he envisions for his self-defense: "As you have rightly become reconciled to the other defendants," Demosthenes pleads, "grant also that reconciliation to me" (*Ep* 2.16).

Cicero exhibits a similar caution in his conciliatory letter to Crassus (*Ad Fam* 5.8).[50] A quarrel had interrupted the reconciliation effected by Pompey earlier in the year (cf. *Ad Fam* 1.9.20). But Cicero does not explore the strife. He begins, instead, by directing attention to the good services which he had recently rendered. The debate in the senate over the allocation of funds to Crassus as governor of Syria has provided Cicero with the opportunity to become the champion of Crassus's honor. Cicero never lacked the will to contribute to Crassus's advancement; only the "many variations of circumstance" have caused him to intermit the service which has been owing to their friendship (*Ad Fam* 5.8.1). But now the occasion has arisen for which Cicero has hoped, and he is sure that he has made it plain to the senate and people of Rome that he is Crassus's very good friend (*Ad Fam* 5.8.2). Only after he has given Crassus assurances of friendship does he come to speak of the present dispute. Even then, the nature of the conflict is not described. He refers only to "certain infringements which have affected our relations." These differences, he asserts, are "surmised rather than real"; they are "mere

---

[49]See the nuanced rhetorical analysis of Goldstein, *The Letters of Demosthenes*, 157-66, who follows the *scholia minora* to Hermogenes in his understanding of these points.

[50]Text in Cicero: *Epistulae ad Familiares*, vol. 1 ed. D. R. Shackleton Bailey (Cambridge: Cambridge University, 1977) 86-88, with commentary, 327-29. Translation in D. R. Shackleton Bailey, *Cicero's Letters to His Friends* (Atlanta: Scholars Press, 1988) 69-71. On the conciliatory purpose of the letter, see D. F. Epstein, *Personal Enmity in Roman Politics 218–43 B.C.* (London: Croom Helm, 1987) 5.

figments of the imagination." Cicero exhorts: "Let them be utterly eradicated from our memories and our lives" (*Ad Fam* 5.8.3). Cicero's treatment of the controversy is controlled by his conciliatory purpose: "Between two men such as you are and I desire to be, whose lot has fallen on the same political ground, I would hope that alliance and friendship will conduce to the credit of both" (*Ad Fam* 5.8.3). Cicero follows the conventions of the genre, even if his real sentiments about Crassus remained negative (cf. *Ad Fam* 4.13.2: *o hominem nequam!*).

Relations between Apollonius of Tyana and his brother Hestiaeus do not appear to have been good.[51] There has been a dispute over money. In the earlier letters, there are judgments and reproaches.[52] Hestiaeus has contributed to the shameful opinion that his brother travels abroad in search of money (*Ep* 35). Apollonius is pained and asks his relation, "How could you judge me so harshly?" (*Ep* 44). For his part, Apollonius believes that kinship should override such difficulties; he longs, like Odysseus, to return to his home and behold the sepulchres of his fathers (*Ep* 44). The next letter makes clear that the overture has been accepted; a reconciliation has occurred (*Ep* 45). Apollonius first assures Hestiaeus of the permanence of their affections: those who are convinced that they are philosophers cannot rightly be supposed to hate their brothers (Ep. 45). What is now uppermost in Apollonius's mind is not their "misunderstanding" (ὑποψία) about money, which was something that they tried to despise even before they became philosophers, but the suspicion and hurt feelings that may have resulted from what he wrote, and from his

---

[51]Text and Latin translation in R. Hercher, *Epistolographi Graeci* (Paris: Didot, 1873) 115-16, 117, 120, 124-25; text and English translation in *Philostratus II: The Life of Apollonius of Tyana. The Epistles of Apollonius*, ed. F. C. Conybeare, LCL (Cambridge MA: Harvard University Press, 1969) 432, 436-40, 448-50, 470. See also R. Penella, *The Letters of Apollonius of Tyana. A Critical Text with Prolegomena, Translation and Commentary* (Leiden: Brill, 1979) 48-51, 54-57, 62-65, 76-79, 108-109, 113-14, 118, 128.

[52]The collection as we have it is not arranged chronologically. There are two clusters of letters to Hestiaeus, *Epp* 44-45 and 72-73, plus two standing alone, *Ep* 35 and *Ep* 55. *Ep* 35 presupposes the charge that Apollonius travels in pursuit of financial gain; cf. *Ep* 45, where the charge is explicitly discussed. Several remarks in Philostratus seem intended as tacit refutations of such a charge, e.g., *Vit Soph* 1.18; 3.33; 8.2.3.

failure to write. It was never Apollonius's intention, he asserts, to cause his brother grief. In proof of his love, Apollonius announces, "I will return to you towards the end of spring" (*Ep* 45).

Marcus Aurelius wrote a letter of apology to his friend and former teacher Herodes Atticus.[53] A quarrel between Herodes and his fellow-Athenians had come before the emperor's court (Philostratus *Vit Soph* 2.1.550-61). The verdict in the case went against the sophist: his freedmen were punished, and Herodes himself appears to have made financial concessions.[54] From self-imposed exile at Oricum in Epirus, Herodes addressed a complaint to the emperor. Thereupon, Marcus wrote to Herodes a letter which has been partly preserved in Philostratus's *Lives of the Sophists*.[55] In a long first section, the emperor dwells upon his present sufferings: he describes the rigors of his winter quarters, and laments the recent death of his wife; he remarks upon his own bad health (*Vit Soph* 2.1.562). The motive of the *commiseratio* is to account for the suspension of his correspondence, of which Herodes had complained, and to establish a basis for reconciliation in the commonality of affliction. Only then does Marcus venture to speak of what has been at issue between them. He assures Herodes of his good-will, then argues that Herodes should not regard himself as unjustly treated (μηδὲ ἡγεῖσθαι ἀδικεῖσθαι) because some of his household have been chastised with a punishment "as mild as possible" (ὡς οἷόν τε ἐπιεικεῖ). About

---

[53]Text and translation in *Philostratus and Eunapius: Lives of the Sophists*, ed. W. C. Wright, LCL (Cambridge MA: Harvard University Press, 1968) 174-75. All of Philostratus *Vit Soph* 2.1.559-63 should be read as background.

[54]Philostratus *Vit Soph* 2.1.561. Something more than the benefactions for which Herodes was famous seems intended by the θεραπεία mentioned in line 93 of the recently discovered letter of Marcus Aurelius to the Athenians; see J. Oliver, *Marcus Aurelius. Aspects of Civic and Cultural Policy In the East*, Hesperia Suppl. 13 (Princeton: Princeton University Press, 1970) 27. Perhaps the "remedy" consisted in the payment of his father's *fideicommissa* to the people of Athens, which Herodes had earlier refused to honor.

[55]Philostratus *Vit Soph* 2.1.562-63; text and translation in *Philostratus and Eunapius: Lives of the Sophists*, ed. W. C. Wright, LCL (Cambridge MA: Harvard University Press, 1968) 174-75. Philostratus states that he extracts from the letter only that which bears upon his narrative.

the compensation to the Athenians that Herodes has been forced to make, the emperor says nothing at all, but allows,

> If I have grieved you in anything, or am still grieving you (εἰ δέ τι λελύπηκα σε ἢ λυπῶ), demand reparation from me in the temple of Athena in your city at the time of the mysteries" (*Vit Soph* 2.1.563).

The principle of composition is plain: one who wished to defend what was said or done in a manner that restored relations, avoided insofar as possible discussion of the source of strife. Only so much is said of the cause of conflict as is necessary in order to explain that it was not the author's purpose to give offence. This simple principle is observed whenever the aim of a writing is conciliatory, whatever the rhetorical species.[56] It is the response appropriate to the situation.[57]

---

[56]Thus, in counselling concord between the cities, Isocrates, *Panegyricus* 129, bows to convention and apologizes for having recalled the enmities between Athens and Sparta, "after having stated at the outset that I intended to speak on conciliation" (προειπὼν ὡς περὶ διαλλαγῶν ποιήσομαι τοὺς λόγους). In his *Letter to the Alexandrians*, the emperor Claudius refuses to make an "exact investigation" (ἀκριβῶς ἐξελέγξαι) of the cause of strife arising between Jews and Greeks; he urges, rather, the parties to cease their "destructive and mutual enmity"; text and translation in *Corpus Papyrorum Judaicarum*, vol. 2, ed. V. Tcherikover and A. Fuks (Cambridge MA: Harvard University Press, 1960) 41, 43. Note Tcherikover's observation on these lines in the commentary (48): "Claudius's refusal to hold an inquiry is due only to his firm decision to stop the hostilities at once and to impose peace on both sides." When Marcus Aurelius endeavors to reconcile the Athenians to their own Herodes, he buries the memory of their present dispute beneath the confident imperial assurance that no impediment to goodwill remains: he asks, "For what could still be lingering in the mind of anyone after the memory of the accusations has been effaced? Now that a remedy has been fully worked out, perhaps it will be possible for the Athenians to love my own Herodes and their own, since nothing else of importance still stands in the way of goodwill" (τί γὰρ ἂν ἔτι ὑποκαθέζοιτο ἐν γνώμηι τινὸς μετὰ τὸ ἀπαλειφθῆναι τὴν ἐπὶ ταῖς αἰτίαις μνήμην; τῆς θεραπείας ἐπὶ πᾶσιν ἐκπεπονημένης ἴσως Ἀθηναίοις ἐξῆν τὸν ἐμὸν καὶ τὸν ἴδιον αὐτῶν Ἡρώιδην στέργειν οὐδενὸς ἔτι ἑτέρου τῆι εὐνοίαι μεγάλου ἀντικρούοντος); text and translation in C. P. Jones, "A New Letter of Marcus Aurelius to the Athenians," *ZPE* 8 (1971): 181-82.

[57]On social situation as a factor in generic composition, see S. Stowers,

The convention is in keeping with the understanding of reconciliation in the Greco-Roman world: reconciliation was held to consist in an act of deliberate forgetfulness. The concept was given decisive articulation in the reconciliation of 403 B.C.E., which ended the Athenian civil war.[58] The agreement was recorded for public consultation and was often cited in antiquity as a model of political enlightenment.[59] Plutarch gives the exact date on which Thrasyboulos and his followers marched back into Athens and claims that the event was still being celebrated in his own day (*Mor* 349F). The famous reconciliation was negatively described as μὴ μνησικακεῖν, not bearing malice, not remembering past wrongs, and positively, in later authors (e.g., Plutarch *Mor* 814B; *Cic* 42.2), as ἀμνηστία, an act of political forgiveness.[60] Valerius Maximus equates the term with *oblivio*.[61] Thus Aristotle states that the political parties "blotted out recriminations with regard to the past" (τὰς περὶ τῶν προτέρων αἰτίας ἐξήλειψαν, *Ath Pol* 40.3).[62] And Andocides praises past generations because "they refused to revive old quarrels" (οὐκ ἠξίωσαν τινι τῶν πρότερον γενομένων μνησικακῆσαι), and urges the men of his own day to equal their ancestors in virtue by "refusing to cherish grievances" (μὴ μνησικακῆσαι, *De Mysteriis* 108-109).[63]

It is now possible to see that Paul conforms to convention in his letter of reconciliation in 2 Cor 1:1–2:13; 7:5-16; 13:11-13: he avoids discussion of the source of strife. The challenge to his authority, which precipitated chs. 10-13, is not mentioned in 1:1-2:13; 7:5-16. The offence is there, in the commendation of the repentance and obedience of the

---

Letter Writing In Greco-Roman Antiquity, LEC 5 (Philadelphia: Westminster, 1986) 56.

[58]See T. Loening, *The Reconciliation Agreement of 403/402 B.C.: Its Content and Application*, Hermes 53 (Stuttgart: Steiner, 1987) 19-21.

[59]E.g., Aristotle *Ath Pol* 39.6; Isocrates 18.3; other references are discussed in Loening, *Reconciliation Agreement*, passim.

[60]Liddell-Scott-Jones, *A Greek-English Lexicon* (Oxford: Clarendon Press, 1968) s.v. ἀμνηστέω, ἀμνηστία.

[61]Valerius Maximus 4.1, ext. 4; Nepos 3.2 also uses *oblivio*.

[62]Text and translation in *Aristotle XX: The Athenian Constitution*, ed. H. Rackham, LCL (Cambridge MA: Harvard University Press, 1981) 112-15.

[63]Text and translation in *Minor Attic Orators I*, ed. K. Maidment, LCL (Cambridge MA: Harvard University Press, 1941).

Corinthians (2:9; 7:7-11); but revolt lies within submission, the way discord lies within harmony.[64] There is a passing reference to the collection in the χάρισμα of 1:11; but former suspicions about its purpose (12:16-18) are present only in the invitation to join in helping Paul by prayer.[65] There are lingering doubts about Paul's sincerity (1:12-14); but the subject is broached in the confidence that his actions will now be understood. Nor are the opponents explicitly mentioned. Paul's missionary rivals figure negatively, as the contraposition in relation to which the unity of Paul and the church is affirmed (1:3-7; 2:10-11).[66] But their influence is not acknowledged; Paul chooses to ignore what he disapproves. Nor is the Corinthian offender named; Paul speaks of "one (who) has given grief" (τις λελύπηκεν, 2:5) and, again, of "the one who did wrong" (ὁ ἀδικήσας, 7:12). But Paul withholds the offender's name, as Demosthenes omits the names of his accusers. The group that supported the attack upon Paul appears only as the "majority" which now imposes a sufficient punishment (2:6).[67] When Paul speaks of himself as the object of mistreatment, he speaks not of "me," but of "the one who was wronged" (ὁ ἀδικηθεῖς), and denies that he wrote on account of wrongdoing (7:12). Paul thus avoids a defensive posture and mitigates the harshness of blame. Like Apollonius of Tyana, Paul affects a deeper concern for the grief he has caused than for the original cause of strife.

The presupposition is simply untenable, that in an epistle whose aim is conciliatory, the author should refer explicitly to the former object of dispute. But this is what the critics assume, when they object that Paul's

---

[64]Kennedy, *The Second and Third Epistles*, 99-100; cf. F. Watson, "2 Corinthians x–xii and Paul's Painful Letter to the Corinthians," *JTS* 35/2 (1984): 340-42.

[65]In 2 Cor 8:1, 7 the collection is referred to as ἡ χάρις. Note the striking similarity between the language of 2 Cor 1:10-11 and Rom 15:30-32, where Paul asks for prayers that his "service" to the church in Jerusalem might prove acceptable to the saints. See Windisch, *Der zweite Korintherbrief*, 48-49.

[66]F. Watson, "2 Cor x–xiii and Paul's Painful Letter to the Corinthians," *JTS* 35/2 (1984): 340-42. Note the growing recognition of the opponents as a factor in the letter of reconciliation in the "Epilogue" to Georgi, *Opponents*, 339-40.

[67]See already Kennedy, *The Second and Third Epistles*, 99-110 and Lake, *The Earlier Epistles*, 170.

account of the "letter of tears" in 2 Cor 2 and 7 fails to agree at crucial points with the content of chs. 10-13. Herewith is removed the final objection to the hypothesis which identifies 2 Cor 10:1–13:10 with the "letter of tears."

PAUL'S LETTER OF RECONCILIATION
IN 2 CORINTHIANS 1:1–2:13; 7:5-16
AND ANCIENT THEORIES OF LITERARY UNITY

INTRODUCTION

Johannes Weiss was the first to suggest that 2 Cor 1:1-2:13; 7:5-16 was once an independent work.[1] Weiss saw that the tone of these chapters varied not only from chapters 10–13, but also from the intervening text, 2:14-7:4. In the latter text, the reconciliation is not apparent, which, in chapters 1–2 and 7, is the presupposition of Paul's joy. On the contrary, Paul must still answer charges that he has wronged, corrupted, and defrauded the Corinthians, and must plead with the Corinthians to open their hearts (2:17; 4:1-2; 6:3-13; 7:2-4). This passage must have been written at the height of the conflict, before the successful conclusion of peace. Then, Paul wrote again in a cordial manner to assure the Corinthians of his confidence, and to remove the lingering traces of doubt. The proof of this analysis Weiss discovered in the connection between 2:13 and 7:5: the account of Paul's anxious search for Titus breaks off at the decisive point (2:13) and resumes only four chapters later (7:5) at the very point where it had broken off.

> This separation of what belongs together is unheard of and intolerable, from a literary point of view, since 2:13 and 7:5 fit onto each other as neatly as the broken pieces of a ring.[2]

Approval of Weiss's hypothesis among critics has been widespread.[3]

---

[1]In his review of A. Halmel, *Der Vierkapitelbrief im zweiten Korintherbrief des Apostel Paulus* (Essen: Baedeker, 1894) in ThLZ 19 (1894): 513-14, elaborated in J. Weiss, *Das Urchristentum*, ed. R. Knopf (Göttingen: Vandenhoeck & Ruprecht, 1917) 245-53; idem, *The History of Primitive Christianity*, 2 vols., ed. F. C. Grant (New York: Wilson-Erickson, 1937) 1:345-53.

[2]Weiss, *Primitive Christianity*, 1:349.

[3]Weiss was followed by A. Halmel, *Der zweite Korintherbrief des Apostels Paulus* (Halle: Niemeyer, 1904); A. Loisy, "Les épîtres de S. Paul," *Revue*

Bultmann made Weiss's discovery the basis of his own analysis and of the lectures he delivered for many years; in time, Weiss's insight shaped Bultmann's understanding of the theology of Paul.[4] Bornkamm explored the significance of Weiss's analysis for the attempt to ascertain the motives of the redactor of 2 Cor.[5] A number of scholars now regard 2 Cor 1:1–2:13; 7:5-16 as an independent work, though some append ch. 8, others ch. 9.[6] The verdict of Georgi is characteristic:

---

d'histoire et de littérature religieuses 7 (1921): 213-50; P.-L. Couchoud, "Reconstitution et classement des lettres de saint Paul," *Revue d'histoire et de littérature religieuses* 87 (1923): 8-34; H. Preisker, "Zur Komposition des zweiten Korintherbriefes," *Theologische Blätter* 5 (1926): 154-57. Note the observation by H. Windisch, *Der zweite Korintherbrief*, KEK 6 (Göttingen: Vandenhoeck & Ruprecht, 1924; repr. 1970) 19: "Die Erkenntnis, dass die beiden Stellen 2:13 und 7:5 genau auf einander passen, wie die Bruchstellen eines Ringes, ist von höchster Wichtigkeit. Es ist erstaunlich, dass die hier vorliegende Schwierigkeit bisher noch von keinem Kommentator ernst genommen worden ist."

[4] Bultmann's lecture notes were eventually published as R. Bultmann, *Der zweite Brief an die Korinther*, ed. E. Dinkler, KEK 6 (Göttingen: Vandenhoeck & Ruprecht, 1976). In the preface, 11-12, Dinkler notes the importance of Paul's reconciliation with the church (in 2 Cor 1:1–2:13; 7:5-16) for Bultmann's own theology: in the figure of the reconciling apostle, Bultmann saw the model of Christian existence as such, in which power is made perfect in weakness, and life is manifested in death.

[5] G. Bornkamm, *Die Vorgeschichte des sogenannten Zweiten Korintherbriefes*, SHAW 1961, 2. Abhandlung (Heidelberg, Winter 1961) 21-23, 29-31; Bornkamm saw that by taking this letter as the frame for the epistle, the redactor sought to inscribe the polemic within a structure in which Paul's authority was restored.

[6] The following scholars now regard 2 Cor 1:1–2:13; 7:5-16 as an independent work: D. Georgi, *Die Gegner des Paulus im 2. Korintherbrief: Studien zur religiösen Propaganda in der Spätantike*, WMANT 11 (Neukirchen-Vluyn: Neukirchener, 1964) 14-25; idem, "Second Letter to the Corinthians," *IDBSup*, 183-86; W. Marxsen, *Einleitung in das Neue Testament* (Gütersloh: Mohn, 1963) 73-77; J.-F. Collange, *Énigmes de la deuxième épître de Paul aux Corinthiens: Étude exégétique de 2 Cor 2.14-7.4*, SNTSMS 18 (Cambridge: Cambridge University Press, 1972) 7-15; P. Vielhauer, *Geschichte der urchristlichen Literatur* (Berlin and New York: de Gruyter, 1975) 150-55; H.-M. Schenke and K. M. Fischer, *Einleitung in die Schriften des Neuen Testaments*, vol. 1, *Die Briefe des Paulus und Schriften des Paulinismus* (Berlin: Evangelische Verlagsanstalt, 1978) 108-20; H. Koester, *Introduction to the New Testament*, vol. 2

The seams in 2:13-14 and 7:4-5 are the best examples in the entire New Testament of one large fragment secondarily inserted into another text. The splits in 2:12/13 and 7:4/5 are so basic, and the connections between 2:13 and 7:5 so obvious, that the burden of proof now lies with those who defend the integrity of the canonical text, and they have not brought any good new arguments to support their claims.[7]

Despite widespread agreement with Weiss's hypothesis, understanding of the basis of the unity which Weiss posited has hardly advanced beyond the metaphorical. In what follows, we shall seek to ascertain whether the coherence that Weiss and others have perceived, when they regard 2 Cor 1:1–2:13; 7:5-16 as a literary whole, can be shown to exist in accordance with Greek and Roman assumptions about literary unity. Ancient literary theorists, from Plato to Hermogenes, employ a limited set of criteria in assessing the unity of a work: completeness (τὸ ὅλον), continuity (συνέχεια), connection (συνάψις), order (σύστασις), symmetry (συμμετρία), and so forth.[8] Does 2 Cor 1:1–2:13; 7:5-16 possess these characteristics in such degree that ancient literary critics would have judged the work to be a unity? Special attention must be devoted to the question of digression, since diversity (ποικιλία) was also regarded as a constituent of coherence.[9] In particular, we must ask

---

(Philadelphia: Fortress, 1982) 53, 126-30; H. D. Betz, *2 Corinthians 8 and 9. A Commentary on Two Administrative Letters of the Apostle Paul*, Hermeneia (Philadelphia: Fortress, 1985) 141-44.

[7]D. Georgi, *The Opponents of Paul in Second Corinthians* (Philadelphia: Fortress, 1986) 335.

[8]For the criteria listed here, see M. Heath, *Unity in Greek Poetics* (Oxford: Clarendon Press, 1989) 153 and passim. The criteria are emphasized in varying degree by the literary theorists: Aristotle insists upon completeness in his analysis of plot in the *Poetica*; critics of historical writing, from Polybius to Lucian, stress continuity; Plato emphasizes appropriate order; writers on rhetoric are concerned about symmetry, as is Diodorus Siculus.

[9]This is the thesis argued by Heath in *Unity in Greek Poetics*. His view is best supported by Dionysius of Halicarnassus, whose theory of style incorporates variety as one of its essential principles (*Comp* 12.43.17-46.15; 19.84.5-87.21). But even Dionysius insists upon the restraint of diversity by appropriateness (καιρός) in *Comp* 12.45.6-21. By way of contrast, see Horace's criticism of

whether the apology for Paul's apostolic office in 2:14-7:4 can be construed as a digression within the narrative of 2:12-13; 7:5-6.[10] Finally, it must be stressed that the criteria of coherence are always relative to genre; that is, the assessment of the unity of a work necessarily involves consideration of the characteristic ends of the genre.[11] An account of the literary genre of 2 Cor 1:1–2:13; 7:5-16 must be given in another place.

I. THE PARALLEL STRUCTURE OF THE SENTENCES

Implicit in Weiss's analogy is a recognition of the parallel structure of the sentences in 2:12-13 and 7:5. In 2:12 Paul begins:

---

variare and incongruous conflations at the beginning of the *Ars Poetica*, and the comments of C. O. Brink, *Horace on Poetry II: The Ars Poetica* (Cambridge: Cambridge University Press, 1971) 104-105.

[10]The explanation of 2 Cor 2:14-7:4 as a theological digression goes back to J. A. Bengel, *Gnomon Novi Testamenti* (1742); trans. *Gnomon of the New Testament*, 3 vols., trans. A. Fausset (Edinburgh: T.&T. Clark, 1877) 2:361: "A most noble digression is here introduced in respect to events which had in the meantime occurred and sufferings which had been endured by him elsewhere." The view is widespread in subsequent scholarship: e.g., C. F. G. Heinrici, *Der zweite Brief an die Korinther*, KEK 6 (Göttingen: Vandenhoeck & Ruprecht, 1900) 36, 251-52; A. Plummer, *A Critical and Exegetical Commentary on the Second Epistle of St. Paul to the Corinthians*, ICC (Edinburgh: T.&T. Clark, 1915) 67; L. J. Koch, *Fortolkning til Paulus' Andet Brev til Korinthierne* (Niva, ²1927) 48-50; C. K. Barrett, *The Second Epistle to the Corinthians*, HNTC (New York: Harper & Row, 1973) 97; N. Hyldahl, "Die Frage nach der literarischen Einheit des Zweiten Korintherbriefes," *ZNW* 64 (1973): 289-306.

[11]On the significance of genre and its relation to unity, see F. Cairns, *Generic Composition in Greek and Roman Poetry* (Edinburgh: Edinburgh University Press, 1972) passim, and Heath, *Unity in Greek Poetics*, 17-18, 20-22, 38, 150-54. See esp. Plato's discussion of order in *Phaedrus* 264c-d: the elements of a work are rightly composed when they are related to the *whole* which they together form; the whole is defined by its end, that is, the effects which it aims at producing (*Phdr* 269c-274b); cf. *Grg* 503e-504a. This is the point of the organic analogy so widespread in ancient criticism: a text should be σωματο-ειδώς, that is, it must have all and only the parts proper to it; cf. Aristotle *Rhet* 1415b7-9; *Rhet Ad Alex* 1436a27-31; 1438b14-29; 1442b28-33; Diodorus 20.1.5; Dionysius *Pomp* 3.14; Lucian *Hist Conscr* 23, 55; Ps.-Longinus 10.1.

But when I came to Troas for the gospel of Christ, and a door was opened to me in the Lord, I did not have rest in my spirit, because I did not find my brother Titus, but taking leave of them, I departed into Macedonia" (Ἐλθὼν δὲ εἰς τὴν Τρῳάδα εἰς τὸ εὐαγγέλιον τοῦ Χριστοῦ καὶ θύρας μοι ἀνεῳγμένης ἐν κυρίῳ, οὐκ ἔσχηκα ἄνεσιν τῷ πνεύματί μου τῷ μὴ εὑρεῖν με Τίτον τὸν ἀδελφόν μου, ἀλλὰ ἀποταξάμενος αὐτοῖς ἐξῆλθον εἰς Μακεδονίαν).

In 7:5 Paul continues:

For even when we came into Macedonia, our bodies had no rest, but we were afflicted in every way: fightings without, fears within" (καὶ γὰρ ἐλ- θόντων ἡμῶν εἰς Μακεδονίαν οὐδεμίαν ἔσχηκεν ἄνεσιν ἡ σάρξ ἡμῶν ἀλλ᾽ ἐν παντὶ θλιβόμενοι· ἔξωθεν μάχαι, ἔσωθεν φόβοι).[12]

Each element of Paul's account in 2:12-13 has its counterpart in 7:5, and often in the selfsame words: the participle which describes the journey (ἐλθών/ἐλθόντων); post-positive conjunction (δέ/γάρ); the phrase supplying the destination (εἰς τὴν Τρῳάδα/εἰς Μακεδο- νίαν); the negative (οὐκ/οὐδεμία); the perfect verb, which vividly depicts the continuation of Paul's distress (ἔσχηκα/ἔσχηκεν); the solace which Paul did not find (ἄνεσις); the respect in which Paul was dis- tressed (πνεῦμα/σάρξ).

Repetition is a figure of Greek prose style, whether of a word, a phrase, or the main clause.[13] There are examples in rhetorical (Lysias 13.96; 31.28; Demosthenes 43.79) and non-rhetorical writers (Plato *Grg* 456D; *Leg* 733B; Xenophon *Cyr* 3.3.26). Sometimes repetition makes an impression of carelessness (e.g. Xenophon *An* 3.5.1); but more often it conveys emotive force. There are parallels to the apostle's practice among the apologetic letters. Demosthenes defends his departure from

---

[12]Text cited according to Nestle-Aland, *Novum Testamentum Graece*, 26th ed. (Stuttgart: Deutsche Bibelgesellschaft, 1979) 475, 482.

[13]See the chapter on repetition in J. D. Denniston, *Greek Prose Style* (Oxford: Clarendon Press, 1952) 78-98, with many examples. Cf. H. Lausberg, *Handbuch der literarischen Rhetorik: Eine Grundlegung der Literaturwissenschaft* (Munich: Hueber, ²1973) 1:608-64.

Athens, in the aftermath of the Harpalus affair, by a series of clauses in which ἐλθεῖν is repeated, with a phrase which names the destination:

Καὶ μὴν τό γ' ἀπελθεῖν οὐκ ἂν εἰκότως ὀργὴν πρός με ποιήσειεν ... εἴς τε γὰρ πόλιν ἦλθον, οὐκ ἐν ᾗ μέγιστα πράξειν αὐτὸς ἔμελλον, ἀλλ' εἰς ἣν καὶ τοὺς προγόνους ἐλθόντας ᾔδειν ... μετελθὼν εἰς τὸ τοῦ Ποσειδῶνος ἱερὸν ἐν Καλαυρείᾳ κάθημαι (Ep 1.17-18,20).[14]

Variations within the same expression transport the aged orator from Athens to a place of refuge, and from Troezen to Poseidon's temple, and from this temple to his native land, to which he daily returns in thought. The repetition describes a circle (κύκλος) in which exile turns to restoration. More apposite still is the repetition of the phrase καὶ ἀφικόμεθα εἰς Μακεδονίαν in a pseudonymous epistle of Euripides: used descriptively at the beginning of the letter (Ep. 5.1), it recurs within the subsequent defense (Ep 5.2,4), and lends coherence to the whole.[15]

Nor is 7:5 the only passage in the letter of reconciliation in which a repetition occurs. Repetition may be said to be the dominant figure. In the *exordium* (1:3-7) a number of words are repeated (παράκλησις, θλίψις, πάθημα) in a *traductio* as complex and as effective as any found in Cicero.[16] The first argument employs a repetition like that of 2:12-13 and 7:5. Paul seeks to assure the Corinthians of the sincerity of his intentions; he has long desired to come to Corinth:

---

[14]Text in N. W. DeWitt and N. J. DeWitt, *Demosthenes VII*, LCL (Cambridge MA: Harvard University Press, 1949) 218, 220. The meaning that μετελθών has here is without parallel in fourth-century prose, as noted by J. Goldstein, *The Letters of Demosthenes* (New York: Columbia University Press, 1968) 245, though the verb is attested in the Attic orators. The catachresis is motivated by the figure of repetition.

[15]Text in R. Hercher, *Epistolographi Graeci* (Paris: Didot, 1873) 277-78.

[16]Nor are these the only terms repeated in 2 Cor 1:3-7; note also πᾶσα and περισσεύει. Cf. Windisch, *Der zweite Korintherbrief*, 36-43. On the frequent employment of the same word, or a number of words (the device known to the Romans as *traductio*), see Cicero *De Or* 3.206; *Rhet ad Her* 4.20. With 2 Cor 1:3-7 compare Plato *Rep* 537e-538a. See the discussion in Denniston, *Greek Prose Style* 80-81.

ἐβουλόμην πρότερον πρὸς ὑμᾶς ἐλθεῖν, ἵνα δευτέραν χάριν σχῆτε, καὶ δι' ὑμῶν διελθεῖν εἰς Μακεδονίαν, καὶ πάλιν ἀπὸ Μακεδονίας ἐλθεῖν πρὸς ὑμᾶς καὶ ὑμῶν προπεμφθῆναι εἰς τὴν 'Ιουδαίαν (1:15-16).

The figure becomes clearer and more exact, when one observes the parenthetical character of the purpose clause (ἵνα δευτέραν χάριν σχῆτε) and the ellipsis of the verb (ἐβουλόμην) in the second sentence (καὶ πάλιν ἀπὸ Μακεδονίας, κτλ.).[17]

It is objected that 7:5 could not have followed 2:13 because of the change from singular to plural and the substitution of σάρξ for πνεῦμα.[18] The repetition, it is suggested, should be exact. It is difficult to know what importance to attach to the transition from singular to plural. It is possible that Paul was accompanied on his journey by one or more missionary associates (cf. Acts 19:22), among whom was likely "the brother" Timothy, co-author of the present work.[19] But singular and

---

[17]The construction of the verses suggested here is anticipated by Halmel, *Der zweite Korintherbrief*, 44-47. Thus Paul is not describing his plan for a "double visit," as customarily assumed, but is expressing his desire, twice formulated, to pay a visit to Corinth. In support of this interpretation, see H. W. Smyth, *Greek Grammar* (Cambridge MA: Harvard University Press, 1956) §1782: "ἐβουλόμην followed by an infinitive may express an unattainable wish." In support of the ellipsis of ἐβουλόμην in 1:16 is the resumption of the term (βουλόμενος) in the following sentence.

[18]This objection seems to have originated with C. K. Barrett, "Titus" in *Neotestamentica et Semitica, Studies in Honor of Matthew Black* (Edinburgh: T.&T. Clark, 1969), repr. in idem, *Essays on Paul* (Philadelphia: Westminster, 1982) 130n.25, 26; followed by W. G. Kümmel, *Introduction to the New Testament* (Nashville: Abingdon, ²1975) 291; F. Watson, "2 Cor x–xiii and Paul's Painful Letter to the Corinthians," *JTS* 35/2 (1984): 336; V. Furnish, *II Corinthians*, AB 32A (Garden City NY: Doubleday, 1984) 393, among others.

[19]Suggested by Windisch, *Der zweite Korintherbrief*, 226. Alternatively, Paul may be following a narrative convention: accounts of sea voyages in ancient literature frequently have the narrative in the first person plural. See, for example, Acts 27; Josephus *Vita* 30.14-16. Cf. E. Plümacher, *Lukas als hellenistischer Schriftsteller: Studien zur Apostelgeschichte* (Göttingen: Vandenhoeck & Ruprecht, 1972) 14n.431; V. Robbins, "By Land and by Sea: The We-Passages and Ancient Sea Voyages," in *Perspectives on Luke-Acts*, ed. C. Talbert

plural alternate freely throughout the letter of reconciliation. In the earlier sections (1:3-7; 1:8-11; 1:12-14) the plural predominates (but note ἐλπίζω in 1:13). But at 1:15 the singular occurs, and continues down to 2:13 (but note ἐλπίζω in 1:24), with occasional incursions of the plural pronoun (in 1:18-21). At 7:5 the plural returns, but gives way immediately to the singular, after the mention of Titus, in 7:7, only in order to surface again, in free alternation with the singular, from 7:12 to the chapter's end.[20] Whether Paul's usage is loose or exact, and whatever the changes in number imply, the transition from singular to plural is no argument against the hypothesis of the continuity of 2:12-13 with 7:5.

Nor does the shift from πνεῦμα to σάρξ, in respect to which Paul had no rest, furnish evidence against the view that 2:13 and 7:5 were originally contiguous. For the terms are not, as elsewhere in Paul, constructed in antithesis.[21] The πνεῦμα here (as in Acts 17:16) is the bearer of the inner life, as it responds to external circumstance, without relation to the ἅγιον πνεῦμα bestowed upon the apostle Paul.[22] The noun σάρξ is used in the neutral sense of the person in his corporeality (cf. 1 Cor 7:28; Gal. 4:13f.; 2 Cor 12:7), of the body that is in need of rest, after a long and anxious strain (cf. Mark 14:38).[23] Taken together, the

---

(Danville VA: Association of Baptist Professors of Religion; Edinburgh: T.&T. Clark, 1978) 216; J. Wehnert, *Die Wir-Passagen der Apostelgeschichte* (Göttingen: Vandenhoeck & Ruprecht, 1989).

[20]Note the first person plural pronoun following a singular verb in 7:9,12, and the change from singular to plural within the same sentence in 7:14. See the comments of Windisch, *Der zweite Korintherbrief*, 226.

[21]Thus, rightly, Barrett, *Essays on Paul*, 130n.26: "πνεῦμα and σάρξ are here (though not usually) almost equivalent psychological terms."

[22]Windisch, *Der zweite Korintherbrief*, 95; W. Bauer, *A Greek-English Lexicon of the New Testament and Other Early Christian Literature* (Chicago: University of Chicago Press, 1979) 675, s.v. πνεῦμα 3b; E. Schweizer, πνεῦμα, *TDNT* 6 (1968) 435.

[23]Windisch, *Der zweite Korintherbrief*, 226; Bultmann, *Der zweite Brief*, 56; E. Schweizer, σάρξ, *TDNT* 7 (1971) 125: "According to 2 Cor 7:5 ἡ σάρξ ἡμῶν = ἡμεῖς, and it expressly embraces inner anxieties too, though external affliction is primary here." That is to say, σάρξ has the meaning often attached to σῶμα; note the parallel in Ps.-Euripides *Ep* 5.1: Καὶ ἀφικόμεθα εἰς Μακεδονίαν, ὦ βέλτιστε Κηφισοφῶν, τό τε σῶμα οὐ

terms designate Paul's being in its totality. Only when the complementary character of the terms is grasped can Paul's artistry be appreciated.[24]

Far from destroying the good connection between 2:13 and 7:5, such minor variations as appear mark 7:5 as the direct continuation, rather than the resumption, of what Paul had written in 2:12-13. The negative pronominal adjective οὐδεμία in 7:5 is an intensification of the simple negative in 2:13, by virtue of its meaning and the part it qualifies.[25] The shift from the dative, τῷ πνεύματι, to the substantive, ἡ σάρξ, in respect to which Paul had no rest, makes the suffering more conspicuous, and at the same time more tangible.[26] The repetition of the perfect verb, after the preceding aorists (in 1:23; 2:1,3), prolongs the period of unrest.[27] The shift from the singular to the plural generalizes the distress. Such changes characterize 7:5 as the direct continuation of 2:13. The thread of care is spun out further.

μοχθηρῶς διατεθέντες.

[24]In 1 Cor 7:34 Paul uses σῶμα and πνεῦμα of the human person in its totality. For σάρξ and πνεῦμα as component of man, see Euripides *Fr.* 971: "Swollen with σάρξ, he expired, releasing the πνεῦμα to the aether." Plutarch occasionally speaks of σάρξ and ψυχή as the human components, *De Exilio* 1.599c; *Ser Num Pun* 17.560c. See in general, E. Schweizer, "Die hellenistische Komponente im neutestamentlichen σάρξ-Begriff," *ZNW* 48 (1957): 237-53. Note the conjecture of R. Jewett, *Paul's Anthropological Terms. A Study of Their Use in Conflict Settings* (Leiden: Brill, 1971) 193: "This striking parallelism between 'flesh' and 'spirit' [in 2 Cor 2:13 and 7:5] would seem to indicate that Paul accepts an anthropological dichotomy similar to that found in Rabbinic tradition."

[25]Smyth, *Greek Grammar*, §§337, 2736.

[26]On the dative, see the parallels in 1 Cor 7:28; 2 Cor 12:7. See further, F. Blass, A. Debrunner, and R. Funk, *A Greek Grammar of the New Testament* (Chicago: University of Chicago Press, 1961) §190(3).

[27]A. T. Robertson, *A Grammar of the Greek New Testament in the Light of Historical Research* (New York: Hodder & Stoughton, 1914) 900-901; followed by Windisch, *Der zweite Korintherbrief*, 95. But see Blass-Debrunner, *A Greek Grammar* §343, who takes ἔσχηκεν as a narrative tense, equivalent to the aorist; so also, with hesitation, J. H. Moulton, *A Grammar of New Testament Greek*, vol. 1, *Prolegomena* (Edinburgh: T.&T. Clark, 1908) 145, 238. This logic probably accounts for the presence of the aorist ἔσχεν in part of the manuscript tradition: P[46] B F G K.

A resumption, after a long digression, should have been handled differently; the return to the abandoned subject should have been clearer and more direct. When Greek authors resume the "continuous theme"[28] of an argument or a narrative, the return is signalled, typically, by an adversative conjunction, such as ἀλλά or δέ, and an expression, such as ταῦτα, which dismisses the digression.[29] Thus, in the third Platonic epistle, the author swerves from the account of Plato's trips to Sicily to reflect upon the tendency of great wealth to engender slanderers.[30] He concludes the digression with the words, "Notwithstanding, I put aside all these considerations and went" (ὅμως δ' οὖν πάντα ταῦτα χαίρειν ἐάσας ἦλθον), and resumes the account where he left off: Ἐλθὼν δέ, οἶσθα γὰρ δὴ σύ πάντα τάντεῦθεν ἤδη γενόμενα (317c-e).[31]

When the digression is longer, and leads further astray, it is climaxed by an "apology": the author begs the readers' indulgence for having

---

[28]The expression ἡ συνεχοῦς μνήμη is found in Menander Rhetor, *Rh Gr* 3.440.27. D. A. Russell and N. G. Wilson, *Menander Rhetor* (Oxford: Clarendon Press, 1981) 213, translate "unbroken commemoration." Cf. τὸ συνεχὲς τῆς διηγήσεως in Polybius 6.2.1, which F. W. Walbank, *A Historical Commentary on Polybius I* (Oxford: Clarendon Press, 1957) 637, translates "the continuous thread of the narrative." Compare Quintilian's *rectium iter* in *Inst Or* 4.2.104: "And if we do introduce a digression, it must always be short and of such a nature that we give the impression of having been forced from our proper course [*recto itinere*] by some uncontrollable emotion."

[29]On the technique of digression in Greek literature, see W. H. Race, "Some Digressions and Returns in Greek Authors," *CJT* 76 (1980): 1-8; Heath, *Unity in Greek Poetics* 21-23, 32-35, 89-98. For the rhetorical theory of digression, see J. H. May, "The *Ethica Digressio* and Cicero's *Pro Milone*," *CJT* 74 (1979): 243-44.

[30]Text and translation in R. G. Bury, *Plato IX: Timaeus, Critias, Cleitophon, Menexenus, Epistles*, LCL (Cambridge MA: Harvard University Press, 1981) 430-33.

[31]Note also the long philosophical digression in Plato *Ep* 7, 341b-345c. The return to the subject is signalled by the statement, πῶς δ' ἠτίμασεν ἐγὼ φράζοιμ' ἄν, and the narrative of the third Sicilian visit is resumed: Οὐ πολὺν χρόνον διαλιπὼν τὸ μετὰ τοῦτο κτλ.

"drifted" from the theme, for being "carried away" by the subject itself.[32] The return is marked by an expression, such as ἐπάνειμι or ἐπαν‌έρχομαι—terms which, in the course of time, acquired an almost tech‌nical sense. Thus, Isocrates concludes his famous encomium of Agamem‌non in the *Panathenaicus* abruptly with an apology:

> But (ἀλλά) I do not know whither I am drifting (φερόμενος). For, because I think all the time that I must add the point which logically follows what I have said before, I have wandered entirely from my subject (παντά‌πασι πόρρω γέγονα τῆς ὑποθέσεως). There is, therefore, nothing left for me to do but to crave indulgence (συγγνώμη) to old age for my forgetfulness and prolixity, faults which are wont to be found in men of my years, and to go back (ἐπανελθεῖν) to the point from which I fell into this garrulous strain. For I think that I now see the point from which I strayed (οἶμαι δ᾽ ἤδη καθορᾶν ὅθεν ἐπλανήθην).[33]

In his "Olympic Discourse" Dio Chrysostom maintains that a concept of god is innate in all men, and that belief is strengthened by observa‌tion.[34] Even senseless creatures recognize god and live according to divine ordinance. At this point, Dio abruptly begins an attack upon the Epicureans for trying to banish god from the world (Or. 12.36-37). After a spirited παρέκβασις, Dio explains

> With those remarks (ταῦτα), my argument digressed (ἐκβάς) of itself; for perhaps it is not easy to check the course of a philosopher's thoughts and speech, no matter what direction they may take. Thus, it is not difficult to run back again (ἀναδραμεῖν), just as on a voyage it is not difficult for

---

[32]Summarized by Race, "Digressions," 1-2; Heath, *Unity in Greek Poetics*, 32-34.

[33]Text and translation in G. Norlin, *Isocrates II*, LCL (Cambridge MA: Harvard University Press, 1982) 426-27. See the extended discussion of this passage by W. H. Race, "*Panathenaicus* 74-90: The Rhetoric of Isocrates' Digression on Agamemnon," *TAPA* 108 (1978): 175-85. Compare Isocrates' digression on Theseus in *Helen* 10.18-38.

[34]Text and translation in J. Cohoon, *Dio Chrysostom II*, LCL (Cambridge MA: Harvard University Press, 1977) 38-41.

skilled helmsmen to get back on course after straying from it a bit" (*Or* 12.38).[35]

Other examples might be adduced.[36] But these suffice to demonstrate that a procedure and a consistent terminology existed for digression and return. Paul might have concluded his "digression" on the glory of the apostolic office (in 2:14–7:4) as Demosthenes concluded his digression on the glories of Athens's past (in *De Cor* 199–211): by arresting the movement of his thought, by confessing that his thought had strayed, and by announcing his intention to return to the subject.[37] But 7:5 displays none of the characteristics of digression and return in Greek literature.[38] On the contrary, Paul continues directly the account of his anxious search

---

[35]See Dio's discussion of digressions in *Or* 7.128–132; he compares himself to a hunter in search of game, who leaves his first trail, when he happens to come upon another that is clearer and fresher.

[36]For example, Plato's famous digression on the philosophical life in *Theaet* 172c–177c. Plato puts the apology for the digression and the return to the subject into the mouth of the interlocutor Theodorus: Ἐμοὶ μὲν τὰ τοιαῦτα, ὦ Σώκρατες, οὐκ ἀηδέστερα ἀκούειν· ῥᾷω γὰρ τηλικῷδε ὄντι ἐπακολουθεῖν. εἰ μέντοι δοκεῖ, πάλιν ἐπανίωμεν (177c). See the discussion in A. Barker, "The Digression in the *Theaetetus*," *Journal of the History of Philosophy* 14 (1976): 457–62. See also Aelius Aristides' defence of oratory in *Or* 2.73–74; he concludes the excursus with the remark, "Incited (κινηθείς) by my argument itself, I have perhaps digressed (ἐξήγαγον) at too great length in this matter (ταυτί). May Plato himself and everyone else grant me pardon (συγγνώμη) for experiencing a feeling which was innate in the argument. But I could not restrain myself, when divine intervention and healing happened to enter the discussion. So I was compelled to mention my own experience as part of the evidence. But I shall return (ἐπάνειμι) once more to the rest of the proof."

[37]Demosthenes returns to the subject at *De Corona* 211 with the words: "However (ἀλλά), in touching upon the achievements of our ancestors, I have passed by some of my decrees and other measures. I will now therefore return (ἐπανελθεῖν) to the point at which I digressed (ἐξέβην)."

[38]Note already the question raised by Windisch, *Der zweite Korintherbrief*, 95, whether 2 Cor 2:14–7:4 is *"als Abschweifung erträglich."* Similarly, Vielhauer, *Geschichte*, 152.

for Titus.[39] The variations in what recurs, such as the change from singular to plural, and the reference of ἄνεσις to the σάρξ rather than to the πνεῦμα, mark 7:5 as the continuation of what Paul had written in 2:12-13.

Metonymic shifts, such as one encounters between 2:13 and 7:5, characterize the letter of reconciliation. By this means, within what is repeated, the apostle's purpose is advanced. In 1:15-16 Paul speaks of his desire (ἐβουλόμην), twice formulated, to come to Corinth. Resuming the verb after an ellipsis, the apostle asks: τοῦτο οὖν βουλόμενος μήτι ἄρα τῇ ἐλαφρίᾳ ἐχρησάμην; ἢ ἃ βουλεύομαι κατὰ σάρκα βουλεύομαι, ἵνα ἦ παρ' ἐμοὶ τὸ ναὶ ναὶ καὶ τὸ οὒ οὔ; (1:17). The parechesis, or phonic resemblance, between βούλομαι and βουλεύομαι, makes possible a substitution on the level of substance of "resolve" for "desire."[40] Similarly, χάρις replaces χαρά (in 1:15), which the preceding discussion (1:3-7) had led one to expect, which surfaces, finally, in opposition to λύπη (2:3), and reappears as a verb

---

[39]One should contrast 2 Cor 2:12-13 with 1 Thess 3:1-8. In the latter passage, Paul departs for a moment from the account of his longing for the recent converts to make a pointed observation about the tribulation they have endured. When Paul could bear his separation from the Thessalonians no longer, he sent Timothy to strengthen their faith (3:1-2). The mention of "tribulations" in 3:3a gives rise to "a pointed treatment of the topic of suffering tribulations in 3:3b-4," thus R. Johanson, *To All the Brethren. A Text-Linguistic and Rhetorical Approach to 1 Thessalonians*, CBNTS 16 (Stockholm: Almqvist & Wiksell International, 1987) 105. Johanson notes the care Paul takes in framing the prophetic utterance in 1 Thess. 3:3b-4: "the reiteration of οἴδατε frames this subsequence at its opening and close in a way that serves both to delimit it and to give emphasis to the importance of what is said: αὐτοὶ γὰρ οἴδατε ὅτι εἰς τοῦτο κείμεθα· καὶ γὰρ ὅτε πρὸς ὑμᾶς ἦμεν, προελέγομεν ὑμῖν ὅτι μέλλομεν θλίβεσθαι, καθὼς καὶ ἐγένετο καὶ οἴδατε." The digression is dismissed in 3:5 by διὰ τοῦτο κτλ. And the resumption is signalled by the temporal adverb and conjunction, ἄρτι δέ, in 3:6.

[40]The point is anticipated by H. Lisco, *Die Entstehung des zweiten Korintherbriefes* (Berlin: Schneider, 1896) 37; Halmel, *Der zweite Korintherbrief*, 53-54. On παρήχησις, see Hermogenes *Inv* 4.7, (Rabe 194.4). On παρονομασία and related figures, see J. Martin, *Antike Rhetorik, Technik und Methode*, HKAW 2/3 (München: Beck, 1974) 304-305; Lausberg, *Handbuch*, §637.

throughout the last section (7:7, 9, 16).[41] Paul's cautious preference for metonymy over metaphor, for contiguity over resemblance, is doubtless determined by the need to defend his sincerity against the charges τῇ ἐλαφρίᾳ χρῆσθαι and κατὰ σάρκα βουλεύεσθαι.[42]

Thus, the parallel structure of the sentences 2:12-13 and 7:5 argues for their contiguity. The similarity is created by the figure of repetition, a device Paul uses frequently in the letter of reconciliation. Variations within what is repeated mark 7:5 as the direct continuation of what Paul had written in 2:12-13. The subtle changes have the effect of intensifying Paul's distress. Comparison of the passages leads one to conclude that when the apostle wrote 7:5 he still had the words of 2:12-13 rather exactly in his mind. If the pieces of the related account had been separated by so many pages, one would expect that, at the point of transition, where Paul resumed his report to the church, he would, at least, have made some reference to the subject of the preceding part. The absence of such binding expressions suggests that 7:5 was originally joined directly onto 2:13.

II. THE CONTINUITY OF THE NARRATIVE

More conclusive proof of the unity of 2:12-13 with 7:5 is the continuity of the narrative which these verses contain. As Weiss discerned, the account of Paul's anxious search for Titus breaks off at the decisive point

---

[41]On χάρις as a substitute for χαρά, see already F. Bleek, "Erörterungen in Beziehung auf die Briefe Pauli an die Korinther," *ThStKr* 3 (1830): 621-22. Part of the manuscript tradition, ℵ[c] B L P 81. 104. 365. 614. 1175. 2464 *al* bo Thdt., has χαράν rather than χάριν. Chrysostom *Homiliae III in Epistolam secundam ad Corinthios*, MPG 61, on 2 Cor 1:15, adopts χάρις as the right reading, but explains it as χαρά: χάριν δὲ ἐνταῦθα τὴν χαρὰν λέγει. Yet there is no basis for the conjecture of Plummer, *Second Epistle*, 32, that a copyist substituted a more spiritual term, as in 3 John 4. χάρις is the better attested reading; χαρά is obviously a scribal correction motivated by 1:24 and 2:3.

[42]On μετωνυμία, or ὑπαλλαγή, and its relation to metaphor, see in general Lausberg, *Handbuch*, §565-71. Paul's cautious preference for metonymy in the letter of reconciliation is of a piece with his repeated qualifications, e.g., 1:24; 7:8, 9.

(2:13) and resumes only four chapters later (7:5) at the very point where it had broken off. A single story of Paul's desire has been pulled apart by a redactor, and that at the moment of greatest suspense. The pieces 2:12-13 and 7:5 form a continuous narrative: the story of the apostle's concern for the outcome of his "letter of tears."

> Thus we seem to be constrained to conclude that at 7:5 we have the original continuation of the account begun in 2:12-13 and that what lies between (2:14-7:4) was no part of it, but a fragment of an earlier work."[43]

What led Weiss, among others, to this conclusion was an assumption about literary unity which goes back, ultimately, to Aristotle. Weiss assumed that an account which was single and continuous conferred literary unity upon its textual expression. Conversely, whatever could be removed or transposed without effect upon the whole was not a part of the text at all, and ought not to have been included. In a famous and influential account of literary unity in the *Poetica*, Aristotle states that a unified work must satisfy the conditions of closure and connectedness (1450b23-34).[44] A "complete praxis" is described as "possessing a beginning, a middle, and an end." These terms are themselves explained by reference to causal connection, whether, that is, an event is seen to be consequent on some other event. A unified work is thus defined as the realization in textual form of a self-contained sequence of events.[45]

Aristotle's theory of literary unity is intended as an account of "how plots (μῦθοι) should be constructed (συνίστασθαι) if a work is to be successful" (1447a9-10).[46] He does not, in other words, profess to offer a universally applicable theory of unity; his concern is for the unity of

---

[43]Weiss, *Primitive Christianity*, 1:348.

[44]See the discussion of "unity" in the *Poetica* by S. Halliwell, *Aristotle's Poetics* (Chapel Hill: University of North Carolina Press, 1986) 96-108; note the useful history of the influence of the *Poetica* on pp. 286-323. Cf. the chapter on Aristotle in Heath, *Unity in Greek Poetics*, 39-55.

[45]On the possession of "a beginning, a middle, and an end" as a criterion of unity, see Aristotle *Met* 1024a1-3.

[46]This is a persistent theme in the *Poetica*; so, in particular, 1450b21-23, 1452b28-30, 1454a13-15.

narrative genres, epic and drama.[47] Yet one senses an Aristotelian prece-
dent in Polybius's faith in the interrelatedness of history and in his use
of the organic analogy (1.3.4-6).[48] He speaks of "the continuous thread
of my narrative" (τὸ συνεχὲς τῆς διηγήσεως, 6.2.1).[49] The same
assumption is at work in Dionysius's criticism of historiography (*Ep
Pomp* 3.13): history should be constructed "on the basis of continuities
inherent in the events themselves" (ταῖς περιοχαῖς τῶν πραγμάτων).[50] Diodorus (16.1.1-2) argues that the historian should, where
possible, follow "self-contained actions from beginning to end" (πράξεις αὐτοτελεῖς ἀπ' ἀρχῆς μέχρι τοῦ τέλους). "Incomplete
actions" (ἡμιτελεῖς πράξεις), "the conclusion of which is uncon-
nected with the beginning" (οὐκ ἔχουσαι συνεχὲς ταῖς ἀρχαῖς
τὸ πέρας), interrupt the interest of the reader. One should aim at "continuity of narrative" (τὸ τῆς διηγήσεως συνεχές).[51] That the
canons of closure and causal connection were broadly applied to the
literature of the period is reflected in the criticism of Callimachus (*Aetia*
fr. 1), that he failed to write poetry that was "single and continuous" (ἐν
ἄεισμα διηνεκές),[52] and in Dio's defense of the maxims of Phocylides
(*Or.* 36.12), which are complete (καὶ ἀρχὴν ἡ ποίησις καὶ
πέρας) and continuous (συνεχῆ), however brief in scope.[53]

---

[47]Note the attempt to infer Aristotle's attitude toward other genres by
Halliwell, *Aristotle's Poetics*, 283-84.

[48]P. Scheller, *De Hellenistica Historiae Conscribendae Arte* (Leipzig: Noske,
1911) 41-43; F. W. Walbank, *Polybius* (Berkeley: University of California Press,
1972) 66-69.

[49]The translation is that of F. W. Walbank, *A Historical Commentary on
Polybius* (Oxford: Clarendon Press, 1957) 637. Cf. T. Cole, "The Sources and
Composition of Polybius VI," *Historia* 13 (1964): 442.

[50]The translation modifies S. Usher, *Dionysius of Halicarnassus: The Critical
Essays in Two Volumes*, LCL (Cambridge MA: Harvard University Press, 1985)
2:379. See the discussion in K. Sacks, "Historiography in the Rhetorical Works
of Dionysius of Halicarnassus," *Athenaeum* 60 (1983): 65-87.

[51]The translation modifies C. Sherman, *Diodorus of Sicily VII*, LCL
(Cambridge MA: Harvard University Press, 1952) 233. See the discussion in
Scheller, *De Hellenistica Historiae*, 44-45.

[52]A. S. Hollis, "Callimachus, *Aetia* fr. 1.9-12," *CQ* 28 (1978) 402-406.

[53]Text and translation, J. W. Cohoon and H. Crosby, *Dio Chrysostom III*,

To be sure, the focus of Aristotle's theory is not on the textual expression, but on the underlying structure of thought.[54] "It is plot which represents the action" (1450a8). "Plot is the end at which tragedy aims" (1450a12-13). Plot (μῦθος) is defined as the order (σύνθεσις or σύστασις) of events (πράγματα) to be narrated (1450a8,12). Thus the "whole" whose conditions he stipulates is not the whole of the tragic text, but the plot which supplies its basic structure. But it would be a mistake to conclude that Aristotle was only concerned with an abstraction. He provides no criteria for assessing plots in abstraction from the texts in which they are realized. His assumption, rather, seems to be that an ordered πρᾶξις confers order on its μῦθος, and this in turn upon the text.[55] Thus the principles which define a well-constructed plot must be applied with equal rigor at the level of the text. This is what Aristotle does in his own discussion of the *Odyssea* (1451a24-30).

Later critics applied Aristotle's principles. Thus Dionysius (*Ep Pomp* 3.14) criticizes Thucydides for "leaving the account of earlier events half-finished and embarking upon others" (ἡμιτελεῖς τὰς πρώτας πράξεις καταλιπὼν ἑτέρων ἅπτεται). "He takes a single subject and divides the one body into many parts" (συμβέβηκε τῷ μὲν μίαν ὑπόθεσιν λαβόντι πολλὰ ποιῆσαι μέρη τὸ ἓν σῶμα). Herodotus, on the other hand, is like a "harmoniously unified body" (σύμφωνον ἓν σῶμα) because, despite the complexity of his subject-matter, his narrative of events is complete and continuous. Here the organic analogy is applied at the level of the text.[56] Diodorus (20.1.1) censures those who in their histories insert over-lengthy speeches, "for they rend asunder the continuity of the narrative" (τὸ γὰρ συνεχὲς τῆς διηγήσεως διασπῶσιν). His criticism is based upon a definition of history (20.1.5): "For the nature of history is simple and self-consistent" (τὸ γὰρ τῆς ἱστορίας γένος ἁπλοῦν ἐστι καὶ συμ-

---

LCL (Cambridge MA: Harvard University Press, 1940) 432-33.

[54]See the discussion in E. Downing, "οἷον ψυχή: An Essay on Aristotle's *mythos*," *Classical Antiquity* 3 (1984): 164-78; Halliwell, *Aristotle's Poetics* 103-107; Heath, *Unity in Greek Poetics*, 39-40.

[55]Heath, *Unity in Greek Poetics*, 40.

[56]Dionysius repeats his criticism of Thucydides' arrangement in *Thuc* 9. See Scheller, *De Hellenistica Historiae*, 43-44.

φυὲς αὐτῷ). Like a "living organism" (ἔμψυχον σῶμα), history loses its charm if it is frequently interrupted. But it is clear and pleasant if it remains "whole" (ὅλη) and "consistent" (συμφυές). This is "proper composition" (ἀναγκαία σύνθεσις).[57]

When Weiss proposed that 2 Cor 2:12-13 and 7:5-6 belonged together originally, it was because he had understood that Paul's account of his anxious journey to meet with Titus was single and continuous. In Troas, the apostle had no rest because he did not find his brother Titus there, so he said farewell to the brethren and went on to Macedonia (2:12-13). This is the beginning (ἀρχή) of Paul's account of an action which he undertook to learn the effect of his "letter of tears." It is a beginning that, as Aristotle says, "is not a necessary consequent of anything else, but after which something else exists or happens as a natural result" (1450b27-28). Thus Paul comes to Macedonia in search of Titus, and even there he finds no rest, only "fightings without and fears within" (7:5). This is the middle (μέσον) which, as Aristotle states, "follows something else and something follows from it" (1450b31). Then Titus arrives with the comforting news of the reconciliation of the church (7:6-7). This is the end (τελευτή), a discovery (ἀναγνώρισις) and a reversal (περιπέτεια), which, as Aristotle says, "results from the actual structure of the plot (σύστασις τοῦ μύθου) in such a way that what has already happened makes the result seem inevitable or probable" (1452a14-20). The plot, like the action which it represents, is self-evidently whole and complete (ὅλη καὶ τελεία). The apostle narrates "a sequence of events which follow one another either inevitably or according to probability" (1451a12-13). This single and continuous narrative confers continuity on the text, implies a text in which the plot is realized. But the treatise on the apostolic office in 2:14-7:4 destroys the unity of the whole. When this discourse is removed or transposed, continuity is restored. Weiss saw that it ought not to have been there at all, but was a fragment of an earlier work.

Critics who resist this conclusion generally dispute the premise that the narrative of Paul's search is single. 2:12-13, it is explained, is a

---

[57]The translation modifies R. M. Geer, *Diodorus of Sicily X*, LCL (Cambridge MA: Harvard University Press, 1954) 144-47. See Scheller, *De Hellenistica Historiae*, 44.

"description of a missionary failure"; 7:5-6, on the other hand, is a "concrete example of comfort in affliction."[58] The sections are viewed as materially disparate. But such an explanation imputes a motive which Paul does not state, and draws inferences from a context whose originality is at issue. Paul nowhere says that his efforts in Troas came to naught, rather that "a door was opened to me in the Lord" (2:12b). That he was not able to make full use of the opportunity does not imply that his preaching met with no response. On the contrary, the phrase with which Paul describes his leave-taking, ἀποταξάμενος αὐτοῖς (2:13), emphasizes how difficult it was for him to separate himself from the newly converted Christians of Troas.[59] Neither the success nor the failure of Paul's preaching is the point at issue, but the concern he felt for the church at Corinth, and the steps he was obliged to take. Thus Paul's arrival in Troas and discovery of an opportunity for effective preaching are described by means of participles (ἐλθών and ἀνεῳγμένης) which supply the circumstances under which the action of the main verbs (ἔσχηκα and ἐξῆλθον) took place: "I had no rest in my spirit...I departed into Macedonia." This is the subject of 2:12-13. It is only the desire to connect the narrative of 2:12-13 with the thanksgiving that follows (2:14f.) which has led interpreters to distort the logic of the syntax and construe 2:12-13 as an account of missionary success or failure.

Nor is 7:5-6 rightly understood as "an example of comfort in the midst of affliction." When an example (παράδειγα, *exemplum*) assumes the form of a narrative, it functions as a digression within the argument: "adducing some past action real or assumed, it serves to persuade the audience of the point that one is trying to make" (Quintilian, *Inst* 5.11.6).[60] But the argument of 2:14-7:4 is whole and complete within

---

[58]Watson, "2 Cor x-xiii," 336-38; so already, N. Dahl, *Studies in Paul* (Minneapolis: Augsburg, 1977) 38; similarly, L. Belleville, "A Letter of Apologetic Self-Commendation: 2 Cor 1:8-7:16," *NovT* 31/2 (1989): 143n.4: "Verses 12-13 deal with divine power overcoming human ineffectiveness in the context of evangelism, while 7:5-6 treat the idea of divine comfort in the midst of human affliction and suffering."

[59]Rightly, Windisch, *Der zweite Korintherbrief*, 95; cf. Acts 18:18; 20:1.

[60]On example in narrative, see Lausberg, *Handbuch*, §415: "Als *narratio* ist das exemplum eine *digressio* innerhalb der *argumentatio*." Cf. Martin, *Antike Rhetorik*, 119.

itself, and is concluded in 7:2-4 with an emotional appeal. Paul does not return to the defense of his apostleship after the supposed "illustration" of comfort in the midst of affliction. He fails to make an application of the argument he has "drawn from without" to support the point he is trying to make (Quintilian, *Inst* 5.11.1; 5.11.44). On the contrary, he continues the discussion of the outcome of his "letter of tears" (7:8-13). The theme of "comfort in the midst of affliction" pervades the letter of reconciliation. It is not the subject in particular of 7:5-6. The attempt to construe 7:5-6 as a concrete example of this idea is motivated by the desire to connect these verses with 7:4, where the terms παράκλησις and θλῖψις occur.[61]

Others concede that the account is single, but deny that the narrative is continuous. 2:14-7:4 is viewed as a digression within the narrative. The mention of Titus in 2:13, so the explanation goes, evoked a hymn of thanks to God (2:14f.), followed by a meditation on the greatness of the gospel and the weakness of the apostle.[62] To be sure, ancient literary theorists permitted digression in narrative. Dionysius of Halicarnassus (*Ep Pomp* 3.11-12) knew that lengthy narratives produced satiety (κόρος) in readers, if they were confined to a single series of events; to avoid this effect, "pauses" (ἀναπαύσεις) should be introduced.[63] Theon (*Prog* 4) maintained, similarly, that digressions (παρεκβάσεις) ought not to be entirely excluded, as in the history of Philistus, since digressions serve to refresh (ἀναπαύειν) the reader.[64] Diodorus (20.1-2) criticized lengthy orations, but did not ban them from history, "since history needs variety (ποικιλία)."

---

[61]H. Lietzmann, *An die Korinther I/II*, HNT 9 (Tübingen: Mohr-Siebeck, 1949)131; Dahl, *Studies in Paul*, 38; M. Thrall, "A Second Thanksgiving Period in II Corinthians," *JSNT* 16 (1982): 109-10; Watson, "2 Cor x–xiii," 338.

[62]H. A. W. Meyer, *Critical and Exegetical Handbook to the Epistles to the Corinthians* (Edinburgh: T.&T. Clark, 1879) 2:179-80; Plummer, *Second Epistle*, 67; E.-B. Allo, *Saint Paul: Seconde Épître aux Corinthiens*, Ebib (Paris: Gabalda, 1956) 45; K. Prümm, *Diakonia Pneumatos* (Vienna: Herder, 1967) 1:76; Kümmel, *Introduction to the New Testament*, 291; Barrett, *Second Epistle*, 97.

[63]Cicero *De Oratore* 2.77. See the discussion in H. D. Westlake, *Essays on the Greek Historians and Greek History* (Manchester: Manchester University Press, 1969) 1-38.

[64]Text in L. Spengel, *Rhetores Graeci II* (Leipzig: Teubner, 1854) 80.27-30.

Yet, ancient theorists required that digressions be related to the subject at hand, and fit smoothly into the context, emerging from the subject and returning to the point by an intelligible train of thought.[65] Thus Dionysius (*Ep Pomp* 6.11) criticized Theopompus for the content and timing of his "insertions" (παρεμβολαί), that are neither "necessary" (ἀναγκαίαι) nor "opportune" (ἐν καιρῷ). Theon (*Prog* 4) criticized those digressions which are of such great length and so remote from the theme, "that it is necessary to be reminded of what was said before" (ὥστε δεῖσθαι πάλιν ὑπομνήσεως τῶν προειρημένων); such digressions "alienate the understanding" (ἀπαλλοτριοῖ τὴν διάνοιαν).[66] Quintilian (4.3.4) permitted digression within narrative, "but only if it fits in well with the rest and follows naturally on what has preceded (*sed si cohaeret et sequitur*), not if it is thrust in like a wedge, parting what should naturally come together." Moreover, Quintilian stipulated that "all such digressions should be brief" (4.3.4).[67]

Practice was naturally less rigorous than theory. One is reminded of the long philosophic digression which interrupts the narrative of the third Sicilian visit in Plato, *Ep* 7 (341b-345c).[68] But it is precisely when one considers such an example that the difference between a true digression and Paul's defense of his apostolic office in 2:14-7:4 becomes visible. For Plato obviously took great pains to embed his thoughts on the philosophic life in the account of his third visit to Sicily.[69] The long digression is introduced by Plato's decision to put the tyrant's interest in philosophy

---

[65]On digression in narrative, see Scheller, *De Hellenistica Historiae*, 43-46; Heath, *Unity in Greek Poetics*, 46-55, 82-89. The most rigorous pronouncement remains that of Aristotle *Poetica* 1451a30-35.

[66]Text in Spengel, *Rhetores Graeci II*, 80.30-81.1.

[67]On digression in the *narratio* of speeches, see the discussion in Lausberg, *Handbuch*, §340-42; Martin, *Antike Rhetorik*, 89-91.

[68]Text in *Platonis Epistulae*, ed. J. Moore-Blunt, BT (Stuttgart: Teubner, 1985) 33-37.

[69]G. R. Morrow, *Plato's Epistles* (New York: Harper & Row, 1962) 66, has shown how essential the philosophical digression is to the argument and how aptly it is fitted into the context. See the discussion in L. Edelstein, *Plato's Seventh Letter* (Leiden: Brill, 1966) 70-120, esp. 109: "Within the framework of the representation of the events in Sicily which the author has constructed, the philosophical digression seems indispensable if the story is to be credible."

to the test (340c-341a). The end of the digression is clearly marked by Plato's admission that his thought had strayed (πλάνω) and by a resumptive reference to Dionysius's failed attempt to write something on the highest truths of nature (344d). Dionysius had emptied his own claims to philosophical competence by the disrespect he had shown the leading authority on the subject (345ac). This remark returns us to the narrative of Plato's third voyage to Sicily, an account of the insults heaped on Plato by Dionysius and his henchmen (345c-350b). Thus the philosophical digression is interwoven with the narrative; there are no breaks or joins; the transitions are the smoothest imaginable.

Precisely those features which characterize a true digression within a narrative are absent from 2:14-7:4. It is difficult to exaggerate the degree of discontinuity between 2:12-13 and 2:14ff. In the preceding paragraph (1:15-22) Paul had tried to explain his failure to carry out a promised visit. Had he followed his plan, his coming would have been an occasion of mutual grief (1:23-24). But he had made up his mind not to make the Corinthians another painful visit (2:1-2). So he wrote a letter instead (2:3). The writing of this letter had distressed him greatly. But he assures the Corinthians that his purpose had not been to cause them grief, but to let them know his abundant love (2:4). Paul next refers to the punishment of the wrongdoer whose actions had been at the root of the difficulty which prevented him from visiting Corinth (2:5-11). Then, in 2:12-13, Paul begins to describe the anxiety that he felt while he waited to hear how the Corinthians had reacted to his letter. At this point the narrative suddenly breaks off. One has to wait until 7:6 to learn what happened. Meanwhile, there breaks forth a thanksgiving to God for the triumph of the knowledge of Christ (2:14f.), a thanksgiving which introduces a defense of Paul's apostleship on the basis of the paradox of the cross. Nowhere in the intervening chapters is there an allusion, however fleeting, to the promised visit, or to the "letter of tears," or to the incident which provoked it, or to Paul's anxious search for Titus in Troas and Macedonia. There is nothing which suggests that Paul's defense of his apostleship in 2:14-7:4 was conceived as a digression within the account of his agitated search for Titus.

None of the efforts to discover a connection between 2:12-13 and 2:14ff. has proven successful. The thanksgiving and the subsequent reflection on the theological basis of Paul's ministry have no point of departure in the apostle's account of the anxiety he felt as he waited for

Titus. The commentators frequently assert that the thanksgiving was evoked by the encounter with Titus, who informed Paul of how his letter had been received.[70] Plummer explains: "The remembrance of the victory of God's cause at Corinth leads Paul on to think of the triumph of the gospel generally, and the very subordinate but glorious share which apostolic missionaries have in that triumph."[71] But all such explanations rely upon the effect of information which is not reported until 7:5-6. One is required to assume that the narrative is broken off before the event has been reported upon which the thanksgiving and all else depends.[72] Why should the apostle break off so suddenly the account of his anxious search for Titus, and so long defer his acknowledgement of the repentance and obedience of the church? The long digression on the apostolic office has no point of departure in the text as it stands, but fractures the surface of the text, like a wedge that is inserted by force.

The resumption of the narrative (in 7:5) is just as abrupt, and its relation to the context just as opaque. In the preceding chapters, Paul had defended his ministry against those who questioned his competence (ἰκανότης) for the task. His confidence, his conduct, and his gospel are at issue, and are defended by an exposition of the theological basis of his ministry. In 6:11-13; 7:2-4 the peroration is found. Paul describes his attitude as a speaker ("My heart is open, my mouth is wide"), contrasts his attitude with that of his readers (6:12), and appeals to the Corinthians to reciprocate his love (6:13). He concludes by recapitulation, enumerating (*enumeratio*) the points of his defense: he declares his innocence (7:2), confesses his love (7:3), and summarizes the boast of his heart (7:4). "Great is my confidence in you, great is my boast on your behalf; I am filled with comfort; with all our affliction, I am overjoyed!" Without question, it is the strongest peroration among the extant letters of Paul. After such a conclusion, one could only expect an epistolary

---

[70]E.g., Heinrici, *Der zweite Brief*, 101-102; R. H. Strachan, *The Second Epistle of Paul to the Corinthians*, MNTC (London: Hodder and Stoughton, 1935) 73; R. V. G. Tasker, *The Second Epistle of Paul to the Corinthians* (London: Tyndale, 1958) 56; F. F. Bruce, *First and Second Corinthians* (London: Oliphants, 1971) 187; Barrett, *Second Epistle*, 97.

[71]Plummer, *Second Epistle*, 67.

[72]So, already, Windisch, *Der zweite Korintherbrief*, 96.

postscript. The last thing one would expect to find is the resumption of a narrative.[73]

Paul's apology for his apostolic office in 2:14-7:4 cannot be construed as a digression within a narrative. It is unrelated to its present context. It breaks the thread of the narrative which runs from 2:13 to 7:5. Paul's explanation of his absence from Corinth, and of the letter he sent to Corinth instead, runs straight from 1:15 to 2:13, and from 7:5 to the chapter's end. The account exhibits the greatest closure, and excludes a discourse on the apostolic office such as now stands, without transition, in the middle of the canonical text. There is no exegetical art capable of discovering in the opening chapters a train of thought which makes the insertion of 2:14-7:4 at this point in the canonical text understandable, or even bearable.

The apostle's account, on the other hand, of his agitated search for Titus in 2:12-13 and 7:5-6 exhibits the closure and causal connection which ancient literary theory requires. It conforms to the criteria of a well-constructed narrative which Lucian of Samosata (*Hist Conscr* 55) articulated.[74] A narrative will possess its "proper virtues," if it progresses smoothly, evenly and consistently, so that it has neither humps nor hollows" (λείως τε καὶ ὁμαλῶς προϊοῦσα καὶ αὐτὴ ὁμοί- ως ὥστε μὴ προὔχειν μηδὲ κοιλαίνεσθαι). Clarity is achieved by "interweaving the subject matter" (συμπεριπλοκὴ τῶν πραγμάτων). Everything will be made "distinct and complete" (ἀπόλυτα καὶ ἐντελῆ), if the incidents are "linked together like a chain" (ἀλύσεως τρόπον συνηρμοσμένον). Thus one avoids discontinuity (μὴ διακεκόφθαι).

---

[73]Contra Furnish, *II Corinthians*, 391-92, who perverts the obvious function of 7:4 by making a new paragraph begin at this point, designating 7:4 "the topic sentence of what follows." A number of scholars stress the verbal connections between 7:2-4 and 7:5: Heinrici, *Der zweite Brief,* 251-52; Lietzmann, *An die Korinther I/II*, 131; M. Rissi, *Studien zum zweiten Korintherbrief,* ATANT 56 (Zürich: Zwingli, 1969) 15-16; Thrall, "Thanksgiving Period," 109-10. But the resemblance is merely verbal; the discontinuity of thought remains.

[74]Text and translation in K. Kilburn, *Lucian VI,* LCL (Cambridge MA: Harvard University Press, 1968) 66-67; see also G. Avenarius, *Lukians Schrift zur Geschichtsschreibung* (Meisenheim: Glan, 1956).

III. The Connecting Particles ΚΑΙ ΓΑΡ

Weiss's final argument in support of a connection between 2:12-13 and 7:5 concerns the role of the particles καὶ γάρ in 7:5. Weiss observed that the connectives had never been explained by the commentators and exegetes; indeed, they are incapable of explanation in their present position in the text. Yet the particles supply an important clue that 7:5 was originally joined directly onto 2:13.[75] Weiss did not provide a detailed account of his understanding of the syntax. But implicit in his observation is an assumption about the role of the connectives: καὶ γάρ confirms what was said before by supplying the grounds, or motive, for action. A point is affirmed, and its range extended. Such a relation is not apparent between the account of Paul's search for Titus (7:5) and the appeal to the Corinthians to open their hearts (7:2-4). But precisely such a relation obtains between 2:12-13 and 7:5. Paul's anxiety is confirmed and accentuated by the continuation of the account of his agitated search for Titus.

Weiss's insight has been variously received. Halmel adopted the suggestion and made it part of his argument for the autonomy of 2:14-7:4.[76] Windisch saw that the function of the particles changed, along with the significance, when καὶ γάρ is connected to 7:4, or as Weiss proposed, to 2:13. As it stands in the canonical text, the particles are meant to explain how Paul came to the attitude exhibited in 7:4; the sense of the phrase would then be *denn nun*. But when they are connected to 2:13, the particles serve to confirm that, on his arrival in Macedonia, Paul found himself dominated by the same anxiety that cut short his work in Troas; the sense would then be *denn auch* or *auch nämlich*.[77] Yet Windisch held that in this case ἀλλὰ καί would have been better; he allowed that the whole introductory phrase might have been slightly modified when 7:5-16 was worked into this context.[78]

---

[75]J. Weiss, *ThLZ* 19 (1894) 514.

[76]Halmel, *Der zweite Korintherbrief*, 58.

[77]Windisch, *Der zweite Korintherbrief*, 226.

[78]Windisch does not explain why ἀλλὰ καί would have been better; presumably he was thinking of those occasions on which ἀλλά is used as a connective or progressive particle, reinforced by καί; or perhaps he sensed an

Bultmann followed Windisch's suggestion, declaring "das γάρ stammt vom Redaktor, der die Stücke der verschiedenen Briefe verbunden hat."[79] Recently, critics have seen in the particles evidence against Weiss's proposal: καὶ γάρ establishes a "logical connection" between the thought of 7:5-6 and the last sentence of 7:4 by giving the reason for Paul's comfort in affliction. As a connection to 2:12-13, καὶ γάρ (in 7:5) is felt to be "awkward."[80]

The divergent interpretations of the scholars have their origin in the ambiguity of the particles themselves. In the present combination of particles, γάρ is normally the connective, and καί means "also," "even" or "in fact."[81] The particle γάρ has two basic uses: confirmatory and explanatory.[82] To be sure, these uses are closely related. But the difference in meaning is significant enough to allow for divergent interpretations. Those who defend the canonical text prefer the explanatory use: καὶ γάρ establishes a logical connection between the last sentence of 7:4 and the apostle's account of the arrival of Titus (in 7:5-6) by supplying the reason for Paul's comfort in affliction. Weiss and his followers, on the other hand, perceived that Paul's purpose was confirmatory: καὶ γάρ reaffirms the anxiety Paul felt, and described in the preceding verse (2:13), by continuing the terse account of his agitated search for Titus.

Although both constructions are possible, the combination of particles καὶ γάρ points in the confirmatory direction. This is evident from the meaning of καί ("also," "even"), and from the frequency of this combination in answers.[83] When a writer employs the combination καὶ γάρ in the middle of a continuous passage, the particles give the impression of a person reaffirming his own statement.[84] Thus καὶ γάρ means "yes,

---

implied οὐ μόνον in 2:12-13, completed by ἀλλὰ καί in 7:5, a familiar construction. On ἀλλὰ καί see J. D. Denniston, *The Greek Particles* (Oxford: Clarendon Press, 1950) 3, 21-22.

[79]Bultmann, *Der zweite Brief*, 56.

[80]Thrall, "Thanksgiving Period," 109-10; Watson, "2 Cor x-xiii," 336.

[81]Denniston, *Greek Particles*, 108-109.

[82]Denniston, *Greek Particles*, 58-60, with examples.

[83]Denniston, *Greek Particles*, lxxiii, 108-10.

[84]Denniston, *Greek Particles*, lxxiii: "If in such cases we do not catch the nuance of dialogue . . . we miss something of the colour of the style."

and," or "and further."[85] In such cases, "the particles are usually followed by a pronoun, or by a word repeated from the preceding speech: sometimes by both."[86]

Such is the use the apostle makes of the particles καὶ γάρ in 7:5. Paul wished to prove to the Corinthians the sincerity of his intentions (1:12). Thus he revealed to the Corinthians the pain he had suffered through the crisis in their relationship. The letter that Paul felt it was necessary to write had been written "out of much affliction and anguish of heart, through many tears" (2:4). The distress continued while he waited to hear how the Corinthians would react to his letter. When Paul came to Troas for the gospel of Christ, and a door was opened to him in the Lord, he did not have rest in his spirit, because he did not find his brother Titus there. So he said farewell to the brethren and went on to Macedonia (2:12-13). At this point in the apostle's account, it is as if his mind ignites; recalling the anxiety he felt, and the opportunity he was obliged to forego, his thought is kindled into a bright flame. Like a man responding to his own protest, or reaffirming his own statement, Paul continues: "Yes, and even when we came into Macedonia, our bodies had no rest, but we were afflicted in every way—fightings without and fears within" (7:5). Like ignition sparks, the particles transfix the image of the apostle's grief upon the memory of his readers.[87] The phrase καὶ γάρ reaffirms the anxiety Paul felt, confirms the account of his state of mind.

This is the use that is made of the particles in other apologetic letters. In Demosthenes' appeal for exoneration, he attempts to stir the pity of the Athenians by alluding to the dire consequences that could follow if they were to fail to bring about his restoration: "Because if my differences with you are really irreconcilable, it would be better for me to be dead" (*Ep* 2.21). As evidence that this is no "idle threat,"[88] Demosthenes

---

[85]Denniston, *Greek Particles*, lxxiii, 109.

[86]Denniston, *Greek Particles*, 109, where Denniston treats καὶ γάρ in answers, and lxiii, where he mentions cases of καὶ γάρ transferred to continuous speech.

[87]Demetrius *De Elocutione* 57: "A particle may often be used to express emotion. . . . If you remove the particle, you will remove the feeling it conveys." He gives as example the words καὶ νύ, which suggest lament and mourning; cf. Denniston, *Greek Particles*, lxxii.

[88]Demosthenes ended his second exile in 322 B.C. by taking poison.

reminds the Athenians that he gave them the opportunity to sentence him to death when he proposed that they investigate the Harpalus affair:

> Indeed, I even put myself in your power (καὶ γὰρ ἐμαυτοῦ κυρίους ὑμᾶς ἐποίησα) and did not run away before my trial, in order that I might not betray the truth, nor place myself beyond the reach of any of you, but that you might deal with me as you pleased (Ep. 2.22).[89]

Demosthenes' decision to submit his fate to the will of the people, right or wrong, to accept the penalty of death, confirms his statement that it would have been better for him to die than to live in exile unreconciled.

The spurious *Ep* 12 of Aeschines presents a defense of the orator's conduct throughout the course of his public career.[90] He was banished from Athens by the cleverness of Demosthenes, but was not, he maintains, convicted of wrong (*Ep* 12.4). The orator's conduct during his exile demonstrates his loyalty: for he selected as his place of exile not Thebes or Thessaly, where he might have heard his country slandered, but Rhodes, a city far away, which bears no ill will towards the men of Athens (*Ep* 12.9-10). Nor, indeed, did he remain there (καὶ γὰρ οὐδ' ἐνταῦθα μείνας), where he might have dwelt comfortably, but withdrew to a little garrison on the opposite mainland, where he lives in genteel poverty (*Ep* 12.11).[91]

Instances of the use of καὶ γάρ and its negative counterpart (οὐδὲ γάρ) in apologetic letters might be multiplied.[92] But the

---

[89]This was a standard rhetorical maneuver for use before the assembly; see Anaximenes in Spengel, *Rhetores Graece I*, 68.8-9.

[90]Text in E. Drerup, *Aeschinis quae feruntur epistolae* (Leipzig: Dieterich, 1904) 69-73. See the discussion of Ps.-Aeschines *Ep* 12 in Goldstein, *The Letters of Demosthenes*, 265-66.

[91]See also Ps.-Aeschines *Ep* 12.4-6, where the author asserts that in exile the orator's true character was revealed to all the Hellenes: "For who does not know that when men must die or when they must flee from the fatherland, then especially they become such as manifest their character." In confirmation of this statement, he says: "For indeed (καὶ γάρ) the things which they once concealed appear clearly in the midst of all."

[92]So, e.g., Plato *Ep* 7.338b. Plato's second visit to Sicily was ended by the outbreak of war (338a). When peace was made, the tyrant sent for him, and kept demanding insistently that he should come (338b). Dion urged Plato to make the

examples cited demonstrate that the common usage was confirmatory and causal, and that the particles affirm the truth of a statement by adducing a motive or describing an action. It is not possible to discover such a relation between 7:5-6 and 6:11-13; 7:2-4. In what sense does Paul's account of his search for Titus confirm his appeal to the Corinthians to reciprocate his love? Only when 7:4 is viewed in isolation is one able to construe 7:5-6 as an explanation of Paul's comfort in the midst of affliction. But then, one must ask whether καὶ γάρ is sufficient to mark 7:5-6 as an explanation of the attitude expressed in 7:4, given the fact that the preceding chapters contain no references to Titus and his mission to Corinth. Does the context not require something stronger? That which justifies Paul's exclamation, "With all our affliction, I am overjoyed!" is the paradoxical word of the cross. The courage which the apostle claims in 2:14-7:4 is not contingent upon the Corinthians' response. It is grounded in the apprehension that "the transcendent power belongs to God" (4:7-12).

Paul's other use of the particles καὶ γάρ in the letter of reconciliation is likewise confirmatory and causal. Earlier, Paul had urged the Corinthians to affirm their love for a certain member who had caused distress to the entire community (2:5-11): they should forgive this person and comfort him, lest he be overwhelmed by excessive sorrow (2:7). Paul seeks to assure the Corinthians that he does not hold anything against the man: "Anyone whom you forgive, I also forgive" (2:10). Then Paul hastens to add: "And indeed (καὶ γάρ) what I have forgiven, if I have forgiven anything, has been for your sakes in the presence of Christ" (2:10). The point of the statement introduced by καὶ γάρ is to confirm that the apostle has forgiven and to disclose the motive for his action. If Paul is reluctant to acknowledge that he has forgiven something, it is

---

voyage, though his own recall had been deferred. The author confirms Dion's advice, supplying the motive for his counsel: "For in truth (καὶ γὰρ δή) constant accounts were pouring in from Sicily how Dionysius was now once more marvellously enamoured of philosophy" (338b). See also Ps.-Aeschines *Ep* 12.14: καὶ γὰρ ὀργίζεσθαι ῥᾳδίως ὑμῖν ἔθος ἐστι καὶ χαρίζεσθαι πάλιν. Cf. Apollonius of Tyana *Ep* 35; Ps.-Euripides *Ep* 5.3 (οὐ γάρ); Demosthenes *Ep* 2.14 (οὔτε γάρ). On οὐδὲ γάρ, see Denniston, *Greek Particles*, 111-12.

because he does not wish to seem to lord it over the Corinthians' faith, but rather to work with them for their joy (1:24).

The other uses of καὶ γάρ in the Pauline corpus are consistent with this interpretation.[93] From the earliest instance to the latest, the particles are confirmatory, and are best translated "for even" or "and in fact." In 1 Thess. 3:3-4, Paul reminds the Thessalonians that persecution is to be their lot: "Indeed, you yourselves know that this is what we are destined for. In fact (καὶ γάρ), when we were with you, we told you beforehand that we were to suffer persecution; so it turned out, as you know." In Rom. 15:1-3, Paul tells the strong Christians to bear with the weak, and not merely to seek to please themselves. He exhorts: "Let each of us please his neighbor for the good purpose of his edification." Paul strengthens his point with the observation: "For even (καὶ γάρ) the Christ did not please himself; but, as it is written, 'The reproaches of those who reproached you have fallen on me.'"

The suggestion that γάρ in 7:5 is a subsequent addition by the redactor is not warranted by the evidence. Paul's use of καὶ γάρ in 7:5 is in keeping with the understanding of the particles in Greek literature generally, and is consistent with his own practice elsewhere. If anything, γάρ is the preferred connective in the letter of reconciliation (note esp. the sentences opening with γάρ in 1:8, 12, 13, 19, 20; 2:1, 2, 4; 7:5, 10, 11). Nor would ἀλλὰ καί have been better, as Windisch suggests. For the idea of contrast, of difference, runs through all the shades of meaning of ἀλλά, from the strongest ("but") to the weakest ("further," "again").[94] This fact holds true, even if ἀλλά is occasionally used as a progressive particle, reinforced by καί.[95] Progressive ἀλλά is rare in prose writers.[96]

IV. THE SYMMETRY OF CHAPTERS 2 AND 7

Once Weiss had grasped the basic connection between 2:13 and 7:5, the coherence of other parts of the text became immediately apparent.

---

[93]Rom 11:1; 15:3; 16:2; 1 Cor 5:7; 8:5; 12:13; 12:14; 14:8; 2 Cor 5:2; 5:4; 13:4; 1 Thess 3:4.

[94]Denniston, *Greek Particles*, 1-2.

[95]Denniston, *Greek Particles*, 21.

[96]Denniston, *Greek Particles*, 22.

The symmetry of chapters 2 and 7 impressed itself upon Windisch.[97] In more than one respect the account begun in 2:1-13 of Paul's dealings with the church at Corinth finds its completion and elaboration in the course of 7:5-16. One learns not only that Paul met with Titus and that his anxiety was relieved (7:6). One also discovers that Titus brought the report of the salutory effect of the letter of tears (7:7, 9, 11), something which is presupposed, but not expressed, in Paul's comments on the punishment of the wrongdoer in 2:5-11. One learns, moreover, that the community has been disobedient to its apostle, that it has treated Paul with disrespect (7:9, 11), so that Paul was obliged to write things that were very painful to the community (7:8), something that is only hinted at in 2:1-4, 9. Accordingly, the community has now repented (7:9-10) and has publicly demonstrated its loyalty to the apostle (7:7, 11-12), something which one could only assume from the statements of 2:2-4, 9. In 7:11-12 one learns that the reprehensible conduct of the community was related, in particular, to the case of a "wrongdoer," something which is implied, but not stated, in Paul's discussion of the τοιοῦτος in 2:5-11, and that consequently the punishment of this person by the community constitutes part of its repentance. Finally, one learns that in the incident which occasioned Paul's painful epistle, an ἀδικήσας and an ἀδικη- θείς were involved, but that Paul's primary object of concern remained his relation with the Corinthian church (7:12), a statement which mirrors and clarifies Paul's earlier assertion in 2:5: "But if anyone has caused pain, he has caused it not to me, but in some measure, not to put it too severely, to you all."

Each moment of the crisis in their relations is taken up again and reconsidered: the purpose of the severe epistle; the incident involving the wrongdoer; the complicity of the community in the affair; the repentance and obedience of the church; the punishment of a community member; the restitution of mutual joy. It is obviously the same situation with which Paul is dealing in chs. 2 and 7, and the same stage in that situa- tion. Yet, one notes a difference in perspective: in 2:1-13 Paul is more concerned with the one who has caused the community grief; but in 7:5- 16 he devotes his attention to the conduct of the community. Thus in ch.

---

[97]Windisch, *Der zweite Korintherbrief*, 224-25, details six ways in which 7:5- 16 completes the discussion begun in 2:1-13.

2 the community plays the role of the jury, advised by Paul; while in ch. 7 the church appears as the party which must defend itself, and Paul plays the role of the merciful judge. Obviously, 7:5-16 is no doublet of the second chapter, but the completion and elaboration of the argument presented there, under a somewhat different aspect.

What marks the shift in Paul's perspective is the encounter with Titus in 7:5-6. The arrival of Paul's emissary is the dramatic center of the work. Before this moment, all is prospect: not only the defense of the severe epistle, made by reference to Paul's motive (2:3-4), but even the obedience of the church, represented as something which Paul must test (2:9). After this moment, all is retrospect: the epistle is seen in its effect (7:8-9); the obedience of the church is now complete, and is something which Titus can recall (7:11, 15-16). Titus embodies in his person the new relationship between Paul and the church. He has already received comfort and joy, the fruit of the reconciliation, and has conveyed these experiences to Paul (7:6-7, 13, 16). His mind has already been set at rest (7:13). Thus it is proper that the encounter with Titus should structure the apostle's account of his dealings with the church at Corinth. It is this which creates the symmetry between intention and fulfillment.

Symmetry (συμμετρία) is one of the criteria by which Greek literary theorists judged the unity of a work.[98] Hermogenes required that all the elements of a text fit together harmoniously and proportionately (τὸ ἐκ πάντων τῶν ποιούντων τὰς ἰδέας αὐτοῦ πάσας . . . εὐάρμοστον καὶ σύμμετρον), like the body's limbs and parts (*Id.* 296.15-298.10).[99] A good composition is characterized by the symmetry of its constituent elements (συμμετρία μελῶν καὶ μερῶν). Dionysius criticized Thucydides for the lack of due proportion in his elaboration of the subject: the apportioning of care and textual space to the various segments of material is unbalanced, follows no discernible plan, and frequently fails to correspond to the intrinsic significance of the events recorded (*Thuc* 13-20). Diodorus repeatedly justifies authorial decisions (e.g., 1.8.10; 1.9.4; 1.41.10) by reference to the necessity of

---

[98]Discussed by Scheller, *De Hellenistica Historiae*, 46-48; C. M. J. Sicking, "Organische Komposition und Verwandtes," Mnemosyne 16 (1963) 237-38; Heath, *Unity in Greek Poetics*, 32-33, 37, 87.

[99]Text in *Rhetores Graeci VI. Hermogenes Opera*, ed. H. Rabe (Stuttgart: Teubner, 1969).

preserving due proportion (στοχαζόμενοι τῆς συμμετρίας). That beauty consists in the συμμετρία of the parts with each other and with the whole was the rhetorical and philosophical consensus.[100]

In practice, Greek authors avoided discussions which threatened to destroy due proportion. This was achieved by consideration of what was proper (πρέπον) and opportune (καιρός).[101] At the end of the prologue in the *Panathenaicus* (12.33-34), Isocrates introduces a *praeteritio* on the poetry of Homer and Hesiod, appealing to what is proportionate (συμμετρία) and appropriate (εὐκαιρία):

> But I perceive that I am being carried beyond the due limits which have been assigned to an introduction (αἰσθάνομαι δ' ἐμαυτὸν ἔξω φερόμενον τῆς συμμετρίας τῆς συντεταγμένης τοῖς προοιμίοις); for it behooves a man of sense not to indulge his resourcefulness, when he has more to say on a given subject than other speakers, but to preserve always the element of timeliness (ἀλλὰ τὴν εὐκαιρίαν διαφυλάτ-τειν) no matter on what subject he may have occasion to speak—a principle which I must observe.

In the *Antidosis* (15.68-69) Isocrates introduces extracts from his early discourse *Ad Nicocles* with an apology for the failure of this work to fulfill the requirements of proportion and connectedness:

> It is not, however, composed in the same style as the other extracts which have been read. For in them each part is always in accord and in logical connection with what goes before (οὗτοι μὲν γὰρ τὸ λεγόμενον ὁμο-λογούμενον ἀεὶ τῷ προειρημένῳ καὶ συγκεκλειμένον ἔχουσιν); but in this, on the contrary, I detach one part from another, and break up the discourse.

---

[100]See, e.g., Chrysippus, *SVF* 3.278.31-34: ὥσπερ τε τὸ κάλλος τοῦ σώματός ἐστι συμμετρία τῶν μελῶν καθεστώτων αὐτῷ πρὸς ἄλληλά τε καὶ πρὸς τὸ ὅλον, οὕτω καὶ τῆς ψυχῆς κάλλος ἐστὶ συμμετρία τοῦ λόγου καὶ τῶν μερῶν αὐτοῦ πρὸς τὸ ὅλον τε αὐτῆς καὶ πρὸς ἄλληλα. Cf. Cicero *Tusc Dis* 4.13.30. Plotinus 1.6.1 characterizes the idea as almost universally held. Cf. Lucian *Hist Conscr* 27-28.

[101]See Plato's treatment of the artistic norm (τὸ μέτριον) as it relates to the length of a discussion in *Polit* 284E5-8: the norm is achieved by consideration of τὸ πρέπον, καιρός, and τὸ δέον. Cf. *Rhet ad Alex* 1436a23-31; Isocrates 15.310-11.

The source of Isocrates' dissatisfaction is neither the content nor the intent of the counsel which he had to offer, but the lack of proportion and logical connection. The epistolary genre imposed a stricter symmetry. In his epistle *Ad Phil* (2.13) Isocrates explains:

> Although I have much more to say, because of the nature of the subject, I will cease; for I think that you and the ablest of your companions will readily add as much as you wish to what I have said. Besides, I fear my advice will be inopportune (ἀκαιρία); for even now I have unawares gradually drifted beyond the due proportion of a letter and run into a lengthy discourse" (καὶ γὰρ νῦν κατὰ μικρὸν προϊὼν ἔλαθον ἐμαυτὸν οὐκ ἐπιστολῆς συμμετρίαν ἀλλ' εἰς λόγου μῆκος ἐξοκείλας).[102]

When an author nevertheless concluded that it was necessary or desirable to digress, he took care to select material which was apt to his theme and proportionate to the rest of his work. Thus Isocrates introduces a digression on Heracles into his *Philip* (5.110) with the observation:

> I have refrained from touching upon his other exploits and have singled out only one—a story which is pertinent and in keeping with what I have said before, while being of a length best proportioned to the subject now in hand (προσήκουσα μὲν καὶ πρέπουσα τοῖς προειρημένοις, τὸν δὲ καιρὸν ἔχουσα μάλιστα σύμμετρον τοῖς νῦν λεγομένοις).

Similarly, Isocrates defends his prolix praise of the constitution of Athens in the *Panathenaicus* (12.135) by saying that, though his discourse will seem unduly long to superficial hearers, a truly discerning audience will find what he has to say "neither burdensome nor untimely, but of due measure and in keeping with what I have said before" (οὔτ' ὀχληρὸς οὔτ' ἄκαιρος, ἀλλὰ σύμμετρος καὶ προσήκων τοῖς πρότερον εἰρημένοις). When Isocrates disregards due proportion (in the digression on Agamemnon in the *Panath.*), he explains:

> I was more concerned about doing justice to the theme than about the symmetry of my speech (ἡ τοῦ λόγου συμμετρία), though I knew full

---

[102]Text and translation in G. Norlin, *Isocrates*, LCL (Cambridge MA: Harvard University Press, 1945).

well that the lack of due proportion (ἡ ἀκαιρία) in my speech would detract from my own reputation" (12.86).[103]

The due proportion and firm connection between 2 Cor 2:1-13 and 7:5-16 are destroyed by the untimely insertion of the discourse on Paul's apostolic office (2:14-7:4). Had Paul wished to include a defense of his apostleship in the letter of reconciliation, one might have expected that he would have created an apology more in keeping with his theme and proportionate to the rest of the work. It is difficult to see why Paul should not have concluded the account of his relations with Corinth, before embarking upon the discussion of a matter which remained at issue. Thus Paul would have succeeded in rounding-off his points and in making connections between one point and another, as ancient critics recommended (e.g., Aristotle, *Rhet* 1414b26; Isocrates 12.24-25).[104] It is incomprehensible that Paul should break off the account of his relations with Corinth so suddenly, and at the most suspenseful moment (2:13), and so long defer his acknowledgement of what the Corinthians had accomplished, of their repentance and obedience, and should then interpose so much defense and so much debate, so much theological reflection—it is incomprehensible. If the pieces of the related account (2:1-13 and 7:5-16) had been separated by so many pages, one would expect that, at the point of transition, where Paul resumed his report to the church, he would, at least, have made some reference to the subject of the preceding part, such as: "Now to conclude the report of Titus," or "Now concerning

---

[103]See the observation on this passage by Heath, *Unity in Greek Poetics*, 33: "All of this is, of course, highly disingenuous. . . . Isocrates is taking pains over his rhetorical *ethos*; he contrives to claim moral credit for an artistic negligence of which he simultaneously implies that he is not guilty. . . . Clearly, we are not to take these rhetorical figures literally; they are devices by which Isocrates works the digression into the continuous texture of his speech, effecting those artful transitions from point to point which he elsewhere declares necessary (12.24; 15.11,68-69), while at the same time engaging the complicity of the reader to whose superior artistic judgement implicit tribute is paid."

[104]Aristotle *Rhet* 1414b26 requires that the parts of a speech have smooth connections (συνάψαι) between them. Isocrates (12.24-25) regards it as inartistic to leave a discussion unfinished; to fail to round off each point and to make connections between one point and the next is slovenly, random (εἰκῇ) composition.

the grief which you have been caused." The absence of such transitions is surprising, and hardly tolerable, if 7:5-16 is the resumption of the second chapter; but it is less noticeable, and ideed is unexpected, if, as Weiss and others have suggested, this section formed the continuation of the account begun in 2:1-13.

Symmetry and connection are restored, and the apparent neglect of καιρός amended, if 7:5-16 is reaffixed to its counterpart in 2:1-13. Thus the following textual sequence results: the letter Paul wrote in place of a visit (2:1-4); the particular case that led Paul to write (2:5-11); the search for Titus and news of the church (2:12-13); the encounter with Titus and his report (7:5-7); the defense of the letter from its effect (7:8-10); the repentence and obedience of the church (7:11); the summary of the correspondence (7:12). As Windisch states, "Unverkennbar ist der Vorteil, den die Umstellung zuwege bringt."[105]

Within Paul's defense of his severe epistle, the encounter with Titus marks the turning point. Paul's search for Titus dramatizes his quest for reconciliation with the church. Thus the search for Titus appropriately structures Paul's apology for his conduct towards Corinth. From this point, the apostle can look forward and back, contriving balance to contrive an whole. If 7:5-16 is more explicit than 2:1-13 in its account of the conduct of the Corinthian church, this corresponds to Paul's conviction that reconciliation defines the new being and all of its relationships.

CONCLUSION

Weiss's original insight retains all of its force: 2:13 and 7:5 "fit onto each other as neatly as the broken pieces of a ring." His proofs, asserted, and partly implied, have been confirmed by detailed examination of Greek literary theory and practice. The parallel structure of the sentences in 2:12-13 and 7:5 argues for their contiguity: the symmetry is established by the figure of repetition, a figure used elsewhere by Paul, and by other Greek authors, to convey the strength and depth of emotion. The account of Paul's anxious search for Titus in 2:12-13 and 7:5-6 is single and continuous; thus it conforms to the criteria of a well-constructed narrative as defined and applied by Greek literary theorists. The particles καὶ γάρ in 7:5 demonstrate that this verse, and the one that follows,

---

[105]Windisch, *Der zweite Korintherbrief*, 225.

were originally joined to 2:13. Only thus does καὶ γάρ in 7:5 recover its affirmative force. The symmetry of 2:1-13 and 7:5-16 argues for their original coherence. Finally, Paul's apology for his apostolic office in 2:14-7:4 cannot be construed as a digression within a narrative: it has no point of departure in what precedes; it makes no connection with what follows. The discourse can be removed or transposed without effect upon the whole. We may conclude that it ought not to have been there at all, but is a fragment of an earlier work. 2 Cor 1:1-2:13; 7:5-16 has been shown to be a coherent work in accordance with Greek and Roman assumptions about literary unity: it possesses the characteristics of connection (σύναψις), continuity (συνέχεια), and symmetry (συμμετρία) in such degree that ancient literary critics would have judged the work to be a unity.[106]

---

[106]More important still for the question of unity are the criteria of order (σύστασις) and completeness (ὅλος). But these can be established for 2 Cor 1:1-2:13; 7:5-16, as for any text, only on the basis of analysis of the arrangement (τάξις) and form (εἶδος) of the work. This lies beyond the scope of the present essay.

PAUL'S DEFENSE OF HIS CHARACTER AND TRUTHFULNESS IN 2 CORINTHIANS 1:17-23

Iuravit autem ipse Apostolus in epistolis suis.
Augustine *De Mendacio* 28

I. AN EXEGETICAL CRUX

There is no thornier crux in the *corpus Paulinum* than the last clause of 2 Cor 1:17—ἵνα ᾖ παρ' ἐμοὶ τὸ ναὶ ναὶ καὶ τὸ οὒ οὔ; The most thorough exegetes, and the most critical, are most conscious of its ambiguity.[1] Not surprisingly, the history of the interpretation of the passage is studded with forced constructions of the syntax and conjectural emendations of the text.[2] It is ironic that a statement that has occasioned such difficulty should be found in an epistle in which Paul contends he writes nothing but what his readers can understand (2 Cor 1:13).

The sources of difficulty are principally three. First and most problematic is the repetition of the particles ναί and οὔ.[3] The difficulty

---

[1]Acknowledged with characteristic honesty by A. Plummer, *A Critical and Exegetical Commentary on the Second Epistle of St. Paul to the Corinthians*, ICC (Edinburgh: T.&T. Clark, 1915) 34: "The exact meaning of what follows is uncertain"; H. Windisch, *Der zweite Korintherbrief*, KEK 6 (Göttingen: Vandenhoeck & Ruprecht, 1924; repr. 1970) 65: "Der Sinn, den Paulus damit verbindet, ist freilich in jedem Falle unklar ausgedrückt."

[2]The history of interpretation is surveyed by C. F. G. Heinrici, *Der zweite Brief an die Korinther*, KEK 6 (Göttingen: Vandenhoeck & Ruprecht, 1900) 76-78; Windisch, *Der zweite Korintherbrief*, 64-66; F. Young, "Note on 2 Corinthians 1:17b," *JTS* 37 (1986): 404-15. On conjectural emendations, see esp. F. Hahn, "Ist das textkritische Problem von 2 Kor 1,17 lösbar?" in *Studien zum Text und zur Ethik des Neuen Testaments*, Festschrift zum 80. Geburtstag von Heinrich Greeven, ed. W. Schrage (Berlin: de Gruyter, 1986) 158-65.

[3]Recognized as a problem by Windisch, *Der zweite Korintherbrief*, 64-65; W. C. van Unnik, "Reisepläne und Amen-Sagen, Zusammenhang und Gedankenfolge in 2. Korinther 1:15-24," in *Studia Paulina honorem Johannis de Zwaan* (Haarlem: Bohn, 1953) 216, 219; D. Wenham, "2 Corinthians 1:17,18: Echo of

of the duplication is clearly reflected in the preference of certain scholars for the shorter reading, ἵνα ᾖ παρ' ἐμοὶ τὸ ναὶ καὶ τὸ οὔ, although this reading is poorly attested (P[46] 0243 vg Pelagius).[4] Even those who remain by the longer text convey the sense of the shorter one, by leaving the second ναί and οὔ untranslated, explaining that the repetition is merely for emphasis, and that the textual discrepancy is insignificant.[5]

A second obstacle to understanding is Paul's use of the article before the words in question.[6] Is the article generic or specific, in the sense "that with which you charge me"? And if the article functions as a quotation mark, to whom are the words to be ascribed? Does Paul refer to things which have been said at Corinth?[7] Or does Paul formulate the implications, employing a well-known figure of speech?[8]

---

a Dominical Logion," *NovT* 28/3 (1986): 273.

[4]A preference for the shorter reading is expressed by H. Grotius, *Annotationes in Novum Testamentum*, vol. 2 (Paris: Sumptibus authoris, 1646) ad loc.; W. Estius, *In omnes Divi Pauli Apostoli Epistolas commentariorum*, vol. 2, editio secunda (Moguntiae: Sumptibus F. Kirchhemii, 1859) ad loc.; W. G. Kümmel in H. Lietzmann, *An die Korinther I/II*, HNT 9 (Tübingen: Mohr-Siebeck, 1949) 197. For discussion of the manuscript evidence, see F. Hahn, "Ist das textkritische Problem von 2 Kor 1,17 lösbar?" in *Studien zum Text und zur Ethik des Neuen Testaments. Festschrift zum 80. Geburtstag von Heinrich Greeven*, ed. W. Schrage (Berlin: de Gruyter, 1986) 158n.2.

[5]So, e.g., Plummer, *Second Epistle*, 34; E.-B. Allo, *Seconde Épître aux Corinthiens*, ÉB (Paris: Gabalda, ²1956) 26; R. Bultmann, *Der zweite Brief an die Korinther*, KEK 6 (Göttingen: Vandenhoeck & Ruprecht, 1976) 43. The RSV translates: "ready to say Yes and No at once."

[6]Recognized as a problem by Plummer, *Second Epistle*, 34; D. Wenham, "2 Corinthians 1:17, 18: Echo of a Dominical Logion," *NovT* 28/3 (1986): 273.

[7]So, A. Menzies, *The Second Epistle of the Apostle Paul to the Corinthians* (London: Macmillan, 1912) 10; H. Chadwick, "'All Things to All Men' (1 Cor IX.22)," *NTS* 1 (1972): 262; mentioned as a possibility by Windisch, *Der zweite Korintherbrief*, 65: "Aber vielleicht hat sich Paulus einer vulgären, in Korinth auf ihn angewandten Redeweise bedient."

[8]So H. A. W. Meyer, *Kritisch exegetisches Handbuch über den zweiten Brief an die Korinther*, KEK 6 (Göttingen: Vandenhoeck & Ruprecht, 1870) 28; Heinrici, *Der zweite Brief*, 77; Windisch, *Der zweite Korintherbrief*, 64.

A third problem is the relationship of vs. 17c to the phrases which immediately precede.[9] To be sure, there is a broad exegetical consensus that the clause ἵνα ᾖ παρ' ἐμοὶ τὸ ναὶ ναὶ καὶ τὸ οὔ οὔ is consecutive rather than final; ἵνα substitutes for the infinitive of result.[10] Thus, the majority of commentators regard the ἵνα-clause as ep-exegetic.[11] But the opacity of the words has led interpreters to disregard the sentence structure, and to construe the last clause of vs. 17 as alternative to the preceding phrases, or even, assuming a brachylogy, as adversative.[12]

---

[9]The problem is discussed by Plummer, *Second Epistle*, 33-34; Windisch, *Der zweite Korintherbrief,* 64; F. Young, "Note on 2 Corinthians 1:17b," *JTS* 37 (1986): 404-15.

[10]Thus, F. Blass and A. Debrunner, *A Greek Grammar of the New Testament and Other Early Christian Literature*, rev. by R. Funk (Chicago: University of Chicago, 1961) §391 (5); E. Burton, *Syntax of the Moods and Tenses in New Testament Greek*, 3rd ed. (Edinburgh: T. & T. Clark, 1898; repr. 1973) §218. See the discussion of the ecbatic use of ἵνα in the New Testament by A. T. Robertson, *A Grammar of the Greek New Testament in the Light of Historical Research* (New York: Hodder & Stoughton, 1914) 997-99. To be sure, J. H. Moulton, *A Grammar of New Testament Greek, I Prolegomena*[3] (Edinburgh: T.&T. Clark, 1908) 210, argued that the ἵνα-clause should be regarded as final. But Turner concedes that the clause is controversial in his continuation of Moulton, *A Grammar of New Testament Greek* III (Edinburgh: T.&T. Clark, 1963) 102.

[11]So, Meyer, *Kritisch exegetisches Handbuch,* 28; Heinrici, *Der zweite Brief,* 77; Plummer, *Second Epistle,* 34; P. Bachmann, *Der zweite Brief des Paulus an die Korinther*, KNT 8 (Leipzig: Deichert, [3]1918) 61-62; Windisch, *Der zweite Korintherbrief,* 64-65; Allo, *Seconde Épître,* 24; J. Hering, *La Seconde Épître aux Corinthiens* (Neuchâtel: Delachaux, 1958) 26; C. K. Barrett, *The Second Epistle to the Corinthians*, HNTC (New York: Harper & Row, 1973) 75-76; Bultmann, *Der zweite Brief,* 43.

[12]This hermeneutical tendency is already apparent in Chrysostom and Theodoret (see below). In the modern period it is represented by K. von Hofmann, *Die heilige Schrift neuen Testaments zusammenhängend untersucht,* 2. Theil, 3. Abteilung: *Der zweite Brief Pauli an die Korinther* (Nördlingen: Beck, [2]1877) 24-25, and Th. Zahn, *Introduction to the New Testament*, vol. 1 (New York: Scribner's, 1917) 343-44, among others. It is critically evaluated by Windisch, *Der zweite Korintherbrief,* 64-65.

Because several factors are ambiguous, the history of interpretation is exceedingly complex. Nevertheless, it is possible to distinguish three broad opinions: (1) the received text yields a satisfactory sense, without recourse to forced constructions of the syntax; (2) the text can be made comprehensible by the accentuation of certain features and the explanation of others; (3) the text is unintelligible as received and requires emendation.

The majority of exegetes assume that a coincidence of affirmation and negation is being described, whether in an ambiguous or a duplicitous sense, so that the phrase might be translated, "ready to say yes and no at once,"[13] or "saying yes with my lips and no with my heart."[14] This interpretation seems to be supported by what Paul says about the apostolic λόγος in the following verse: οὐκ ἔστιν ναὶ καὶ οὔ.[15] Thus, Paul would seem to be denying the charge of having changed his plans, of having altered his words, in accordance with his own interests.

The traditional interpretation seems so sensible in context, that one may easily fail to see how many assumptions it employs, or how much of the concreteness of expression must be sacrificed to make the general sense of the sentence plain.[16] It is assumed, in the first place, that vs. 17c

---

[13]So the majority of commentators, among them most noteworthy: Heinrici, *Der zweite Brief,* 77; Plummer, *Second Epistle,* 34; Bachmann, *Der zweite Brief,* 61-62; Windisch, *Der zweite Korintherbrief,* 65; Allo, *Seconde Épître* 24; Hering, *Seconde Épître,* 26; Barrett, *Second Epistle,* 75-76; Bultmann, *Der zweite Brief,* 43; H.-J. Klauck, *2. Korintherbrief* (Würzburg: Echter, 1986) 24. So also W. Bauer, *A Greek-English Lexicon of the New Testament and Other Early Christian Literature,* rev. W. F. Arndt, F. W. Gingrich and F. W. Danker (Chicago: University of Chicago Press, 1979) 533: "that my 'yes' should at the same time be 'no.'"

[14]Thus, Windisch, *Der zweite Korintherbrief,* 65: "Ja im Munde und Nein im Herzen," referring to Baba Mezia 49a, where the words are a comment upon Lev 19:36.

[15]So, Menzies, *Second Corinthians,* 10; Plummer, *Second Epistle,* 34; Lietzmann, *An die Korinther,* 197; Windisch, *Der zweite Korintherbrief,* 65; Allo, *Seconde Épître,* 26; W. C. van Unnik, "Reisepläne und Amen-Sagen, Zusammenhang und Gedankenfolge in 2. Korinther 1:15-24," in *Studia Paulina in honorem Johannis de Zwaan* (Haarlem: Bohn, 1953) 219.

[16]The point is made by Windisch, *Der zweite Korintherbrief,* 64, and by F. Young, "Note on 2 Corinthians 1:17b," *JTS* 37 (1986): 404-406.

is clarified by vss. 18 and 19, where ναὶ καὶ οὔ constitutes the predicate.[17] But this overlooks the distinction that Paul establishes, signalled by the adversative conjunction (δέ) in vs. 18a, between a discourse that proceeds from the faithfulness of God and speech which results from human indifference.[18] The apostolic word about Jesus the Messiah is unequivocal (1:19); human promises, by contrast, inhabit an obscure and unstable realm, remote from the clarity of truth. The expression τὸ ναὶ ναὶ καὶ τὸ οὔ οὔ belongs, with the rest of vs. 17, to Paul's formulation of the charges against him; it must be comprehended within its own context, without assuming that Paul is saying the same thing when he uses similar, but less ambiguous language in rebuttal.[19]

Second, it is assumed that the repetition of the particles is merely for emphasis. Some omit the second ναί and οὔ in paraphrase: for example, "The Corinthians say he is vacillating, that Yes and No are much the same to him."[20] Others state explicitly, "The repetition gives emphasis."[21] W. C. van Unnik explains the ναὶ ναί and οὔ οὔ as a Semitic idiom, an iterative use for the sake of emphasis: "immer wieder ja und immer wieder nein."[22] To be sure, there are instances of the

---

[17]So, explicitly, Menzies, *Second Corinthians*, 10; Bachmann, *Der zweite Brief*, 61-62; Lietzmann, *An die Korinther*, 197; Hering, *Seconde Épître*, 26; tacitly assumed by many others.

[18]Rightly, Heinrici, *Der zweite Brief*, 78. Windisch, *Der zweite Korintherbrief*, 66, describes vs. 18 as the "Abweisung" of the reproach against Paul in the preceding verse. van Unnik, "Reisepläne und Amen-Sagen," 218, also senses the contrast and endeavors to explain the connection between vs. 17c and vs. 18ff. by reference to the Rabbinic argument *qal wa-homer*, Barrett, *Second Epistle*, 76, postulates: "[Paul's] 'Yes, yes' and 'No, no' lead him off into a theological digression."

[19]So, rightly, Meyer, *Kritisch exegetisches Handbuch*, 28; Heinrici, *Der zweite Brief*, 77-78; F. Young, "Note on 2 Corinthians 1:17b," *JTS* 37 (1986): 406.

[20]Menzies, *Second Epistle*, 10; similarly, H.-J. Klauck, *2. Korintherbrief* (Würzburg: Echter, 1986) 24: "so dass mein Ja auch ein Nein sein kann."

[21]Plummer, *Second Epistle*, 34; similarly, Windisch, *Der zweite Korintherbrief*, 65; Allo, *Seconde Épître*, 24; Kümmel in Lietzmann, *An die Korinther*, 197, preferring the shorter text of P[46] and the Vulgate.

[22]W. C. van Unnik, "Reisepläne und Amen-Sagen, Zusammenhang und Gedankenfolge in 2. Korinther 1:15-24," in *Studia Paulina in honorem Johannis*

intensive use of the particles in ancient literature, Greek as well as Jewish;[23] and *epanadiplosis* is not unknown in the New Testament.[24] But what must be tested is the assumption that the repetition is merely for emphasis, and not for some other purpose (such as asseveration).

Third, it is assumed that Paul means to describe a simultaneity of expression. This assumption is the great weakness of the majority interpretation—that it depends upon a thought, "at once" or "simultaneously," which remains unexpressed.[25] German commentators insert the words *zugleich* or *zusammen*.[26] English exegetes introduce the phrases "at the

---

de Zwaan (Haarlem: Bohn, 1953) 219-20, 222; followed by F. Zeilinger, *Krieg und Friede in Korinth. Kommentar zum 2. Korintherbrief des Paulus. Teil 1. Der Kampfbrief, Der Versöhnungsbrief, Der Bettelbrief* (Vienna: Böhlau, 1992) 192. Against van Unnik's suggestion, see the observation of F. Hahn, "Ist das textkritische Problem von 2 Kor 1,17 lösbar?" in *Studien zum Text und zur Ethik des Neuen Testaments*, Festschrift zum 80. Geburtstag von Heinrich Greeven, ed. W. Schrage (Berlin: de Gruyter, 1986) 161n.8: "Das ist ganz unwahrscheinlich, da Paulus griechisch denkende Leser voraussetzt."

[23]Instances of repetition of ναί for emphasis: Sophocles *OC* 1743: the Chorus observes, μέγ᾽ ἄρα πέλαγος ἐλάχετον τι; Antigone responds, ναὶ ναί. Theocritus *Idyll* 4.54: Battos asks, ἦ ῥά γε λεύσσεις; Corydon answers, ναὶ ναί, τοῖς ὀνύχεσσιν ἔχω τέ νιν· ἄδε καὶ αὐτά; text in *The Greek Bucolic Poets*, LCL, ed. J. M. Edmonds (London: Macmillan, 1912) 56. Whether other instances of the doubling of ναί (e.g., Alciphron 4.13.8; *PGM* 1.90) are intensive or asseverative must be determined by examination of the context; see below. Examples of repetition of יֵשׁ and הֵן for emphasis are collected by H. L. Strack and P. Billerbeck, *Kommentar zum Neuen Testament aus Talmud und Midrasch*, vol. 1 (München: Beck, 1922) 337.

[24]See in general F. Blass and A. Debrunner, *A Greek Grammar of the New Testament and Other Early Christian Literature*, trans. and ed. R. Funk (Chicago: University of Chicago Press, 1961) §493.

[25]So, already, Lietzmann, *An die Korinther*, 103; Windisch, *Der zweite Korintherbrief*, 65; F. Young, "Note on 2 Corinthians 1:17b," *JTS* 37 (1986): 406.

[26]So, e.g., C. F. G. Heinrici, *Das zweite Sendschreiben des Apostel Paulus an die Korinther* (Berlin: Hertz, 1887) 112; idem, *Der zweite Brief*, 77: "d.h. damit bei mir das Bejahen und das Verneinen zusammen sei, damit ich je nach Befinden der fleischlichen Selbstbestimmung zusage und wieder absage; heute Ja und morgen Nein, oder Ja und Nein gleichsam in einem Athem"; W. Bousset,

same time" or "in the same breath."[27] Sometimes the assumption is made explicit. Menzies states: "The notion 'at the same time' is not expressed in the Greek text, but has to be supplied."[28] And Barrett acknowledges: "The words 'at the same time' . . . are essential to the argument, but have to be introduced into the text."[29] Against this assumption, Lietzmann objected, "aber die Hauptsache «zugleich» ist nicht gesagt."[30]

Finally, the charge that results from the conventional interpretation is not coordinate with the accusations of vacillation and self-interestedness contained in the preceding phrases: ambiguity is something less than irresponsibility and opportunism, even if it is deliberate, just as duplicity is something more.[31]

Caught between the weakness of the majority interpretation and the difficulty of the majority text, interpreters have found themselves driven to adopt unusual constructions of the syntax. A construction that goes back to Chrysostom proposes to treat the second ναί and the second οὔ as predicates, and so to translate, "so that with me yes might be yes and no no."[32] This distinction is sometimes coupled with an emphasis upon

---

Der zweite Brief an die Korinther, in J. Weiss, *Die Schriften des Neuen Testaments II* (Göttingen: Vandenhoeck & Ruprecht, ²1908) 170: "so dass es bei mir bald Ja Ja und bald Nein Nein heisst"; similarly, H. D. Wendland, *Die Briefe an die Korinther*, NTD 7 (Göttingen: Vandenhoeck & Ruprecht, 1968) 170; Bultmann, *Der zweite Brief*, 43: "so dass ich zu gleicher Zeit Ja und Nein gesagt hätte."

[27]E.g., Menzies, *Second Corinthians*, 10; Plummer, *Second Epistle*, 34; H. L. Goudge, *The Second Epistle to the Corinthians* (London: Hodder & Stoughton, 1927) ad loc.; P. Hughes, *Paul's Second Epistle to the Corinthians*, NICNT 8 (Grand Rapids: Eerdmans, 1962) ad loc.; F. F. Bruce, *1 and 2 Corinthians*, NCB/NT 7 (Grand Rapids: Eerdmans, 1971) ad loc.

[28]Menzies, *Second Corinthians*, 10.

[29]Barrett, *Second Epistle*, 75-76.

[30]Lietzmann, *An die Korinther*, 103; similarly, Windisch, *Der zweite Korintherbrief*, 165.

[31]So, already, Heinrici, *Der zweite Brief*, 77; Windisch, *Der zweite Korintherbrief*, 65: "Bewusste Unaufrichtigkeit wäre dann dem Paulus vorgeworfen worden, was stärker ist als leichtsinn."

[32]*S. Joannis Chrysostomi Interpretatio omnium Epistolarum Paulinarum per Homilias facta*, tom. 3, ed. F. Field (Oxford: Bibliotheca Patrum, 1845) 37-38. On this interpretation in older scholarship (Theophylactus, Erasmus, Bengel, et

the phrase παρ' ἐμοί, thought to imply a contrast with παρὰ τῷ θεῷ, so that Paul would seem to be defending himself against the charge of having acted arbitrarily, and not in response to divine impulse.[33] The ellipsis which this interpretation assumes leaves room for various reconstructions of the charge against Paul and the nature of his response.

Theodoret (*PG* 82, 381D-4A), followed by Erasmus and Bengel,[34] construes the charge as one of obstinancy: Paul stubbornly pursues his own purposes, without regard for the Corinthians' well-being. By insisting that his yes means yes, Paul is "carnally consistent,"[35] but is oblivious to the promptings of the Spirit. The problem with this interpretation is that the resulting accusation is inconsistent with the charge of ἐλαφρία in the preceding phrase.[36] As Estius noted long ago, *levitatis et inconstantiae, non autem pertinaciae crimen hic a se depellere studet.*[37] To translate "so that my yes should be yes, my no, no" makes the end of the verse contradict the beginning, instead of proving it.[38] Nor does a

---

al.), see Heinrici, *Der zweite Brief,* 78.

[33]J. C. K. von Hofmann, *Die heilige Schrift neuen Testaments zusammenhangend untersucht* II/3: *Der zweite Brief Pauli an die Korinther* (Nördlingen: Beck, ²1877) 24ff.; followed by Th. Zahn, *Introduction to the New Testament,* vol. 1 (Edinburgh: T.&T. Clark, 1909) 343-44; A. Schlatter, *Der zweite Brief an die Korinther,* Erlauterungen zum Neuen Testament II (Stuttgart: Calwer, 1909) 228, 229-30; idem, *Paulus, der Bote Jesu. Eine Auslegung seiner Briefe an die Korinther* (Stuttgart: Calwer, ²1956) 479; F. Young, "Note on 2 Corinthians 1:17b," *JTS* 37 (1986): 404-15.

[34]Desiderius Erasmus, *Paraphrasis in duas epistolas Pauli ad Corinthios* (Lovanii, 1519) ad loc., repr. in idem, *Opera Omnia,* vol. 7 (Lugduni Batavorum: Petrus van der Aa, 1706); idem, *In Novum Testamentum Annotationes,* ab ipso auctore iam postremum recognitae (Basel: Apud Io. Frobenium, 1542) ad loc.; J. A. Bengel, *Gnomon of the New Testament,* vol. 2 (Edinburgh: T.&T. Clark, 1877) 355; cf. G. B. Winer, *A Treatise on the Grammar of New Testament Greek* (Edinburgh: T.&T. Clark, 1882) 576.

[35]The words are Bengel's in his *Gnomon of the New Testament,* vol. 2 (Edinburgh: T.&T. Clark, 1877) 355.

[36]So, Bachmann, *Der zweite Brief,* 61-62.

[37]W. Estius, *In omnes Divi Pauli Apostoli Epistolas commentariorum,* editio secunda (Dvaci: Ex Officina Typographica Baltzaris Bellevi, 1614) ad loc.

[38]So Menzies, *Second Corinthians,* 10.

charge of inflexibility fit the facts: it was Paul's change of plan (cf. 1:23), not his fixity of purpose, which gave rise to the Corinthians' suspicions.[39]

Closer to Chrysostom's understanding is the interpretation of Karl von Hofmann:[40] the Corinthians demanded of the apostle that he keep his promises under all circumstances, a demand which Paul rejected as conformity to a human standard of conduct (κατὰ σάρκα βουλεύ-εσθαι). Paul denies that he possesses the authority to issue unconditional promises; his plans are always subject to divine overruling. It rests with God to determine whether Paul's yes and no have validity. Thus Paul concedes, by implication, that he failed to keep his promise, but transfers responsibility for the change of plan to God. This interpretation is reflected in the translation of the NEB: "Or do I, when I frame my plans, frame them as a worldly man might, so that it should rest with me to say 'yes' and 'yes' and 'no' and 'no'?" Appealing to Chrysostom, Francis Young suggests the rendering: "Or do I make plans at the human level so that yes being yes and no being no rests in my hands?"[41]

It should be obvious that this interpretation employs almost as many assumptions as the conventional reading it is intended to replace. First, one must assume that the clause in question is not epexegetic of vs. 17a, but formulates a different issue, the issue of personal responsibility. Indeed, Young denies that vs. 17b implies a charge of the Corinthians at all, but gives expression to the apostle's conviction that he cannot be ex-

---

[39]As noted by Plummer, *Second Epistle*, 34; Windisch, *Der zweite Korintherbrief*, 65; Allo, *Seconde Épître*, 24.

[40]J. C. K. von Hofmann, *Der zweite Brief Pauli an die Korinther*, Die heilige Schrift neuen Testaments zusammenhängend untersucht 2/3 (Nördlingen: Beck, [2]1877) 24ff.; critically evaluated by Windisch, *Der zweite Korintherbrief*, 64-65.

[41]F. Young, "Note on 2 Corinthians 1:17b," *JTS* 37 (1986): 415, summarizing the sequence of thought in 1:15ff. as follows: "I planned to visit Corinth on the way to Macedonia and on the way back. Do you imagine my wish to do this arose from fickleness? Or that I make my plans in a worldly way so that yes being yes and no being no depends upon me? Neither is true. It is simply that I am single-minded in following God's purposes. Not that God is changeable—as far as the Gospel is concerned he is utterly reliable and has given a magnificent yes to all his promises in Christ."

pected to carry out his intentions when they are overruled by God.[42] Second, one must assume that the phrase παρ' ἐμοί implies a contrast with παρὰ τῷ θεῷ. Indeed, it is upon the implied contrast that the emphatic position of παρ' ἐμοί depends. And third, one must assume an extraordinary conciseness of expression. Each assumption must be tested.

The assumption that vs. 17b is not epexgetic of the preceding phrase is contradicted by the structure of the sentence. The sentence takes the form of a rhetorical question; more precisely, it consists of two interrogatives, followed by a consecutive clause which formulates the implications of the failings that have been alleged.[43] The conjunction ἤ in vs. 17b "does not introduce an alternative to the previous question, but substitutes instead another question which is more specific and intended to anticipate the answer to the first."[44] It should be translated "or rather," "or precisely."[45] The conjunction ἵνα in vs. 17c substitutes for the infinitive of result;[46] thus Paul endeavors to formulate the conclusion which it seems necessary to draw about conduct which seems irresponsible and oppor-

---

[42]Ibid., 412.

[43]On the structure of the sentence and the relationship of the clauses, see Blass-Debrunner, *Greek Grammar*, §391 (5); Windisch, *Der zweite Korintherbrief*, 64; Bultmann, *Der zweite Brief*, 43.

[44]H. W. Smyth, *Greek Grammar* (Cambridge MA: Harvard University Press, 1956) §2860, adducing Plato *Ap.* 26B: λέγε ἡμῖν πῶς με φῂς διαφθείρειν τοὺς νεωτέρους; ἢ δῆλον δὴ ὅτι . . . θεοὺς διδάσκειν μὴ νομίζειν οὓς ἡ πόλις νομίζει; L. I. Rückert, *Der zweite Brief Pauli an die Korinther* (Leipzig: Köhler, 1837) ad loc., explains ἢ by reference to *aut* of the Vulgate; followed by A. Klöpper, *Commentar über das zweite Sendschreiben des Apostel Paulus an die Gemeinde zu Korinth* (Berlin: Reimer, 1874) ad loc., and Heinrici, *Der zweite Brief*, 77, who describes the relation between the clauses as follows: "Paulus nimmt dann mit dem ersten auf den Bestimmten Fall, mit dem zweiten auf sein Verfahren überhaupt Rücksicht."

[45]Smyth, *Greek Grammar*, §2860.

[46]A. N. Jannaris, *An Historical Greek Grammar* (London, 1897) §1758, §1951, with examples; E. Burton, *Syntax of the Moods and Tenses in New Testament Greek*, 3rd ed. (Edinburgh: T.&T. Clark, 1898; repr. 1973) §218; Robertson, *Grammar*, 997-99; Blass-Debrunner, *Greek Grammar*, §391(5); S. J. Case, *Studies in Early Christianity* (New York: Century, 1928) 51-57; Bauer, *Greek-English Lexicon*, 378.

tunistic. The sentence aims, through each of its clauses, at a more precise definition of what the Corinthians find problematic about Paul's behavior. Nothing suggests that Paul introduces an alternative issue in vs. 17b.

Nor does anything in vs. 17 suggest that Paul begins at this point to express his own convictions.[47] Close examination of the language reveals that Paul refers throughout to the Corinthians' accusations. That the first clause embodies the Corinthians' verdict is acknowledged by all interpreters. The particle ἄρα, by which the phrase is introduced, marks it as an inference from Paul's conduct.[48] Μήτι grants the possibility of what is imputed, while implying that the opinion is not correct.[49] Then, there is the singularity of the term ἐλαφρία, a hapax legomenon in early Christian literature.[50] It is "light-mindedness" or "levity."[51] With the article, and in connection with χρῆσθαι, it means "to behave in a thoughtless manner," or "to act irresponsibly."[52] The sense of the rhetorical question, τοῦτο οὖν βουλόμενος μήτι ἄρα τῇ ἐλαφρίᾳ ἐχρησάμην,

---

[47]As argued by F. Young, "Note on 2 Corinthians 1:17b," *JTS* 37 (1986): 412-15.

[48]Heinrici, *Der zweite Brief*, 76; Blass-Debrunner, *Greek Grammar*, §440(2); Windisch, *Der zweite Korintherbrief*, 63; Bauer, *Greek-English Lexicon*, 1037; Smyth, *Grammar*, §2787.

[49]Robertson, *Grammar*, 1190; Blass-Debrunner, *Greek Grammar*, §427(2); §440(2); Heinrici, *Der zweite Brief*, 76; Windisch, *Der zweite Korintherbrief*, 63; Bauer, *Greek-English Lexicon*, 520.

[50]Bauer, *Greek-English Lexicon*, 248; ἐλαφρία is a late word and seldom of occurrence (Aretaeus p. 162,10; Hesychius), an abstract substantive built from the adjective ἐλαφρός, which Paul also uses in 2 Cor 4:17; on the formation of the word, see C. A. Lobeck, *Phrynichus* (Leipzig: Teubner, 1820) 343; on the ethical dimension of its meaning, see the texts cited in *F. Passow's Wörterbuch der griechischen Sprache völlig neu bearbeitet von W. Crönert* (Göttingen, 1912) esp. Polybius 6.56.11; cf. Heinrici, *Der zweite Brief*, 77; Windisch, *Der zweite Korintherbrief*, 64.

[51]Heinrici, *Der zweite Brief*, 77: "Leichtfertigkeit"; Windisch, *Der zweite Korintherbrief*, 64: "Leichtsinn"; Bauer, *Greek-English Lexicon*, 248: "vacillation, levity"; Barrett, *Second Epistle*, 75: "fickleness."

[52]On this construction, compare Thucydides 1.68; Job 16:10 (LXX); 2 Cor 3:12. Windisch, *Der zweite Korintherbrief*, 64n.2, translates "leichtsinnig handeln"; Victor Paul Furnish, *II Corinthians*, AB 32A (Garden City NY: Doubleday, 1984) 132, 134: "act irresponsibly."

would then be: "When I wanted to do this, was I really behaving in a thoughtless manner, as you say?" To the Corinthians, the apostle's failure to visit Corinth as promised, acknowledged finally in 1:23, appeared to be the result of ἐλαφρία: he had taken his promise to them too lightly; he had not considered seriously enough the consequences of his failure to carry out what he had promised.

That the next question alludes to the Corinthians' verdict is rendered likely by three factors. First, there is the conjunction ἤ, which, as we have seen, coordinates with the previous query and makes its meaning more specific. Then, there is the *paronomasia* βούλεσθαι/βουλεύεσθαι: the verb βουλεύομαι in vs. 17b plays upon βουλόμενος in the preceding phrase, which resumes ἐβουλόμην from vs. 15.[53] The point of the *paronomasia* is plain: it bridges the gulf that the Corinthians have detected between Paul's intention and his resolve. Finally, there is the phrase κατὰ σάρκα. To be sure, κατὰ σάρκα is a Pauline formulation.[54] But the Corinthians have evidently adopted Paul's usage and have turned it, like a sword, against him; for in 10:2-3 the apostle reveals that some suspect him of acting in a worldly manner (κατὰ σάρκα περιπατοῦντες).[55] Moreover, Paul counters the charge of fleshly calculation in

---

[53]So, rightly, Windisch, *Der zweite Korintherbrief*, 62, 63: "Mit τοῦτο οὖν βουλ. knüpft Paulus an v. 15f. an." Part of the manuscript tradition (D E K a b Ambst and the *textus receptus*) substitutes βουλευόμενος for βουλόμενος in vs. 17a; but βουλόμενος is far better attested: P⁴⁶ ℵ A B C F G I^Vid P Ψ 0243. 6. 33. 81. 104. 1175. 1739. 2464 *al* lat co; see *Novum Testamentum Graece*, vol. 2, ed. C. von Tischendorff (Lipsiae: Giesecke & Devrient, 1872) 574, whence the reading was taken into Nestle-Aland. On the wordplay βούλεσθαι/βουλεύεσθαι, see H. Lisco, *Die Entstehung des zweiten Korintherbriefes* (Berlin: Schneider, 1896) and A. Halmel, *Der zweite Korintherbrief des Apostel Paulus. Geschichtliche und Literarkritische Untersuchungen* (Halle: Niemeyer, 1904) 53-54.

[54]The phrase κατὰ σάρκα occurs 18 times in the authentic Pauline letters, usually with a negative connotation—e.g., 1 Cor 1:26; 2 Cor 10:2,3; 11:18; Gal. 4:23,29; Rom. 8:4,5,12,13. See W. Schauf, *Sarx* (Münster: Aschendorff, 1924) 126ff.; R. Jewett, *Paul's Anthropological Terms. A Study of Their Use in Conflict Settings* (Leiden: Brill, 1971).

[55]The comparison is rightly made by Windisch, *Der zweite Korintherbrief*, 64; Bultmann, *Der zweite Brief*, 43. It gains in force if chaps. 10–13 were written before 1–9, as many scholars believe; for this hypothesis, see A. von Hausrath,

the characterization of his conduct in the προθέσις of the epistle: οὐκ ἐν σοφίᾳ σαρκικῇ ἀλλ' ἐν χάριτι θεοῦ (1:12b). Beneath the apparent vacillation, the Corinthians sensed a graver failing: they suspected Paul of calculation with a view to what was personally expedient.

Following on these accusations, the ἵνα-clause serves to formulate the conclusion which it seems necessary to draw about conduct which seems irresponsible and opportunistic. Nothing suggests that its force is restricted to the immediately preceding phrase. Rather, ἵνα embraces and explicates the attitude of heart and mind described as τῇ ἐλαφρίᾳ and κατὰ σάρκα βουλεύεσθαι.[56] Paul seeks to deepen understanding of the defect in character that the terms "vacillation" and "self-interestedness" suggest.

Throughout the course of vs. 17, Paul alludes to the Corinthians' verdict. The rhetorical questions in which their judgments are formulated signal, as elsewhere in Paul's epistles, his emotional involvement with the matter at hand.[57] Paul knows that their suspicions are unfounded; he contrasts their opinion of his conduct with the desire which he repeatedly felt, by the resumption of the verb (of vs. 15f.) with the demonstrative

---

Der Vier-Capitel-Brief des Paulus an die Korinther (Heidelberg: Bassermann, 1870) and J. H. Kennedy, *The Second and Third Epistles of St. Paul to the Corinthians* (London: Methuen, 1900), with the subsequent elaborations of J. Weiss, *The History of Primitive Christianity*, 2 vols., trans. F. C. Grant (New York: Wilson & Erikson, 1937) 1:323ff., and G. Bornkamm, *Die Vorgeschichte des sogenannten Zweiten Korintherbriefes,* SAH 1961, 2. Abhandlung (Heidelberg: Winter, 1961), repr. with an addendum in his *Geschichte und Glaube II, Gesammelte Aufsätze IV* (München: Kaiser, 1971) 162-94.

[56]So, Windisch, *Der zweite Korintherbrief,* 64-65; Bultmann, *Der zweite Brief,* 43: "der ἵνα-Satz expliziert offenbar das τῇ ἐλαφρίᾳ und κατὰ σάρκα."

[57]Such questions abound in chaps. 10–13, where Paul must defend his legitimacy: 11:7, 11, 22, 23, 29; 12:13, 15, 18, 19; 13:5; see also 1 Cor 1:20; 4:7; 6:1-7; 9:1, 4-6; 12:29-30; 14:36; Rom 8:31-35. See the discussion in J. Weiss, "Beiträge zur paulinischen Rhetorik," *Theologische Studien, B. Weiss zu seinem 70. Geburtstag dargebracht* (Göttingen: Vandenhoeck & Ruprecht, 1897) 165-247; R. Bultmann, *Der Stil der paulinischen Predigt und die kynisch-stoische Diatribe* (Göttingen: Vandenhoeck & Ruprecht, 1910; repr. 1984) 85-86; on this verse in particular, see Furnish, *II Corinthians,* 134.

pronoun, τοῦτο βουλόμενος.[58] But he does not dismiss their evaluation; he brings their accusation to speech, employing the Corinthians' words. Nothing suggests that he begins to formulate his own convictions in vs. 17b. Rather, the transition to Paul's response to the charges is clearly marked by the adversative conjunction δέ in vs. 18a.[59] From this point on, Paul begins to contrast the simplicity and sincerity of the apostolic λόγος with the equivocal character of human utterances.

The assumption that παρ' ἐμοί carries special weight in the sentence is not supported by the norms of Greek word order: "*Unemphatic pronouns tend to follow immediately on the verb, as do other parts of the sentence governed by the verb, especially when the subject is expanded.*"[60] The New Testament supplies examples of unemphatic

---

[58]So, Halmel, *Der zweite Korintherbrief*, 43-54, who argues that ἐβουλόμην πρότερον (vs. 15) should be construed together, so that what Paul makes known in vss. 15-16 is not the plan for a "double visit," but the desire which he repeatedly felt to come to Corinth. In support of this interpretation, see Smyth, *Greek Grammar*, §1782: "ἐβουλόμην followed by an infinitive may express an unattainable wish." On the relationship of vss. 15-16 to Paul's question in vs. 17, τοῦτο οὖν βουλόμενος κτλ., Halmel, *Der zweite Korintherbrief*, 43-54, and Windisch, *Der zweite Korintherbrief*, 63-64.

[59]Rightly, Erasmus, *Paraphrasis*, ad loc.: "Sed non fallit Deus . . ."; Heinrici, *Der zweite Brief*, 78: "Das δέ führt den Gegensatz (vielmehr) gegen das mit der vorherigen Frage verneinte Verhältnis ein"; Windisch, *Der zweite Korintherbrief*, 66. On adversative δέ in general, see Blass-Debrunner, *Greek Grammar*, §447; Smyth, *Greek Grammar*, §2834-35; J. D. Denniston, *The Greek Particles*, 2nd ed. (Oxford: Clarendon, 1987) 165-68.

[60]Blass-Debrunner, *Greek Grammar*, §472, with reference to Luke 1:11; cf. J. D. Denniston, *Greek Prose Style* (Oxford: Clarendon, 1952) 44-45; K. J. Dover, *Greek Word Order* (Cambridge: Cambridge University Press, 1960). On the unemphatic position of παρ' ἐμοί in this vs., see Heinrici, *Der zweite Brief*, 78; Bachmann, *Der zweite Brief*, 62; F. Hahn, "Ist das textkritische Problem von 2 Kor 1,17 lösbar?" in *Studien zum Text und zur Ethik des Neuen Testaments. Festschrift zum 80. Geburtstag von Heinrich Greeven*, ed. W. Schrage (Berlin: de Gruyter, 1986) 163n.12: "Die gelegentlich erwogene Betonung von παρ' ἐμοί (im Sinne von παρ' ἐμοί ἐστιν, «es steht bei mir»), so dass hier der Vorwurf aufgenommen sei, Paulus habe selbstherrlich und nicht aus Gottes Antrieb heraus gehandelt, scheidet aus. Der Ton der Aussage liegt eindeutig auf dem Schlussglied."

pronouns following the verb, probably under the influence of the Semitic suffix pronoun.[61] Nor is it upon the sentence structure that interpreters depend who regard παρ' ἐμοί as an emphatic element,[62] but upon the assumption of an implied contrast with the unexpressed thought παρά τῷ θεῷ. Hofmann makes the assumption explicit.[63] But it plays a large part in Young's interpretation as well. Young explains: "Those who operate κατὰ σάρκα, conforming to worldly standards and expectations, are precisely those who depend upon themselves and plan for the future without being open to unexpected promptings of the Spirit. The wise after this world dare not be so irresponsible as to take no thought for the morrow. To operate κατὰ σάρκα, then, is to assume that one has power over one's own life, 'so that it might rest in my hands that yes be yes and no no.'"[64] As the quotation makes plain, the assumption that παρ' ἐμοί implies a contrast with παρὰ τῷ θεῷ is not grounded in analysis of the text as such, but is suggested by analogy with the thought of James 4:13f. Hofmann, again, makes the comparison explicit.[65] But James lies in the back of Young's mind as well, for it shapes the language of his paraphrase. Surely one's assumptions about what a passage implies should be grounded in analysis of the passage itself, and not in perceived analogy with the content of another text!

Third, the minority interpretation assumes an extraordinary conciseness of expression. One recalls how Hofmann and his followers reconstructed the dialogue that led up to Paul's utterance: the Corinthians demanded of the apostle that he keep his promises under all circumstances, a demand which Paul rejected as βουλεύεσθαι κατὰ σάρκα. Persuaded that decisions in the realm of the Spirit could only be made pro-

---

[61]N. Turner in Moulton, *A Grammar of New Testament Greek*, vol. 3 (Edinburgh: T.&T. Clark, 1963) 349.

[62]As Young acknowledges in "Note on 2 Corinthians 1:17b," *JTS* 37 (1986): 409: "Ultimately, the proof of the point that παρ' ἐμοί bears weight in the sentence lies not so much in the sentence structure as in the better exegetical sense it permits."

[63]Hofmann, *Der zweite Brief*, 25; followed by Schlatter, *Paulus, der Bote Jesu*, 479; see the critique by Heinrici, *Der zweite Brief*, 78.

[64]F. Young, "Note on 2 Corinthians 1:17b," *JTS* 37 (1986): 412; similarly, Schlatter, *Der zweite Brief*, 229-30.

[65]Hofmann, *Der zweite Brief*, 25; critique in Heinrici, *Der zweite Brief*, 78.

visionally, Paul insists that God alone determines whether his yes and no have validity.[66] Now, ellipsis can naturally go far in an epistle, "where the writer can count on knowledge which the recipient shares."[67] But one may question whether the best informed reader could have understood an argument expressed so concisely. Had Paul wished to persuade the Corinthians that adherence to his promise, not his failure to keep it, constituted fleshly calculation, must he not have endeavored to state his case with greater force and clarity, especially as, throughout the paragraph, the sincerity of his statement is the point at issue?[68]

But let us grant the hypothesis—vs. 17b is a case of ellipsis. One need only attempt to supply what is lacking to see that the assumption is untenable. The copula has been omitted, of course, between τὸ ναί as the subject and ναί as the predicate, and similarly with τὸ οὔ and οὔ.[69] Such an ellipsis is conventional,[70] even if it is infelicitous.[71] But one must also understand an unexpressed infinitive (εἶναι) in the prepositional phrase παρ' ἐμοί.[72] In the resulting sentence, both παρ' ἐμοί and the second ναί and οὔ must be construed as predicates.[73]

---

[66]Hofmann, *Der zweite Brief*, 24-25; Zahn, *Introduction*, 1:343-44; Schlatter, *Der zweite Brief*, 228-30; F. Young, "Note on 2 Corinthians 1:17b," *JTS* 37 (1986): 411-15.

[67]Blass-Debrunner, *Greek Grammar*, §481.

[68]Windisch, *Der zweite Korintherbrief*, 64-65.

[69]Hofmann, *Der zweite Brief*, 24-25; Zahn, *Introduction*, 1:343; F. Young, "Note on 2 Corinthians 1:17b," *JTS* 37 (1986): 407.

[70]Blass-Debrunner, *Greek Grammar*, §127-28, §480.

[71]Windisch, *Der zweite Korintherbrief*, 65: "Unwahrscheinlich ist bei einem Stilisten wie Paulus auch die Scheidung von Nαί ναί und Οὔ οὔ in Subjekt und Pradikat—er hätte dann gesagt ἵνα τὸ ναί ᾖ ναί παρ' ἐμοί καὶ τὸ οὔ oder ähnlich."

[72]F. Young, "Note on 2 Corinthians 1:17b" *JTS* 37 (1986): 407-408: "παρ' ἐμοί would then be predicative . . . it is possible to understand an unexpressed εἶναι." Cf. F. Hahn, "Ist das textkritische Problem von 2 Kor 1,17 lösbar?" in *Studien zum Text und zur Ethik des Neuen Testaments* ed. W. Schrage (Berlin; de Gruyter, 1986) 163n.12.

[73]Acknowledged by F. Young, "Note on 2 Corinthians 1:17b," *JTS* 37 (1986): 408: "There is a slight difficulty with this in the case of the longer form of text, since at first sight it does not seem easy to give due weight to both points at once, treating both παρ' ἐμοί and the second ναί and οὔ as

The awkwardness of the resulting sentence will prove unbearable for many interpreters.[74] And yet, how much must still be assumed! Must not a stylist of Paul's ability have expressed himself with greater clarity?

A final point must be made against the view that Paul is disclaiming personal responsibility for saying yes and no in vs. 17b. Is it not improbable that Paul would seek to excuse his change of plan by an appeal to divine overruling, when a few verses later, in 1:23 and 2:1, he insists that the change of plan was his own considered decision (ἔκρινα γὰρ ἐμαυτῷ), and adduces the decision as evidence of his love for the Corinthians?[75]

Upon close examination, the view that Paul is excusing his change of plan by transferring responsibility from himself to God has little to recommend it, although it is represented by such illustrious interpreters as Chrysostom in the early church and Theodor Zahn in the modern one. This way of construing the text is supported by neither the syntax nor the context. It is almost as arbitrary as Luther's translation of 1522, which puts a question mark after κατὰ σάρκα βουλεύομαι, then adds the thought *nequaquam*, assuming that ἵνα ᾖ κτλ. is adversative to the preceding phrase: "oder sind meyne anschlege fleyschlich? Nicht also/sondern bey mir ist ia/ia und neyn ist neyn."[76]

The knot of the text is tied so tightly that a number of interpreters have seen no alternative but to draw the sword of conjectural emendation.[77] The oldest and best known proposal is that of Markland,[78] subse-

---

predicates."

[74]Menzies, *Second Corinthians*, 10; Plummer, *Second Epistle*, 34; Bachmann, *Der zweite Brief*, 62; Windisch, *Der zweite Korintherbrief*, 65.

[75]Allo, *Seconde Épître*, 24; D. Wenham, "2 Corinthians 1:17, 18: Echo of a Dominical Logion," *NovT* 28/3 (1986): 273n.7.

[76]In the revision of the Luther Bible of 1956 and 1984 the passage reads: "Oder ist mein Vorhaben fleischlich, so dass das Ja Ja bei mir auch ein Nein Nein ist?" See the comments of Heinrici, *Der zweite Brief*, 78.

[77]The conjectures are surveyed by Windisch, *Der zweite Korintherbrief*, 65; F. Hahn, "Ist das textkritische Problem von 2 Kor 1,17 lösbar?" *Studien zum Text und zur Ethik des Neuen Testaments*, ed. W. Schrage (Berlin: de Gruyter, 1986) 158-61.

[78]W. Bowyer, *Critical Conjectures and Observations on the New Testament, collected from various Authors* (London, 1782) 351.

quently adopted by Baljon: ἵνα ᾖ παρ' ἐμοὶ τὸ ναὶ οὐ καὶ τὸ οὐ ναί.[79] Nissen inserts the negative after ἵνα, thus: ἵνα μὴ ᾖ παρ' ἐμοὶ τὸ ναὶ ναὶ καὶ τὸ οὐ οὔ.[80] More recently, Hahn suggests that Paul must have written ἵνα ᾖ παρ' ἐμοὶ τὸ ναὶ ναὶ καὶ οὔ, finding this contrast in vss. 18-20.[81]

The attraction of such radical solutions lies in the consonance which they establish between the text as conjectured and the context as described. This is hardly surprising, since the wording of the conjecture is in each case derived from an understanding of the context. Hahn justifies his conjecture with the argument "dass vom Kontext her ναί und ναὶ καὶ οὔ die Alternativbegriffe sind, wie sich aus v. 18-20a ergibt."[82] Hahn escapes from the nets of an unintelligible text into a hermeneutical circle hardly less confining. But one must question whether one ought to derive an emendation of vs. 17c from vss. 18-19, where ναὶ καὶ οὔ constitutes the predicate.[83] Does this suggestion take sufficient account of

---

[79]J. M. S. Baljon, *De Tekst des Brieven van Paulus aan de Romienen, de Corinthiërs en de Galatiërs als voorwerp van de conjecturaalkritiek beschouwd* (Utrecht: J. van Boekhoven, 1884) 141; also his *Novum Testamentum Graece* (Groningen: Wolters, 1898) ad loc.; see also P. Schmiedel, *Die Briefe an die Thessalonicher und an die Korinther*, HCNT 2.1 (Tübingen: Mohr-Siebeck, [2]1892) 214-15.

[80]Th. Nissen, "Philologisches zum Text des Hebraeer-und 2. Korinther-briefes," *Philologus* 92 (1937) 247-48.

[81]F. Hahn, "Das Ja Paulus und das Ja Gottes. Bemerkungen zu 2 Kor 1,12-2,1," in *Neues Testament und christliche Existenz. Festschrift für Herbert Braun* (Tübingen: Mohr-Siebeck, 1973) 229-39, esp. 234-37; idem, "Ist das textkritische Problem von 2 Kor 1,17 lösbar?" in *Studien zum Text und zur Ethik des Neuen Testaments. Festschrift zum 80. Geburtstag von Heinrich Greeven*, ed. W. Schrage (Berlin: de Gruyter, 1986) 158-65.

[82]F. Hahn, "Ist das textkritische Problem von 2 Kor 1,17 lösbar?" in *Studien zum Text und zur Ethik des Neuen Testaments*, ed. W. Schrage (Berlin: de Gruyter, 1986) 159, reasoning backwards from the ναὶ ἐν αὐτῷ of vs. 19 to the response of the community, τὸ ἀμὴν τῷ θεῷ: "Geht man davon aus, ergibt vs. 17c keinen klaren Sinn, vielmehr müsste dort vorausgesetzt werden: ἵνα ᾖ τὸ ναὶ ναὶ καὶ οὔ was ich meinerseits als Konjektur vorgeschlagen habe."

[83]Hahn acknowledges what he has done in an explanatory note to his conjecture, ibid., 159n.5: "Das ναὶ καὶ οὔ ist hier ebenso wie in v.18

the adversative conjunction in vs. 18a? Is it clear that the Corinthians had the same contrast in mind which Paul develops in reply to their charges? Nor can Hahn give a convincing account of how the received text might have arisen.[84] Markland's conjecture is also tempting: it confers good sense upon the sentence by rearranging its elements.[85] Paul would then be charged with dishonesty. But is such a charge appropriate to things which Paul had merely planned and purposed? Must Paul not then have written λαλῶ or γράφω, rather than βουλεύομαι?[86]

Nissen's conjecture has much to commend it from a technical point of view, since it is easy to imagine how the received text might have arisen from an error in reading.[87] But the conjecture is meaningful in

---

Pradikatsnomen." See the warning against too easy assimilation of vs. 17c, with its diplasiasmus, to vs. 18 in Heinrici, *Der zweite Brief*, 77 and in H.-J. Klauck, *2. Korintherbrief* (Würzburg: Echter Verlag, 1986) 24.

[84]F. Hahn, "Das Ja des Paulus und das Ja Gottes. Bemerkungen zu 2 Kor 1,12–2,1," in *Neues Testament und christliche Existenz* (Tübingen: Mohr-Siebeck, 1973) 234-37, posits the early influence of James 5:12b upon the manuscript tradition of 2 Cor 1:17c: the copyist, he suggests, mistook 2 Cor 1:17c for an abbreviated citation of the dominical logion on swearing and expanded the text in accordance with the form of the saying found in the Epistle of James; thus the majority text. The minority text resulted from assimilation to the wording of vs. 18. Responding to the objection of Heinrich Greeven, that it is hardly imaginable that the Epistle of James should have exercised such influence upon the early manuscript history of 2 Cor., Hahn appeals to the strength of the oral tradition of Jesus' sayings, referring to Justin *Apol.* 1.16.5, idem, "Ist das textkritische Problem von 2 Kor 1,17 lösbar?" in *Studien zum Text und zur Ethik des Neuen Testaments*, ed. W. Schrage (Berlin: de Gruyter, 1986) 164n.16.

[85]For this reason it is preferred by J. M. S. Baljon, *De Tekst der Brieven van Paulus aan de Romienen, de Corinthiërs en de Galatiërs als voorwerp van de conjecturalkritiek beschouwd* (Utrecht: J. van Boekhoven, 1884) 141; idem, *Theologisch Tijdschrift* 20 (1887): 437; P. Schmiedel, *Die Briefe an die Thessalonicher und an die Korinther*, HCNT 2/1 (Tübingen: Mohr-Siebeck, 21892) 214-15; see the apparatus to Nestle-Aland, 26th ed., and the discussion in Allo, *Seconde Épître*, 24-25.

[86]Windisch, *Der zweite Korintherbrief*, 65.

[87]So, Heinrich Greeven in F. Hahn, "Ist das textkritische Problem von 2 Kor 1,17 lösbar?" in *Studien zum Text und zur Ethik des Neuen Testaments*, ed.

context, only if one also assumes that the second ναί and οὔ function as predicates.[88] Even so, the charge is not rightly expressed; for it is not the accuracy of Paul's yes and no that is the point at issue, but his failure to carry out what he had promised.[89]

It is no argument against such emendations that manuscript support is entirely wanting. The historical critic will not hesitate to emend the text of the New Testament when the situation warrants. The same principles apply to criticism of the Christian scriptures as to other ancient literature.[90] But before adopting one conjecture or another, we should make a thorough investigation of ancient literature for parallels to Paul's expression. Only then shall we know whether the text can be satisfactorily explained, or whether it requires emendation.

Recently, Peter Marshall has suggested that Paul's words, τὸ ναί ναί καὶ τὸ οὔ οὔ, are intended to recall the stock description of the flatterer, whose inconstant character is revealed by his readiness to agree with what another has said.[91] In his play, *The Eunuch* (251-53), Terence allows Gnatho to describe his practise of accommodation: "Whatever they say I praise; if again they say the opposite, I praise that too. If one says no, I say no; if one says yes, I say yes (*negat quis nego; ait aio*). In fact, I have given orders to myself to agree with them in everything."[92] Cicero (*De amic* 25.93) comments upon Gnatho's self-disclosure in illustration of the inconstancy that undermines friendship. In the process, Cicero employs several terms which echo the language of the Pauline passage: the

---

W. Schrage (Berlin: de Gruyter, 1986) 162: "MHHΠ mit den acht aufeinanderfolgenden Hasten bietet dem abirrenden Auge eine hinlänglich glatte Rutschbahn, an deren Ende nur der nach dem ἵνα zu erwartende Konjunktiv ᾖ samt dem vor APEMOI nicht entbehrlichen Π erfasst wurde."

[88]See the discussion by Kümmel in Lietzmann, *An die Korinther*, 197.

[89]Windisch, *Der zweite Korintherbrief*, 65; Bultmann, *Der zweite Brief*, 43n.15.

[90]Rightly, J. Strugnell, "A Plea for Conjectural Emendation in the New Testament," *CBQ* 36 (1974): 555-58.

[91]P. Marshall, *Enmity in Corinth: Social Conventions in Paul's Relations with the Corinthians*, WUNT 23 (Tübingen: Mohr-Siebeck, 1987) 318-19; the suggestion is adopted by V. Furnish, *II Corinthians*, 135, 144-45.

[92]Text and translation in *Terence*, vol. 1, LCL, ed. J. Sargeaunt (Cambridge MA: Harvard University Press, 1912).

flatterer is "fickle and falsehearted"; his soul is "changeable and manifold"; his hypocrisy "destroys sincerity" (*De amic* 25.91-92).[93] Given these parallels, it seems reasonable to conclude that some in Corinth have accused Paul of flattery. Nor is this an improbable result: some may have interpreted Paul's desire to conciliate (evident, above all, in 2 Cor 5:11-6:13; 7:2-4) as evidence of a changeable character.[94]

Yet, nowhere in the context of vs. 17 does Paul reflect the charge of flattery. Insincerity has been alleged, and a certain complexity of purpose (1:12). But such attitudes seem expressions of volition rather than compliance. To be sure, insincerity and flattery have something in common, namely, inconstancy. The flatterer is the inconstant friend.[95] It is inconstancy which creates the similarity between the language which Terence ascribes to the flatterer and the words which Paul applies to himself. Nor is the similarity exact: the flatterer's "yes" is always a response to a "yes" which someone else has said; while the apostle's "yes" is the reaffirmation of something he has said himself. It is the double affirmation (or double denial) which reveals the defect in Paul's character. Within the need to reiterate lies the flaw which the Corinthians have sensed, and have experienced as equivocation.

Before entering upon our investigation, we may summarize the results of previous research. First, the longer text is to be preferred to the shorter one.[96] The manuscript evidence is unambiguous: the shorter reading is

---

[93]Cicero *De amic* 17.64-18.65, where "fickleness" (*levitas*) is contrasted with "loyalty" (*fides*); cited by Marshall, *Enmity in Corinth*, 319n.156.

[94]On the flatterer as one who tries to conciliate, see Plutarch *Mor* 52A-53A (describing Alcibiades); Aristotle *Eth Nic* 4.6.1. See the discussion in H. Chadwick, "'All Things to All Men' (1 Cor IX.22)," *NTS* 1 (1955): 261-75, esp. 262-63.

[95]Cicero *De amic.* 25.95; Plutarch *Mor* 59Cff., 97A-B. See the discussion in Marshall, *Enmity in Corinth*, 78-90. On the philosopher as flatterer, see Paul's own account in 1 Thess 2:1-8 and the discussion by A. Malherbe, "Gentle as a Nurse: The Cynic Background to 1 Thessalonians 2," *NovT* 12 (1970): 203-17; repr. as chap. 3 of his *Paul and the Popular Philosophers* (Minneapolis: Fortress, 1989) 35-48.

[96]Rightly, Meyer, *Kritisch exegetisches Handbuch*, 28; Heinrici, *Der zweite Brief*, 77; Barrett, *Second Epistle*, 69n.3; Bultmann, *Der zweite Brief*, 43n.15; Furnish, *II Corinthians*, 134.

poorly attested.[97] The longer text is the *lectio difficilior*. The shorter reading probably resulted from assimilation to vss. 18 and 19.[98]

Second, the last clause of vs. 17 is epexegetic of the preceding phrases. So much is indicated by the conjunction ἵνα, which substitutes for the infinitive of result, and by the overall structure of the sentence, which aims at a more precise definition of what the Corinthians find problematic about Paul's behavior. Whatever meaning is assigned to the expression ἵνα ᾖ παρ' ἐμοὶ τὸ ναὶ ναὶ καὶ τὸ οὒ οὔ, it must be consistent with the preceding phrases, whose consequences it explicates.[99]

Third, the articles indicate that the words ναὶ ναί and οὒ οὔ are quotations, of whatever provenance.[100] This fact has sometimes been acknowledged by interpreters;[101] but it deserves to be taken more seriously in the search for Paul's meaning. It is possible that Paul echoes what had been said at Corinth.[102] But the words make the impression of a fixed

---

[97]The shorter reading, τὸ ναὶ καὶ τὸ οὔ, is supported by few mss.: P[46] 0243 6 424[c] vg Pelagius; for two further witnesses, see F. Hahn, "Ist das textkritische Problem von 2 Kor 1,17 lösbar?" in *Studien zum Text und zur Ethik des Neuen Testaments*, ed. W. Schrage (Berlin: de Gruyter, 1986) 159n.2. The longer text is supported by the best majuscules, ℵ B A C D, as well as the important minuscules, 33 and 81.

[98]B. M. Metzger, *A Textual Commentary on the Greek New Testament* (London & New York: United Bible Societies, 1975) 576; Barrett, *Second Epistle*, 69n.3; Furnish, *II Corinthians*, 134.

[99]Meyer, *Kritisch exegetisches Handbuch*, 28; Heinrici, *Der zweite Brief*, 78; Menzies, *Second Corinthians*, 10; Plummer, *Second Epistle*, 34; Windisch, *Der zweite Korintherbrief*, 65; Allo, *Seconde Épître*, 24; Bultmann, *Der zweite Brief*, 43.

[100]For Paul's use of τό to introduce quotations, see 1 Cor 4:6; Gal 5:14; 6:9; Rom 13:9; cf. C. F. D. Moule, *An Idiom Book of New Testament Greek* (Cambridge: Cambridge University Press, 1959) 110-11. On the use of τό as a quotation mark generally, see Bauer, *Greek-English Lexicon*, 552.

[101]Menzies, *Second Corinthians*, 10; Plummer, *Second Epistle*, 34.

[102]Menzies, *Second Corinthians*, 10; Windisch, *Der zweite Korintherbrief*, Chadwick, "'All Things to All Men' (1 Cor IX.22)," *NTS* 1 (1972): 262; M. J. Harris, *Expositor's Bible Commentary*, vol. 10 (Grand Rapids: Eerdmans, 1976) 324.

formula.[103] The conjunction (ἵνα) and the structure of the sentence suggest that Paul formulates the implications of what has been alleged by employing a well-known figure of speech.

Finally, the duplication of the particles ναί and οὔ must be recognized as the source of hermeneutical difficulty. It is the critics' discomfort with this aspect of the sentence that, consciously or unconsciously, lies behind the various errors in exegetical judgment: the preference for the shorter reading, the attempt to construe the second ναί and οὔ as predicates, the tendency to omit the second ναί and οὔ in translation. The last named tendency reflects the assumption that the repetition is for emphasis. It is this assumption that must be tested. Duplication serves other purposes in ancient literature, purposes which, like the Corinthians' suspicions, relate to issues of truth and character.

II. The Source of the Formula

In the final clause of vs. 17, the apostle endeavors to formulate the conclusion which it seems necessary to draw about conduct which seems irresponsible and opportunistic. Only, the fault is not described abstractly, but by means of a phrase which, judging from its formulaic character, must have been well-known to the Corinthians: τὸ ναὶ ναὶ καὶ τὸ οὔ οὔ.

Precisely such a formula appears in discussions of oath taking in the Sermon on the Mount (Matt. 5:37) and in the Epistle of James (5:12).[104]

---

[103]Meyer, *Kritisch exegetisches Handbuch*, 28; Heinrici, *Der zweite Brief*, 77; Windisch, *Der zweite Korintherbrief*, 64, speaks of "eine allgemein übliche oder sprichwörtliche Redeweise": F. Hahn, "Ist das textkritische Problem von 2 Kor 1,17 lösbar?" in *Studien zum Text und zur Ethik des Neuen Testaments*, ed. W. Schrage (Berlin: de Gruyter, 1986) 163, speaks of "eine bereits erstarrten Formel."

[104]See the commentaries on these passages by G. Strecker, *Die Bergpredigt: Ein exegetischer Kommentar* (Göttingen: Vandenhoeck & Ruprecht, 1985) 80-84; U. Luz, *Das Evangelium nach Matthäus* (Mt 1–7), EKK 1/1 (Zürich: Benziger, 1985) 279-90; M. Dibelius, *James: A Commentary on the Epistle of James*, Hermeneia, rev. by H. Greeven (Philadelphia: Fortress, 1976) 248-51; F. Mussner, *Der Jakobusbrief*, HTKNT 13/1 (Freiburg: Herder & Herder, ²1967).

The parallel has often been noted by interpreters,[105] but is readily dismissed,[106] because of the difference in attitude toward oath taking that is apparent. For it is not only the case that a prohibition of oaths is lacking in Paul, he begins the following paragraph (1:23) by calling God to witness against him![107] Thus, scholars have concluded that the parallel is insignificant, because the apostle's point is different.[108] If they refer to the parallel at all, it is only in order to illustrate the iterative use of the particles for emphasis.[109]

---

[105]Meyer, *Kritisch exegetisches Handbuch*, 28; Heinrici, *Der zweite Brief*, 77; Windisch, *Der zweite Korintherbrief*, 64: ἵνα ἦ παρ' ἐμοὶ τὸ ναὶ ναὶ καὶ τὸ οὖ οὖ erinnert sofort an Mt. 5:37 oder Jak. 5:12"; Allo, *Seconde Épître*, 24; Héring, *Seconde Épître*, 26; W. C. van Unnik, "Reisepläne und Amen-Sagen. Zusammenhang und Gedankenfolge in 2. Korinther 1:15-24," in his *Sparsa Collecta* I (Leiden: Brill, 1973) 147; Bultmann, *Der zweite Brief*, 43.

[106]Plummer, *Second Epistle*, 34; Allo, *Seconde Épître*, 24; Héring, *Seconde Épître*, 26; van Unnik, *Sparsa Collecta I*, 147: "Zusammenhang mit dem Jesuswort in Matthäus v.37 ist ausgeschlossen, denn die Situation ist ganz verschieden"; Barrett, *Second Epistle*, 76; F. Hahn, "Ist das textkritische Problem von 2 Kor 1,17 lösbar?" in *Studien zum Text und zur Ethik des Neuen Testaments*, ed. W. Schrage (Berlin: de Gruyter, 1986) 159.

[107]On Paul's use of an oath in 1:23, see Windisch, *Der zweite Korintherbrief*, 74; G. Stählin, "Zum Gebrauch von Beteuerungsformeln im Neuen Testament," *NovT* 5 (1962): 131. On the possibility that 1:18 (πιστὸς ὁ θεὸς ὅτι) is also a mild oath, see Hofmann, *Der zweite Brief*, 26; Lietzmann, *An die Korinther*, 103; Windisch, *Der zweite Korintherbrief*, 66; G. Stählin, "Zum Gebrauch von Beteuerungsformeln im Neuen Testament," *NovT* 5 (1962): 131; Bultmann, *Der zweite Brief*, 43; Furnish, *II Corinthians*, 135. Paul frequently calls God to witness his oath: 1 Thess 2:5,10; Gal 1:10; 2 Cor 11:31; Phil 1:8; Rom 1:9; 9:1.

[108]Plummer, *Second Epistle*, 34; van Unnik, *Sparsa Collecta I*, 147; Barrett, *Second Epistle*, 76: "'Yes, yes' and 'No, no' . . . recall James v.12; Matt. v.37, though Paul's point is different"; G. Stählin, "Zum Gebrauch von Beteuerungsformeln im Neuen Testament," *NovT* 5 (1962): 130; G. Dautzenberg, "Ist das Schwurverbot Mt. 5,33-37; Jak. 5,12 ein Beispiel für die Torakritik Jesu?" *BZ* 25 (1981): 63-64.

[109]Plummer, *Second Epistle*, 34; Windisch, *Der zweite Korintherbrief*, 64-65; Bultmann, *Der zweite Brief*, 43; Bauer, *Greek-English Lexicon*, 533; Luz, *Evangelium nach Matthäus*, 286n.46.

In assessing the importance of this parallel, it is important to identify clearly what is the point at issue. Some argue, for example, that Paul's use of an oath in 2 Cor 1:23 violates the prohibition of swearing common in early Christian paraenesis.[110] Others deny that Paul is using the kind of oath prohibited by Matt 5:33ff.[111] But whether Paul contravenes a communal norm, or merely questions its application to his plans for the future, his attitude toward oath-taking in general is not the point at issue. Nor is it immediately relevant whether Paul's formulation reflects acquaintance with the dominical logion.[112] Some would argue, again, that the apostle alludes directly to a saying of Jesus.[113] Others explain that Paul seeks to correct the Corinthians' misunderstanding of Jesus' saying, so that what Paul picks up is not Jesus' saying as such, but Jesus' saying as used by his opponents against him.[114] Still others insist that a connection with Jesus' saying is excluded by differences in attitude and situation.[115] What seems more likely is that early Christian tradition as a whole (Matt 5:37; James 5:12; 2 Cor 1:17) reflects acquaintance with a formula widely used in asseveration.[116] As Windisch observed: "Bekannt-

---

[110]Zahn, *Introduction*, 343, 595; H. Chadwick, "'All Things to All Men' (1 Cor IX.22)," *NTS* 1 (1972): 262; C. Dietzfelbinger, "Die Antithesen der Bergpredigt im Verständnis des Matthäus," *ZNW* 70 (1979): 10.

[111]G. Stählin, "Zum Gebrauch von Beteuerungsformeln im Neuen Testament," *NovT* 5 (1962): 131; D. Wenham, "2 Corinthians 1:17,18: Echo of a Dominical Logion," *NovT* 28,3 (1986): 276-78.

[112]Rightly, Windisch, *Der zweite Korintherbrief*, 64.

[113]P. Feine, *Jesus Christus und Paulus* (Leipzig: Hinrichs, 1902) 252; G. Stählin, "Zum Gebrauch von Beteuerungsformeln im Neuen Testament," *NovT* 5 (1962): 130; O. Bauernfeind, *Eid und Frieden* (Stuttgart: Kohlhammer, 1956) 113.

[114]M. J. Harris, *Expositor's Bible Commentary*, vol. 10 (Grand Rapids: Eerdmans, 1976) 324; D. Wenham, "2 Corinthians 1:17,18: Echo of a Dominical Logion," *NovT* 28,3 (1986): 275.

[115]Plummer, *Second Epistle*, 34; Allo, *Seconde Épître*, 24; Héring, *Seconde Épître*, 26; van Unnik, *Sparsa Collecta I*, 147; Barrett, *Second Epistle*, 76.

[116]So, already, Meyer, *Kritisch exegetisches Handbuch*, 28: "Der Artikel bezeichnet das ναὶ ναὶ und das οὒ οὒ als bekannte und solenne Formeln der bejahenden und verneinenden Betheuerung (wie sie es auch im Judentum waren)"; similarly, Heinrici, *Der zweite Brief*, 77; Windisch, *Der zweite Korintherbrief*, 64.

schaft mit dem Herrenwort braucht indes bei Paulus nicht angenommen
zu werden, da das ja ja und nein nein eine allgemein übliche oder
sprichwörtliche Redeweise sein wird."[117] In any case, it is evident that
allusion to a dominical logion is not the point at issue.

What must be determined is simply this: whether the formal parallel
between 2 Cor 1:17 and Matt 5:37, etc. provides insight into the meaning
of Paul's words, and why he employs them in this context. The words
"yes, yes" and "no, no" appear in Hellenistic Jewish literature and in the
works of Rabbinic Judaism as a formula that may be substituted for an
oath.[118] The formula gained currency in early Christianity after it was
adopted by Jesus. The doubling of the particles was one of several ways
of seeking to establish the truth of one's statement by employing what
amounts to an oath.[119] Such formulae predominated among persons whose

---

[117]Windisch, *Der zweite Korintherbrief,* 64.

[118]See the parallels to Matt 5:37 adduced by Wettstein and Strack-Billerbeck:
J. Wettstein, *Novum Testamentum Graecum,* Tomus 1 (Amsterdam: Dommerian,
1752; repr. Graz, 1962) 308; H. L. Strack and P. Billerbeck, *Kommentar zum
Neuen Testament aus Talmud und Midrasch, Erster (Doppel-) Band: Das
Evangelium nach Matthäus* (München: Beck, 1922) 336-37. A number of
commentators regard ναί ναί and οὔ οὔ as formulae to be used in place of
an oath: H. Holtzmann, *Die Synoptiker,* HCNT 1/1 (Tübingen: Mohr-Siebeck,
³1901); E. Klostermann, *Das Matthäusevangelium,* HNT 4 (Tübingen: Mohr-
Siebeck, ²1927); Strecker, *Die Bergpredigt,* 84: "Die doppelte Verneinung oder
Bejahung ist in jüdischer Literatur als Beteuerungsformel belegt"; see also
G. Dautzenberg, "Eid IV: Neues Testament," *TRE* 9 (1982): 381; Dibelius,
James, 250-51. Many of the relevant texts are assembled by K. Berger, *Die
Amen-Worte Jesu: Eine Untersuchung zum Problem der Legitimation in apoka-
lyptischer Rede* (Berlin: de Gruyter, 1970) 9-12; reviewing the evidence for the
use of ναί as a *Schwurpartikel,* Berger (p. 9-10) concludes: "Ferner wird ναί
zu Beginn von Schwüren und bekräftigenden Aussagen verwendet, dann also im
Sinne von «fürwahr». Die gleiche Funktion hat doppeltes ναί, das ausser zur
Bekräftigung auch bei Imperativen und Gebeten verwendet wird." See below for
discussion of 2 Enoch 49:2; b.Sheb. 36a; Megillah 32a-b and other relevant texts.

[119]Other formulae devised by Jews and Jewish Christians as substitutes for an
oath include ναί, ἀμήν (Rev 1:7), ἀμὴν ἀμήν (Test Abr Rec A 20;
John 13:16, 20, 21; 21:18; etc.), ἀληθῶς λέγω ὑμῖν ὅτι . . . (Luke 9:27;
12:44; 21:3; etc.), ἐν ἀληθείᾳ λέγω ὑμῖν ὅτι . . . (Test Dan 2:1). See
the discussion of these formulae below and in G. Dalman, *The Words of Jesus*

scrupulousness led them to suppress the name of the deity, so as to avoid taking a downright oath. The Sermon on the Mount (Matt 5:33-37) ascribes to Jesus the teaching:

Do not swear at all, neither by heaven, . . . nor by earth, . . . nor by Jerusalem. . . . But let your word be 'yes, yes' or 'no, no'; for whatever is more than these comes of evil" (μὴ ὀμόσαι ὅλως· μήτε ἐν τῷ οὐρανῷ, . . . μήτε ἐν τῇ γῇ, . . . μήτε εἰς Ἱεροσόλυμα, . . . ἔστω δὲ ὁ λόγος ὑμῶν ναὶ ναί, οὒ οὔ· τὸ δὲ περισσὸν τούτων ἐκ τοῦ πονηροῦ ἐστιν).[120]

The Epistle of James (5:12) repeats the injunction, without attribution to Jesus: μὴ ὀμνύετε μήτε τὸν οὐρανὸν μήτε τὴν γῆν μήτε ἄλλον τινὰ ὅρκον· ἤτω δὲ ὑμῶν τὸ ναὶ ναὶ καὶ τὸ οὒ οὔ, ἵνα μὴ ὑπὸ κρίσιν πέσητε.[121] Interpreters have made much of the difference in syntax, separating ναὶ ναί and οὒ οὔ as subject and predicate, and translating, "But let your yes be yes and your no be no."[122]

(Edinburgh: T.&T. Clark, 1902) 226-29; Zahn, *Introduction*, 595; E. Peterson, ΕΙΣ ΘΕΟΣ, *Epigraphische, formgeschichtliche und religionsgeschichtliche Untersuchungen* (Göttingen: Vandenhoeck & Ruprecht, 1926) 167, 179, 232-33, 325; G. Stählin, "Zum Gebrauch von Beteuerungsformeln im Neuen Testament," *NovT* 5 (1962): 115-43; Berger, *Die Amen-Worte Jesu*, 4-9, 95ff.

[120]On the history of the tradition found in Matt 5:34b-37, see H. Wrege, *Die Überlieferungsgeschichte der Bergpredigt*, WUNT 9 (Tübingen: Mohr-Siebeck, 1968) 73-74; P. Minear, "Yes or No: The Demand for Honesty in the Early Church," *NovT* 13 (1971): 1-3, 7; Strecker, *Die Bergpredigt*, 84.

[121]On the isolation of this vs. in its context, see W. Beyschlag, *Kritisch-exegetisches Handbuch über den Brief des Jacobus*, KEK 15 (Göttingen: Vandenhoeck & Ruprecht, 1897) ad loc.; H. Windisch, *Die katholischen Briefe*, HNT 4/2 (Tübingen: Mohr-Siebeck, 1911) ad loc.; see in general Dibelius, *James*, 248-51.

[122]So, B. Weiss, *Der Jakobusbrief und die neuere Kritik* (Leipzig: Deichert, 1904) ad loc.; H. Windisch, *Die katholischen Briefe*, 3rd ed. by H. Preisker, HNT 15 (Tübingen: Mohr-Siebeck, ³1951) ad loc.; Dibelius, *James*, 249: "The clause must be read: 'Let your "yes" be true and your "no" be true.'" Cf. G. Stählin, "Zum Gebrauch von Beteuerungsformeln im Neuen Testament," *NovT* 5 (1962): 118: "Euer Ja sei ein einfaches Ja, euer Nein ein einfaches Nein."

So construed, the saying becomes an injunction to truthfulness which makes swearing superfluous.[123]

But the saying does not seem to have been understood in this way by the early church. Justin Martyr (*Apol* 1.16.5) presents the saying in a form that resembles the version found in the Epistle of James in respect to the disputed phrase, while resembling Matthew's version in other respects: μὴ ὀμόσητε ὅλως· ἔστω δὲ ὑμῶν τὸ ναὶ ναὶ καὶ τὸ οὒ οὔ· τὸ δὲ περισσὸν τούτων ἐκ τοῦ πονηροῦ.[124] The final observation, "whatever is more than these comes of evil," indicates clearly that the clause ἔστω δὲ ὑμῶν τὸ ναὶ ναὶ καὶ τὸ οὒ οὔ is understood to contain a formula to be used in place of an oath, not an exhortation to absolute truthfulness.[125] The same form of the saying is found in Clement of Alexandria (*Strom* 5.99.1), the Pseudo-Clementine

---

[123]G. Hollmann and W. Bousset, *Der Jakobusbrief* (Göttingen: Vandenhoeck & Ruprecht, ³1917) ad loc.; Dibelius, *James*, 250-51 and 249n.50, citing the interpretation of Theophylactus: ἀντὶ τοῦ, ἡ κατάθεσις ὑμῶν βεβαία καὶ ἐπὶ βεβαίου, καὶ ἡ ἀπαγόρευσις ὑμῶν ὡσαύτως. Cf. P. Minear, "Yes or No: The Demand for Honesty in the Early Church," *NovT* 13 (1971): 6. A number of interpreters understand Matt 5:37 in the same way: Bauer, *Greek-English Lexicon*, 533 s.v. ναί: "a clear 'yes,' a clear 'no' and nothing more"; E. Kutsch, "Eure Rede aber sei ja ja, nein nein," *EvT* 20 (1960): 206-18; G. Stählin, "Zum Gebrauch von Beteuerungsformeln im Neuen Testament," *NovT* 5 (1962): 119-20; Luz, *Das Evangelium nach Matthäus*, 286: "«Ja, ja» meint nicht anderes als: ein wirkliches Ja, ein Ja, das gilt und Bestand hat."

[124]Text in *Justinus' des Philosophen und Märtyrers Apologien*, ed. J. Pfattisch (Münster: Aschendorff, 1933) 17; cf. W. Bousset, *Die Evangeliencitate Justins des Märtyres in ihrem Wert für die Evangelienkritik von neuem untersucht* (Göttingen: Huth, 1891) 71; Dibelius, *James*, 250.

[125]Conceded by Dibelius, *James*, 250n.52: "To be sure, the final words treat the clause 'let your yes . . . ' as if it contained the short formula of affirmation (to be used in place of an oath)." J. Schniewind, *Das Evangelium nach Matthäus* (Göttingen: Vandenhoeck & Ruprecht, 1968) *ad* Matt. 5:37 argues strongly that the twofold ναί and οὒ are intended as substitutes for an oath; similarly, A. Meyer, *Das Rätsel des Jacobusbriefes* (Giessen: Töpelmann, 1930) 85; C. Dietzfelbinger, "Die Antithesen der Bergpredigt im Verständnis des Matthäus," *ZNW* 70 (1979): 10; Strecker, *Bergpredigt*, 84.

Homilies (3.55.1; 19.2.4), and Epiphanius (*Haer* 19.6.2).[126] What is assumed in each case is the ellipsis of the word ὅρκος (or λόγος) from the sentence, ἔστω δὲ ὑμῶν τὸ ναὶ ναὶ καὶ τὸ οὔ οὔ.[127] This interpretation is the one followed in a particular stream of the manuscript tradition of the Epistle of James (ℵ* 8 25 33^mg 1243 vg^cl sy^p bo), where ὁ λόγος is supplied after δέ, and in the catenae and scholia, where the words ναὶ ναί, οὔ οὔ are taken to substitute for an oath (ἀντὶ τοῦ ὅρκου).[128]

The logic of the substitution becomes clearer when one examines the theory and practise of oath taking in Hellenistic Judaism.[129] Philo reminds

---

[126]See also Clement *Strom* 7.67.5. Cf. A. Resch, "Miscellen zur neutestamentlichen Schriftforschung," *ZWL* 9 (1888): 283ff.; Dibelius, *James*, 250n.53. Note the judgment of P. Minear, "Yes or No: The Demand for Honesty in the Early Church," *NovT* 13 (1971): 7: "Justin's version is nearest the nucleus (of the saying)."

[127]O. Procksch, "Das Eidesverbot Jesu Christi," *Thüringer Kirchliches Jahrbuch* 12 (1907): 21; Belser, *Die Epistel des heiligen Jakobus* (Freiburg: Herder. 1909) *ad* James 5:12; O. Bauernfeind, *Eid und Frieden* (Stuttgart: Kohlhammer, 1956) 99, 123; D. Wenham, "2 Corinthians 1:17, 18: Echo of a Dominical Logion," *NovT* 28/3 (1986): 272. It is possible that the ellipsis is reflected in 2 Cor 1:18 with its ὁ λόγος ἡμῶν . . . οὐκ ἔστιν ναὶ καὶ οὔ.

[128]Nestle-Aland, *Novum Testamentum Graece*, 26th ed. (Stuttgart: Deutsche Bibelgesellschaft, 1983) 597; see the scholion of Cyril in the catena, ed. J. A. Cramer, *Catenae Graecorum Patrum in Novum Testamentum*, vol. 8 (Oxford: Oxford University, 1840) and Theophylactus, *Epistola catholica Sancti Jacobi apostoli*, MPG 125, 1188-89; see also the scholia gathered from various manuscripts by C. F. Matthäi, *SS. Apostolorum Septem Epistolae Catholicae* (Riga, 1782) 195; cf. Dibelius, *James*, 249n.49.

[129]Hellenistic Jewish writers condemn the making of many oaths (Sir 23:9-11) and the taking of false oaths (Ps-Phocylides 16), but stop short of an absolute prohibition of swearing, such as was attributed to Pythagoras (Diogenes Laertius 8.22; Iamblichus *Vit Pyth* 47). According to Josephus (*BJ* 2.135), the Essenes generally avoided swearing, but were required to take a solemn oath upon initiation into the sect (*BJ* 2.139, 142). Philo urges the avoidance of oaths (*Decal* 84) and warns against use of the divine name (*Spec leg* 2.2ff.), while not prohibiting swearing as such. See the discussion in R. Hirzel, *Der Eid: Ein Beitrag zu seiner Geschichte* (Leipzig: Hirzel, 1902) 6, 11, 15-18, 26-27, 64, 88-89, 99-100, 109-10; S. Lieberman, *Greek in Jewish Palestine* (New York: Jewish

his readers of the obvious (*De Sac. Abelis et Caini* 93): "Men have recourse to oaths to win belief, when others deem them untrustworthy" (τοῦ γε μὴν πιστευθῆναι χάριν ἀπιστούμενοι καταφεύγουσιν ἐφ᾽ ὅρκον ἄνθρωποι).[130] The best course would be not to swear at all (*Decal* 84): "The good man's word should be his oath (λόγος ὅρκος ἔστω), firm (βέβαιος) and unswerving" (*De spec leg* 2.1.2). "But if occasion should force one to swear, then the oath should be by a father or mother, their good health and welfare, if they are alive, their memory, if they are dead" (*De spec leg* 2.1.2). In no case should one swear by God himself, since his nature is unknowable (*Leg all* 3.207). One must be content to swear by God's name (*Leg all* 3.207-208). But even God's name should not be used lightly (*De spec leg* 2.1.2-5). Philo regards as worthy of praise those persons who, when they are forced to swear, demonstrate their unwillingness by adding nothing to their "yes" or "no": "Such people are in the habit of saying 'yes, by ____' (νὴ τόν) or 'no, by ____' (μὰ τόν), and by thus breaking off, suggest the clear sense of an oath without actually making it" (*De spec leg* 2.1.4).[131] Philo nevertheless allows mundane substitutes for the divine name: "But a person may add to his 'yes' or 'no' if he wish, not indeed the highest and most venerable and primal cause, but earth, sun, stars, heaven, the whole universe" (*De spec leg* 2.5). Similarly, the Mishnah and Talmud of tractate *Shebuot* allow heaven and earth as substitutes for the divine name in taking an oath (*mSheb* 4:13; *bSheb* 35b).[132]

Theological Seminary, 1942) 125-26; J. Schneider, ὀμνύω, *TDNT* 5:176-80; Dibelius, *James*, 248-49.

[130]Text and translation of Philo from F. H. Colson, *Philo*, 10 vols., LCL (Cambridge MA: Harvard University Press, 1937). Cf. I. Heinemann, "Philos Lehre vom Eid" in *Judaica: Festschrift zu H. Cohens siebzigstem Geburtstage* (Berlin: Cassirer, 1912) 109-18; J. Schneider, ὀμνύω, *TDNT* 5:179-80.

[131]Philo is perhaps thinking of Socrates, to whom Plato attributes such an oath in *Gorgias* 466E; see below. But the formula was current in Philo's Egypt; see E. R. Goodenough, *The Jurisprudence of the Jewish Courts in Egypt: Legal Administration by the Jews under the Early Roman Empire as described by Philo Judaeus* (New Haven: Yale University Press, 1929) 43n.46, 44-45, 47n.48.

[132]Cf. A. Wünsche, *Neue Beiträge zur Erläuterung der Evangelien aus Talmud und Midrasch* (Göttingen: Vandenhoeck & Ruprecht, 1878) 59; for other substitutes and "handles," see S. Lieberman, *Greek In Jewish Palestine* (New

Among the expressions added by convention to one's affirmation or denial as substitutes for the divine name, one encounters simply a second "yes" or "no," in repetiton. Such a double affirmation as a substitute for an oath is found in the *Book of the Secrets of Enoch*.[133] The product of a Hellenistic Jew who lived in Egypt, probably in Alexandria, *2 Enoch* is contemporary with the Pauline epistles.[134] In *2 Enoch* 49:1 the author has Enoch instruct his sons in the taking of an oath:

> I swear to you, my children, but I swear not by any oath, neither by heaven nor by earth, nor by any other creature which God created. The Lord said: "There is no oath in me, nor injustice, but truth. If there is no truth in men, let them swear by the words 'yea, yea,' or else 'nay, nay.'"[135]

Enoch proceeds to swear in this fashion, using the double affirmation: "And I swear to you, yea, yea, that there has been no man in his mother's womb, but that etc." (2 *Enoch* 49:2).

In Rabbinic literature, as well, the words "yes, yes" and "no, no" are taken to imply an oath. Thus in tractate *Shebuot*, Raba explains that "yes" alone is not an oath: "But that is on condition that he said 'no, no' twice or 'yes, yes' twice . . . and, then, since 'no' has to be said twice to mean an oath, so, too, 'yes' must be said twice to mean an oath" (*bSheb*

York: Jewish Theological Seminary, 1942) 115-43, esp. 121, 137.

[133]Though originally written in Greek, *The Book of the Secrets of Enoch* (*2 Enoch*) has been preserved only in Slavonic; translation and notes in *The Apocrypha and Pseudepigrapha of the Old Testament*, vol. 2: *Pseudepigrapha*, ed. R. H. Charles (Oxford: Clarendon Press, 1964) 425-69. The text is first cited in connection with 2 Cor 1:17 by Windisch, *Der zweite Korintherbrief*, 64; followed by Bultmann, *Der zweite Brief*, 43.

[134]On the authorship and date of *2 Enoch*, see Charles, *Apocrypha and Pseudepigrapha*, 2:429. The authenticity of 49:1-2 is called into question by C. Bottrich, *Weltweisheit, Menschheitsethik, Urkult: Studien zum slavischen Henochbuch* (Tübingen: Mohr/Siebeck, 1992) 117: "In ihrer jetzigen Gestalt aber wurden die Verse wohl von christlicher Hand nach dem ntl. Wortlaut über-arbeitet." Contrast the verdict of Windisch, *Der zweite Korintherbrief*, 64: "kaum christliche Interpolation."

[135]See the observation by Conybeare in Charles, *Apocrypha and Pseudepig-rapha*, 2:460n.1: "This appears to be a Jewish commonplace."

36a).[136] The assumption that a double affirmation substitutes for an oath underlies the discussion of omens in *Megillah* 32a-b: R. Shefatiah said in the name of R. Johanan: "Whence do we know that we may avail ourselves of a chance utterance [as an omen]? Because it says, 'And thine ears shall hear a word behind thee saying.' This applies, however, only if . . . it says 'yes, yes' or 'no, no'."[137]

In each case, the repetition of "yes" or "no" serves to establish the truth of what is said. Like an oath, the double-affirmation provides assurance in light of human unreliability (cf. Cicero *De offic* 3.104; Philo *De Sac. Abelis et Caini* 92-93).[138] The repetition guarantees that the "yes" of the speaker is truly "yes," as his "no" is truly "no" (cf. *Midr Ruth* 3:18).[139] Whatever the difference in form and syntax between 2 Cor 1:17 and James 5:12, the thought is essentially the same: the "yes" of the righteous should be truly "yes," and the "no" should be "no" (cf. *Sifra*

---

[136]Translation in *The Talmud of Babylonia: An American Translation*, vol. 27b: *Tractate Shevuot*, ed. J. Neusner (Atlanta: Scholars Press, 1992); cf. Strack-Billerbeck, *Kommentar* 1:336.

[137]Text and translation in *The Hebrew-English Edition of the Babylonian Talmud: Ta'anith*, ed. J. Rabbinowitz (London: Soncino, 1984; cf. Strack-Billerbeck, *Kommentar* 1:337.

[138]On the nature and function of oath, see R. Hirzel, *Der Eid: Ein Beitrag zu seiner Geschichte* (Leipzig: Hirzel, 1902) 4ff.; J. Schneider, ὅρκος, *TDNT* 5:458. On the double affirmation fulfilling the same function, see J. Mann, "Oaths and Vows in the Synoptic Gospels," *AJT* 21 (1917): 260; P. Minear, "Yes or No: The Demand for Honesty in the Early Church," *NovT* 13 (1971): 10-13; Berger, *Die Amen-Worte Jesu*, 10-11.

[139]See also *Mekilta*, Tractate Bahodesh 5 and 6; text and translation in *Mekilta de-Rabbi Ishmael*, vol. 2, ed. J. Lauterbach (Philadelphia: Jewish Publication Society of America, 1933) 230, 238; *Baba Metzia* 49a: "But it is to teach you that your 'yes' should be just and your 'no' should be just"; translation in I. Epstein, ed., *The Babylonian Talmud* (London: Soncino, 1952).

Lev 19:36; *Midr Ruth* 3:18; *The Two Books of Jeu* 43).[140] Both forms of the saying struggle against the inconstancy of human nature.

The double affirmation seems to have developed from the standard use of the particles in oaths and asseverations.[141] In classical Greek, μά is the particle used in oaths and asseverations, with the accusative of the deity or the thing by which one swears.[142] In itself, μά is neither affirmative nor negative, but is made so by prefixing ναί or οὔ.[143] Μά

---

[140]*Sifra. Commentar zu Leviticus aus dem Anfange des III. Jahrhunderts*, ed. R. ben David, with Masoret ha-Talmud by J. H. Weiss (Vienna: Schlossberg, 1862); see the comment of S. Schlechter, "Rabbinic Parallels to the New Testament," *JQR* 12 (1900): 426: "Thus when interpreting Lev. 19:36, the Rabbis somehow managed to derive from it the law of 'let your speech be yea, yea; nay, nay.'" On *Midr. Ruth* 3:18, see Strack-Billerbeck, *Kommentar* 1:336. *The Two Books of Jeu* is a Coptic gnostic writing; text in C. Schmidt, *Gnostische Schriften in koptischer Sprache aus dem Codex Brucianus*, TU 8,1-2 (Leipzig: Hinrichs, 1892) 102; translation by V. MacDermot in *The Books of Jeu and the Untitled Text in the Bruce Codex*, ed. C. Schmidt (Leiden: Brill, 1978) 133: "And before all things, command him to whom you will give the mysteries not to swear falsely, nor to swear at all, . . . nor to invoke the name of the archons, nor the name of their angels over any matter, . . . but to let their yea be yea, and their nay be nay."

[141]There is no comprehensive investigation of ναί or οὔ, such as Denniston provides for other Greek particles. Texts illustrating the use of ναί and οὔ in oaths and asseverations are collected in *A Greek-English Lexicon*, ed. H. Liddell and R. Scott, rev. H. Jones (Oxford: Clarendon Press, 1978) 1070, s.v. μά; 1159, s.v. ναί. See also Wettstein, *Novum Testamentum* 1:308 *ad* Matt. 5:37; Bauer, *Greek-English Lexicon*, s.v. ναί, 5; Berger, *Die Amen-Worte Jesu*, 9-12. Berger's account of the development of the double affirmation as a formula to be used in place of an oath differs from my own in positing the existence of this function in profane Greek. I cannot find a clear instance of the double ναί as a substitute for an oath outside of Hellenistic Judaism (inclusive of early Christianity and Rabbinic Judaism). The duplication of the particle in Archilochus 99 [Diehl²], ναὶ ναὶ μὰ μήκονος χλόην, is probably due to the meter; cf. A. Adkins, *Poetic Craft in the Early Greek Elegists* (Chicago: University of Chicago Press, 1985) 33-54.

[142]Liddell-Scott-Jones, *Greek-English Lexicon*, 1070; Smyth, *Greek Grammar*, §2894.

[143]Liddell-Scott-Jones, *Greek-English Lexicon*, 1070.

means properly "in truth" or "verily."[144] Thus, ναὶ μὰ Δία is "Yes, in truth, by Zeus"; οὐ μὰ Δία is "No, in truth, by Zeus."[145]

Examples of the use of adverbs of swearing are found in Greek literature of all periods—in poetry and in prose, and especially in colloquial discourse.[146] In one of Pindar's *Nemean Odes*, he praises Aristagoras as a person of local athletic distinction and suggests that he might have won the prize at Olympia, but for the timidity of his parents. Upon this declaration, the poet takes an oath: "Yes, verily, I swear that (ναὶ μὰ γὰρ ὅρκον), in my judgment, he would have returned with greater glory than his rivals" (Pindar *NO* 11.24).[147] In Aristophanes' *Acharnians*, an ambassador claims to have been served oxen "baked whole in the oven" at the court of the king. When the honest citizen, Dicaeopolis, scoffs at his claim, the braggart calls the deity to witness: "Yes, in truth, by Zeus (ναὶ μὰ Δί'), he served us a bird three times the size of Cleonymus, too" (Aristophanes *Ach* 88).[148]

Similarly, οὐ μά is found in negation. Thus, Electra blames Clytemnestra for her troubles: "The fault is yours, not mine; for yours are the acts, and mine but the words that show them forth" (Sophocles *El* 624-25). Clytemnestra underscores her denial with an oath: "But no, in truth, by our lady Artemis (ἀλλ' οὐ μὰ τὴν δέσποιναν Ἄρτεμιν), you shall regret your boldness when Aegisthus comes again" (Sophocles

---

[144]Smyth, *Greek Grammar*, §2894.

[145]Smyth, *Greek Grammar*, §1596, 2922. See also νή asseverative with the accusative of the deity invoked, Liddell-Scott-Jones, *Greek-English Lexicon*, 1173; Smyth, *Greek Grammar*, §1596, 2923; νὴ Δία is especially common in prose. Cf. Hirzel, *Der Eid*, 11-22.

[146]Liddell-Scott-Jones, *Greek-English Lexicon*, 1070. Cf. Hirzel, *Der Eid*, 1-40. Compare Denniston's account of the function of ἦ μήν in J. Denniston, *The Greek Particles* (Oxford: Clarendon Press, 1987) 350: "ἦ μήν introduces a strong and confident asseveration, being used both in direct and indirect speech. It is most frequently employed in oaths and pledges."

[147]Text and translation in *The Odes of Pindar*, ed. J. Sandys, LCL (Cambridge MA: Harvard University Press, 1978) 430-31.

[148]Text in *Aristophanis Comoediae*, vol. 1, ed. F. W. Hall and W. M. Geldart (Oxford: Clarendon Press, 1976) 8. See also Plato *Rep.* 407B: Ναὶ μὰ τὸν Δία, ἦ δ' ὅς. On ναὶ μήν in asseverations, see the texts assembled by Berger, *Die Amen-Worte Jesu*, 11n.17.

El. 626-27).[149] In Aristophanes' *Knights*,[150] Paphlagon emerges from his house determined to thwart the plans of his enemies: "No, in truth, by the Twelve Gods (οὔ . . . μὰ τοὺς δώδεκα θεούς), you two won't get away with this long-standing conspiracy of yours against the people!" (*Eq* 235-36). In the prologue to the *Theatetus*, Terpsion asks Euclides if he can repeat the conversation he once heard between Socrates and Theatetus. Euclides replies: "No, in truth, by Zeus (οὐ μὰ τὸν Δία), not as it fell from their lips! But I made some notes at the time, and so . . . " (Plato *Tht.* 142e).[151]

In keeping with the elliptical nature of the language, μά is frequently used alone, chiefly in negation when a negative follows (e.g., μὰ Δί' οὐκ εἶδον ἐμαυτοῦ ἀμείνω ὑλοτόμον, *IG*² 1.1084; μὰ τὴν πατρῴαν ἑστίαν, ἀλλ' οὐχ ὕβρει λέγω τάδ', Sophocles *El* 881; μὰ τοὺς παρ' "Αιδη νερτέρους ἀλάστορας, οὗτοι ποτ' ἔσται τοῦτο, Euripides *Med* 1059; μὰ τὸν 'Απόλλω, οὐκ, Aristophanes *Thesm* 269; μὰ τὴν γῆν, μὴ σύγε δῷς, Anaxilas 9; μὰ δαίμονας, οὐκ ἀπὸ ῥυσμοῦ εἰκμάζω, Callimachus *Epigr* 44; μὰ τὸν Δία, δὲ οὐδὲ νομίζω, *IG*² 2.1099.30; μὰ σέ, Καῖσαρ, οὐδείς σε νικᾷ, Dio Cassius 61.20), but also when a negative precedes (e.g., οὐδ' ὄναρ, μὰ τὰς Μοίρας, Herodotus 1.11), especially when the negative is found in a question (e.g., οὐκ αὖ μ' ἐάσεις; μὰ Δί', ἐπεὶ κἀγὼ πόνηρός εἰμι, Aristophanes *Eq.* 336).[152] In later Greek, μά also stands alone in affirmation (thus, for example, δακρύω μὰ σέ, δαῖμον, *Annales du Service des Antiquites de l'Egypte* 27.32; μὰ τὴν "Αρτεμιν 'Ακοντίῳ γαμοῦμαι. Aristaenetus 1.10).[153]

---

[149]Text and translation in *Sophocles*, vol. 2, ed. F. Storr, LCL (Cambridge MA: Harvard University Press, 1939) 172-73.

[150]Text in *Aristophanis Comoediae*, vol. 1, ed. F. W. Hall and W. M. Geldart (Oxford: Clarendon Press, 1976) 63.

[151]Text in *Platonis Opera*, vol. 1, ed. I. Burnet (Oxford: Clarendon Press, 1977) 256.

[152]Liddell-Scott-Jones, *Greek-English Lexicon*, 1070; Smyth, *Greek Grammar*, §1596. See also Arsitophanes *Ran.* 1374-75: μὰ τὸν ἐγὼ μὲν οὐδ' ἂν εἴ τις ἔλεγέ μοι τῶν ἐπιτυχόντων, κτλ.

[153]Liddell-Scott-Jones, *Greek-English Lexicon*, 1070. See also Achilles Tatius 8.5.

Conversely, μά is sometimes omitted after ναί. The interplay of word and action in Aristophanes' *Wasps* (1435-40) illustrates the use of the affirmative particle in oath taking.[154] Philokleon stops an accuser on his way to court and offers to arrange a better settlement (*Vesp* 1421). Unpersuaded, the accuser begins to walk away, accompanied by his summons witness (*Vesp* 1435). At the words μὴ φεῦγ᾽, he turns around, only to find that Philokleon wants to tell a "Sybaritic" tale: "In Sybaris a woman once broke a jar" (*Vesp* 1435-36). In illustration, Philokleon strikes the accuser on the head. The gesture provokes the accuser to cry, "I call on you to witness this" (ταῦτ᾽ ἐγὼ μαρτύρο-μαι), a standard phrase used in claiming that an offence has been committed.[155] Taking up the accuser's words, Philokleon concludes the tale: "So the one to whom the jar belonged called someone to witness. Whereupon, the Sybarite woman said: 'If, in truth, by Kore (εἰ ναὶ τὰν Κόραν), you had forgotten this calling people to witness, and had hurried up and brought a bandage, you'd have been more sensible" (*Vesp.* 1438-40).[156]

Similarly, μά is omitted after οὐ. Oaths play a large part in the *Oedipus Tyrannus*, where life hangs from the truthfulness of what has been said. Creon is suspected by Oedipus of plotting against his royal person. He opposes the malicious slander by uttering a solemn oath: "May I never prosper, but die accursed, if I in any way am guilty of this charge" (Sophocles *OT* 644-45).[157] Seeking to reconcile the friends, Jocasta adds her adjuration: "O, for the gods' sake, believe him Oedipus,

---

[154]Text and commentary in *Aristophanes Wasps*, ed. D. M. MacDowell (Oxford: Clarendon Press, 1971) 117-18.

[155]Ibid., 317; cf. J. Werres, "Die Beteuerungsformeln in der attischen Komödie" (diss., Bonn, 1936).

[156]The translation is that of A. H. Sommerstein, *The Comedies of Aristophanes*, vol. 4: *Wasps* (Warminster: Aris & Phillips, 1983) 139. Other examples of ναί in oaths without μά: Epicharmus 81: ναὶ τὸν Ποτιδᾶν; Euripides *Med.* 1277: ναί, πρὸς θεῶν, ἀρήξατ᾽· ἐν δέοντι γαρ; Xenophon *HG* 4.4.10: Ναὶ τὼ σιώ, ὦ Ἀργεῖοι, ψευσεῖ ὑμὲ τὰ σίγμα ταῦτα, χωρεῖν ὁμόσε; Herodas 1.86: ναὶ Δήμητρα; Theocritus 4.47; 5.141; 6.21: ναὶ τὸν Πᾶνα.

[157]Text and translation in *Sophocles*, vol. 1, ed. F. Storr, LCL (New York: Putnam's Sons, 1939) 62-63.

first for the sake of this awful oath by the gods, then for mine, and for theirs who stand before you" (*OT* 646-48). The chorus urges the king to relent, to respect a man whose probity is known to all, and who has now confirmed the truth of his words by taking such a fearful oath (*OT* 649, 651). Asked to explain why he should let the matter rest, the chorus of Theban elders replies: "You should never cast dishonor in accusation by means of an unproven tale upon a friend who has called down a curse upon his head" (τὸν ἐναγῆ φίλον μήποτ' ἐν αἰτίᾳ σὺν ἀφανεῖ λόγῳ σ' ἄτιμον βαλεῖν, *OT* 656-57).[158] That is, since Creon now rests under the ban of the gods by whom he has just said ἀραῖος ὀλοίμην, κτλ. (*OT* 644), he need not be further dishonored.[159] Oedipus then accuses the elders of seeking his death or banishment through their proposal (*OT* 658-59). The elders hide from the accusation under a solemn oath of their own: "No, by the foremost god of all the gods (οὐ τὸν πάντων θεῶν θεὸν πρόμον), Helios, may I die by the uttermost doom, unblest, unfriended, if such a thought was ever mine!" (*OT* 660-64).[160]

In colloquial discourse, especially in Attic,[161] the name of the deity was often suppressed due to scrupulousness or indifference.[162] In the

---

[158]The translation offered here rests upon the comments of R. Jebb in his edition of *The Oedipus Tyrannus* (Cambridge: Cambridge University Press, 1920) 75.

[159]Sophocles *OT* 644, referring to Aeschines *In Ctes* 110: γέγραπται γὰρ οὕτως ἐν τῇ ἀρᾷ· εἴ τις τάδε, φησί, παραβαίνοι, . . . ἐναγής, φησιν, ἔστω τοῦ Ἀπόλλωνος ("let him rest under the ban of Apollo"): as Creon would rest under the ban of the gods by whom he had sworn.

[160]Compare Sophocles *OT* 1087-88: εἴπερ ἐγὼ μάντις εἰμὶ καὶ κατὰ γνώμαν ἴδρις, οὐ τὸν Ὄλυμπον ἀπείρων, ὦ Κιθαιρών, οὐκ ἔσει τὰν αὔριον κτλ.; Sophocles *Ant* 758-59: ἄληθες; ἀλλ' οὐ τόνδ' Ὄλυμπον, ἴσθ' ὅτι, χαίρων ἐπὶ ψόγοισι δεννάσεις εμε; Sophocles *El* 1063-64: ἀλλ' οὐ τὰν Διὸς ἀστραπὰν καὶ τὰν οὐρανίαν Θέμιν.

[161]See the explanation of Gregorius Corinthus, ed. G. H. Schaefer (Leipzig, 1811) 150: τὸ ἐλλειπτικῶς ὀμνύειν . . . Ἀττικόν ἐστι. Cf. Liddell-Scott-Jones, *Greek-English Lexicon*, 1070.

[162]On the range of motives for the suppression of the name of the deity, whether scrupulousness, indecision, or indifference, see Hirzel, *Der Eid*, 90-103, esp. 96n.2; Smyth, *Greek Grammar*, §1596, 2894. Note the observation of the

Gorgias, Socrates and Polus debate whether politicians exercise more power in the state than anyone else.[163] Socrates answers "No": for they do not do what they wish, but only what seems best to them (*Grg* 466D-E). Baffled and enraged by this distinction, Polus insists that doing what one thinks best is a great power to have (*Grg* 466E). To express the magnitude of his denial, Socrates resorts to an oath: Μὰ τὸν – οὐ σύ γε (*Grg* 466E).[164]

An epigram of Strato in the *Anthologia Palatina* illustrates the suppression of the name of the deity to avoid taking an outright oath: "If Cleonicus does not come now, I will never receive him in my house! No, in truth, by —, I will not swear (οὐ μὰ τὸν – οὐκ ὀμόσω). For if he did not come owing to a dream he had, and then does appear tomorrow, it is not all over with me because of the loss of this one day" (*AP* 12.200-203).[165]

Socrates' famous oath "by the dog" (μὰ τὸν κύνα) was interpreted in antiquity as a substitute for the divine name.[166] Philostratus the

---

scholiast to Aristophanes *Ran* 1374-75 (μὰ τόν): οὕτως ἔθος ἐστὶ τοῖς ἀρχαίοις ἐνίοτε μὴ προστιθέναι τὸν θεὸν εὐλαβείας χάριν. Cf. *Aristophanis Comoediae*, vol. 2, ed. F. W. Hall and W. M. Geldart (Oxford: Clarendon Press, 1978) 154. See also Suidas, s.v. ναὶ μὰ τόν· ῥυθμίζει ὁ λόγος πρὸς εὐσέβειαν, ed. G. Bernhardy (Halle, 1853) col. 944.

[163]Text and translation in *Plato*, vol. 3, ed. W. Lamb, LCL (Cambridge MA: Harvard University Press, 1946) 324-25.

[164]On Socrates' motive for avoiding the name of the deity, see the comments of E. R. Dodds, *Plato: Gorgias* (Oxford: Clarendon Press, 1959) 234. Perhaps Plato was influenced by the Pythagorean teaching reported by Diogenes Laertius 8.22: μηδ' ὀμνύναι θεούς.

[165]Text and translation in *The Greek Anthology*, vol. 4, ed. W. R. Paton, LCL (Cambridge MA: Harvard University Press, 1979) 384. Other examples of the suppression of the name of the deity: Callimachus fr. 66d, ναὶ μὰ τόν in *Fragmenta nuper reperta*, ed. R. Pfeiffer (Bonn: Hanstein, 1923); Aelian *De Nat. An.* 3.19, βάσκανον δὴ τὸ ζῷον ἡ φώκη, ναὶ μὰ τόν in *Aelian: On the Characteristics of Animals*, vol. 1, ed. A. F. Scholfield, LCL (Cambridge MA: Harvard University Press, 1958) 178.

[166]Aristophanes *Vesp* 83; Plato *Grg* 466C. See Hirzel, *Der Eid*, 100-104 on Socrates' oath and 90-104 on the Ῥαδαμάνθυος ὅρκος generally. See also E. R. Dodds, *Plato: Gorgias* (Oxford: Clarendon Press, 1959) on 482B 5; cf. R. Hoerber, "The Socratic Oath by the Dog," *CIJ* 58 (1963): 268-69.

sophist explains (*Vit Apol* 6.19): "He swore by such objects not as gods, but in order to avoid swearing by the gods" (ὤμνυ γὰρ ταῦτα οὐχ ὡς θεούς, ἀλλ' ἵνα μὴ θεοὺς ὀμνύοι).[167] The oath "by the cabbage" (μὰ τὴν κράμβην) was common in comedy.[168] One of the guests at Athenaeus' banquet quotes Ananius as saying: καὶ σὲ φιλέω, ναὶ μὰ τὴν κράμβην (*Deip* 9 . 370B).[169]

In everyday life, on the streets and in the markets, Greeks swore ἐκ τοῦ παρατυχόντος, by whatever was at hand (ἀνὰ χεῖρας):[170] by the caper plant (μὰ τὴν κάππαριν), by the goose (μὰ τὸν χῆν), by the vegetables (μὰ τὰ λάχανα).[171] One may doubt whether, in such cases, religious scruple was determinative, but rather ease, indifference and established custom.[172] Suidas describes as "a jesting oath" (ὅρκος ἐπὶ χλευασμῷ) a line from the elegist Archilochus (108): "Yes, yes, by the green of the poppy" (ναὶ ναὶ μὰ μήκωνος χλόην).[173] Eustathius attests that elliptical oaths were employed throughout antiquity.[174]

---

[167]Cited by Lieberman, *Greek In Jewish Palestine*, 126. See also Proclus *in Alc* 234.9.

[168]E.g., Epicharmus 25 in *Comicorum Graecorum Fragmenta,* ed. G. Kaibel (Berlin, 1899) 88; Eupolis 74 in *Comicorum Atticorum Fragmenta*, vol. 1, ed. T. Kock (Leipzig, 1880) 258.

[169]Text in *Athenaeus: Deipnosophistae*, ed. C. Gulick, LCL (Cambridge MA: Harvard University Press, 1978).

[170]Eustathius, *Commentarii ad Homeri Iliadem et Odysseam* (Leipzig, 1825) on *Il.* 1.234, p. 77; cf. Hirzel, *Der Eid*, 25n.1.

[171]See the texts assembled by P. Meinhardt, *De forma et usu iuramentorum* (Frommanni: Pohle, 1892) 74ff., 77; cf. Hirzel, *Der Eid*, 96n.2. Lampon, for example, swears "by the goose" in Aristophanes *Aves* 521. Cf. Suidas s.v. Ῥαδαμάνθυος ὅρκος: πολλοὶ γὰρ πρὸς λάχανα ὀμνύουσιν.

[172]Meinhardt, *De forma et usu iuramentorum*, 23; Hirzel, *Der Eid*, 96n.2.

[173]Text and translation in *Elegy and Iambus*, vol. 2, ed. J. M. Edmonds (New York: Putnam's Sons, 1931) 158-59.

[174]Eustathius *Com. ad Hom.* to *Il.* 19.396, p. 209; see also Suidas s.v. μὰ τὰ λάχάνα. Cf . Hirzel, *Der Eid*, 96n.2. Lieberman, *Greek in Jewish Palestine*, 127-28, suggests that Jews heard such oaths from their neighbors and adopted the practice; he argues that *Mishnah* Nedarim 2:5 treats the case of one who vows "by the fishing net," while *Tosefta* Sanhedrin 5:1, 422 mentions an oath "by the figs."

As the foregoing examples show, great flexibility of expression was permitted in taking an oath. The verb of swearing (ὀμνύω, ὄμνυμι) was usually ellipsed.[175] Either of the particles might be omitted. The name of the deity might be suppressed. It was doubtless the strength of established custom which made such flexibility possible. With all the omissions and suppressions, the structure of swearing remained the same: an adverb, affirmative or negative, followed by an asseverative particle, which governs the accusative of the thing by which one swears, after the ellipsis of the verb.[176] The asseverative particle serves to confirm the truth of what has been averred.[177] Given such flexibility, it is not difficult to understand how the double affirmation developed.

Nor was the doubling of the particles the only means which pious Jews of the period discovered for employing what amounts to an oath. Hebrew ἀμήν is coupled with ναί by the author of the Apocalypse (1:7) to confirm the truth of a prophetic utterance, its asseverative force enhanced by its foreignness.[178] The double ἀμήν attributed to Jesus by the author of the Fourth Gospel serves to corroborate the statements which it prefaces.[179] Dalman reconstructs Jesus' motives:

---

[175]Smyth, *Greek Grammar,* §2894.

[176]Ibid., §1596.

[177]Ibid., §2894.

[178]Cf. Berger, *Die Amen-Worte Jesu,* 6: "handelt es sich in v. 7 um einen Satz, der inhaltlich den futurischeschatologischen Aussagen entspricht, der weithin den synoptischen Amen-Worten eignet: die «prophetische» Aussage wird durch den Sprecher selbst bekräftigt." See also Rev. 22:20, where ἀμήν is the response of the ἐκκλησία to the divine "yes." On the equivalence of ναί and ἀμήν, see the comment of Oecumenius on Rev. 3:14: ἰσοδυναμεῖ τοῦτο τῷ τάδε λέγει ὁ ἀληθινός ... ἀμὴν γάρ ἐστιν τὸ ναί, in H. C. Hoskier, ed., *The Commentary of Oecumenius on the Apocalypse of John* (Ann Arbor: University of Michigan Press, 1928) 64. In the *Acts of Thomas* 121, a voice is heard from heaven which says ναί, ἀμήν in confirmation of the words which Judas has spoken over Mygdonia at her baptism: ἐδέξω σου τὴν σφραγῖδα κτίσαι σεαυτῇ ζωὴν αἰώνιον; Greek text in R. A. Lipsius et M. Bonnet, *Acta Apostolorum Apocrypha,* pars II, vol. II: Acta *Philippi et Acta Thomae accedunt Acta Barnabae,* ed. M. Bonnet (Lipsiae, 1903) 231.

[179]The double ἀμήν is placed before the sayings of Jesus 25 times in John's Gospel; see esp. John 13:16, 20, 21, which may be pre-Johannine. The

Clearly an enforcement of what he said by a mere appeal to its truthfulness was not felt to be sufficient by Jesus. With that end in view, no other resource remained open for him than an averment with the use of an oath, after the manner, say, in which Yohanan ben Zakkai (ca. 80 A.D.) confirmed a principle of his teaching before his pupils with 'by your life' (*Pes d Rab Kah* 40b). But an oath had been pronounced by Jesus (Matt 5:37) as displeasing to God; he had therefore to seek for some other mode of emphasis, and found it in the solemn 'amen'. This is not an oath, yet more potent than a simple 'verily,' because it gives the hearer to understand that Jesus confirms his own statement in the same way as if it were an oath or a blessing. Thus did he fulfill his own injunction to make the simple 'yea, yea' take the place of an oath.[180]

In such cases, ἀμήν is not a liturgical acclamation or a doxological response, but a confirmation and an assurance; ἀμήν retains its "original inward meaning,"[181] its full asseverative force.[182]

---

single ἀμήν is found in the Synoptic gospels (30 times in Matthew, 13 in Mark, 6 in Luke, replaced by ἀληθῶς in 9:27; 12:44; 21:3 and by ἐπ' ἀληθείας in 4:25). The double ἀμήν of John's Gospel is probably influenced by the O.T. usage (אָמֵן אָמֵן in Num 5:22; Ps 89:93; Neh 8:6, usually translated as γένοιτο in the LXX). The double ἀμήν is also found in the Qumran literature, e.g., 1QS 2.10, 18, and in *Test Abr Rec A* 20. See the discussion in Strack-Billerbeck, *Kommentar* 1:242-44; R. Bultmann, *The Gospel of John: A Commentary* (Philadelphia: Westminster, 1971) 105n.2; Berger, *Die Amen-Worte Jesu*, 4, 17, 95-116.

[180]Dalman, *The Words of Jesus*, 228-29. Dalman's conclusion is disputed by H. Schlier, ἀμήν, *TDNT* 1:337. Berger attributes a greater role to apocalyptic tradition in Hellenistic Judaism, *Die Amen-Worte Jesu*, 18: "Die Amen-Worte Jesu können in bezug auf ihre Einleitung nur auf dem Boden des Griechisch sprechenden Judentums formuliert worden sein, da die Verwendung des Amen an dieser Stelle nur aus griech. Sprachgebrauch erklarbar ist. Die ausser-ntl Belege in Test, Abr. wie auch die in Apc wiesen bereits in den gleichen Bereich, in dem auch grosse Teile der synoptischen Tradition ihren Ursprung haben: in den lebendiger, vorwiegend apokalyptischer Tradition unter hellenisierten Juden. Das Amen zu Beginn von Jesus-Worten ist ein besonders typisches Produkt dieser Vermischung jüdischer und griechischer Elemente."

[181]H. Schlier, ἀμήν, *TDNT* 1:337.

[182]G. Quell, ἀλήθεια, *TDNT* 1:232n.1 (on אמת); Berger, *Die Amen-Worte*

Several cases that have been regarded as repetitions of the particles for emphasis are discovered, upon closer examination, to be related to the invocation of the deity.[183] Thus in the first of the *Papyri Graecae Magicae*, in the πρᾶξις of Pnouthis for acquiring a daimon as an assistant (*PGM* I.42-195), "yes, yes" appears at the climax of the spell as a summons to the deity:

> And you address inducive words to the god: 'I shall have you as a friendly assistant, a beneficent god who serves me whenever I say, 'Quickly, by your power already on earth, yes yes, appear to me, god!' (τάχος, τῇ σῇ δυνάμει ἤδη ἔ[γγ]αιος, ναὶ ναί, φαῖνέ μοι, θεέ).[184]

In what follows, the words which summon the deity are referred to as an "oath" of the god: "And you yourself speak, while reclining, about what you propose, quickly. Test this oath of the god (πειρῶ δὲ θεοῦ τὸν ὁρκισμὸν αὐτόν) on [what] you wish."[185] This usage seems to have influenced the prayer of Judith in the Septuagint (*Jud* 9:12): ναὶ ναὶ ὁ

Jesu, 15-18.

[183]Luz, *Das Evangelium nach Matthäus*, 286 n.46, gives as instances of "intensivierendes ναὶ ναί," *PGM* 1.90; Aristophanes *Nub* 1468; Theocritus *Idyll* 4.54; Archilocus fr. 99 [Diehl²]; Petronius *Sat* 25.1; 2 Cor 1:17. A similar list of texts are cited by G. Stahlin, "Zum Gebrauch von Beteuerungsformeln im Neuen Testament," *NovT* 5 (1962): 119n.2, as examples of doubling for emphasis.

[184]Text in *Papyri Graecae Magicae: Die Griechischen Zauberpapyri* I, ed. K. Preisendanz, 2nd ed. (Stuttgart: Teubner, 1973) 6-8. The translation offered here differs from that of E. O'Neil in *The Greek Magical Papyri in Translation, Including the Demotic Spells*, ed. H. D. Betz (Chicago: University of Chicago, 1986) 5, in respect to the term πρόπεμπε, which O'Neil renders "preliminary (?)," explaining his choice in n. 20: "πρόπεμπε with an inanimate (and esp. abstract) object is poetic. Here the prefix seems to have its literal meaning: 'first,' hence 'preliminary words.'" The translation "inducive" seems more appropriate to the general sense of the verb, which is "to send forth," "to escort"; the words serve to "conduct" the daimon into the presence of the magician, as offerings are carried in procession to the gods (Aeschylus *Pers* 622), or as a corpse is accompanied to the grave (Aeschylus *Th* 1064; Plato *Leg* 800E; Plato *Mx* 236D).

[185]Text and translation in *Papyri Graecae Magicae: Die Griechischen Zauberpapyri* I. See also *PGM* 1.204-205; Peterson, ΕΙΣ ΘΕΟΣ, 233 (an amulet with inscription).

θεὸς τοῦ πατρός μου καὶ θεὸς κληρονομίας Ισραηλ, δέσποτα τῶν οὐρανῶν καὶ τῆς γῆς, κτίστα τῶν ὑδάτων, βασιλεῦ πάσης κτίσεώς σου, σὺ εἰσάκουσον τῆς δεήσεώς μου.[186] Even when the doubling of the particle serves to emphasize the speaker's response, the context sometimes includes an oath or an invocation of the deity. In the *Clouds*, Strepsiades repents (too late) of having cast away the gods for Socrates. He invites Pheidippides to join him in a return to ancestral piety. When Pheidippides hesitates, Strepsiades urges: "Yes yes, come reverence paternal Zeus!" (ναὶ ναί, καταιδέσθητι πατρῷον Δία, Aristophanes *Nu* 1468).[187] One of Alciphron's courtesans avers:

I should prefer to lie on this green grass rather than on those rugs and soft coverlets. By Zeus (νὴ Δια), you know, dinner parties here, amid the beauty of green fields and under the open sky, are more delightful than in town" (Alciphron *Ep* 4.13.7).[188]

Her companions employ the double affirmation to signal their assent to her oath: "'Yes, yes, you speak truly,' the others said" (ναὶ ναί, λέγεις καλῶς, ἔφασαν *Ep* 4.13.7).[189] Whether in oath, invocation, or

---

[186]Text in *Septuaginta*, editio minor, ed. A. Rahlfs (Stuttgart: Deutsche Bibelstiftung, 1935) 989-90; cited by Berger, *Die Amen-Worte Jesu*, 11n.16.

[187]Text and translation in *Aristophanes*, vol. 1, ed. B. Rogers, LCL (Cambridge MA: Harvard University Press, 1938).

[188]Text and translation in *The Letters of Alciphron, Aelian and Philostratus*, ed. F. Fobes, LCL (Cambridge MA: Harvard University Press, 1979) 286-87.

[189]Ibid. See also *Anth Pal* 9.341, Ναὶ ναί, Πὰν συρικτά, καὶ εἰς αἴγειρον ἐκείναν σοί τι κατὰ φλοιοῦ γράμμ' ἐκόλαψε λέγειν (attributed to Glaucus); *Anth Pal* 12.45, ναὶ ναὶ βάλλετ', Ἔρωτες· ἐγὼ σκοπὸς εἰς ἅμα πολλοῖς κεῖμαι (attributed to Posidippus); *Anth Pal* 12.166, ναὶ πάντως τέφρην θέσθε με κάνθρακιήν· ναί, ναί, βάλλετ', Ἔρωτες· ἐνεσκληκὼς γὰρ ἀνίαις, ἐξ ὑμέων τοῦτ' οὖν εἴ γέ τι, βούλομ' ἔχειν (attributed to Asclepiades); text of citations from *The Greek Anthology*, vol. 3, ed. W. R. Paton, LCL (Cambridge MA: Harvard University Press, 1983) 184, 302, 366. A final example of the doubling of ναί is Callimachus 6.63: Demeter speaks angrily to Erysichthon, king of Triopldae—ναὶ ναί, τεύχεο δῶμα, κύον, κύον, ᾧ ἔνι δαῖτας ποιήσεις, text in *Callimachus: Hymns and Epigrams*, ed. A. W. Mair, LCL (Cambridge MA:

response, the double affirmation represents the attempt to establish the truth of one's utterance; it stages the struggle of language against the inconstancy of human nature.

It is the inconstancy of human nature which makes the double affirmation necessary. As Enoch explains to his sons, it is because there is no truth in men that they must swear by the words "yes, yes" and "no, no" (2 Enoch 49:1). Human beings are untrustworthy and insincere; oaths give warrant for their sincerity (Philo De Sac. Abelis et Caini 93). "God knows no change of will," Philo observes, "but ever holds fast to what he has purposed without alteration. Human beings, on the contrary, are ready to change on account of instability (διὰ τὴν ἀβεβαιότητα), whether it be in them or outside them" (Quod Deus immut. 26).[190] Philo proceeds to give examples of mutability:

> Often when we have chosen our friends and been familiar with them for a short time, we turn from them, though we have no charge to bring against them, and count them amongst our enemies, or at least as strangers. Such action proves the facile levity of ourselves, how little capacity we have for holding to our original judgments. But God has no such fickleness. Or again, sometimes we are minded to hold to the standards we have taken, but we find ourselves with others who have not remained constant, and thus our judgments perforce change with theirs (Quod Deus immut 27-28).

The cause of mutability, Philo recognizes, is mortality, the limitation of our senses and our knowledge: "A mere man cannot foresee the course of future events or the judgments of others; but to God, as in pure sunlight, all things are manifest" (Quod Deus immut 29). Philo challenges his readers (De Plant 81-84) to choose whatever science or art they wish, and the person who is best or most approved in it: one invariably finds that the claims of the science are not made good by what the "expert" knows or does; the one fails of the other not by short but by long distances. "It is impossible to obtain perfection in respect of any science

Harvard University Press, 1977) 128; this approximates a curse; on the oath as a curse, see Hirzel, Der Eid, 137-41; S. H. Blank, "The Curse, the Blasphemy, the Spell, the Oath," HUCA 23/1 (1950–1951): 73-96.

[190]Text and translation in Philo, vol. 3, ed. F. H. Colson, LCL (Cambridge MA: Harvard University Press, 1968) 22-23.

or art whatever" (De Plant 83).[191] The power of apprehension does not reside in the mind: sight is not found in the eyes, nor hearing in ears (De Plant 83). Rather, the power of apprehension springs from "the seed of certitude" (τὸ βέβαιον) sown upon the organs by God. That is why, if one wishes certitude in apprehension, as in statement, one must "call God to witness." Philo observes, ironically, that on account of our mortal limitations, "there is no point on which it is more possible to take a sure oath than upon the fact that no subject of knowledge whatever is found to have reached the goal of perfection in the person who is expert in it" (De Plant. 82). "In us the mortal is the chief ingredient. We cannot escape our inborn infirmities. We creep within our covering of mortality, like snails into their shells" (De Sac. Abelis et Caini 95).

Initially difficult to understand, Paul's words τὸ ναὶ ναὶ καὶ τὸ οὖ οὖ describe with formulaic clarity the equivocal character of everything human. The formula gives dramatic expression to the ambiguity of the situation in which Paul finds himself as a result of the Corinthians' suspicions. Paul says: You suspect me of acting insincerely; you accuse me of vacillation and self-interestedness; you deem me untrustworthy. As a result, I am like a man who must continually seek to establish the truth of his statements by employing what amounts to an oath.

It is Paul's genius that he applies to all of his statements a formula which, in common practise, was meant to warrant disputed ones. The generalization is founded, in Paul's case, not upon a Platonic dualism, as in Philo, but upon an eschatological dualism, actuated by the coming of Christ.[192] All human utterances are equivocal, Paul believes, even those which aim at the truth; just as all human moral efforts are ineffectual, even those which aim at the good (Rom. 7:18-25). The double affirmation, which exposes inconstancy, at the same time that it seeks to transcend it, is the paradigm of all human utterances. In this insight, Paul is one with the most acute linguistic philosopher of our day: "The 'yes, yes' must be cited, must recite itself, to bring about the alliance of affirmation with itself, to bring about its ring."[193] Human language

---

[191]Ibid., 254-55.

[192]R. Bultmann, Theology of the New Testament, vol. 1 (New York: Scribner's, 1951) 199-203.

[193]J. Derrida, "Pas," Gramma 3/4 (1976), where the ré-cit of double affirmation is analyzed; the quotation is taken from a later summary of "Pas" in

mirrors mutability: at best, it can only repeat, recite, reiterate, in effort to establish itself. But the interval exposes a void upon which singularity cannot be founded, creates a difference from which sameness can never emerge. That Paul is not lost in the void, that he is not rent by the difference, is owing to the faithfulness of God: πιστὸς δὲ ὁ θεός, κτλ. (2 Cor 1:18). Philo likewise concludes discussions of oath-taking with assurances of divine trustworthiness (*De Plant* 85-93; *De Spec leg* 2. 10-11). Human beings have recourse to oaths to win belief, Philo observes, "but God is faithful in his speech as elsewhere" (ὁ δὲ θεὸς καὶ λέγων πιστός ἐστιν, *De Sac. Abelis et Caini* 93). Philo formulates the difference between the human and the divine thus: οὐ γὰρ δι' ὅρκον πιστὸς ὁ θεός, ἀλλὰ δι' αὐτὸν καὶ ὁ ὅρκος βέβαιος (*De Sac. Abelis et Caini* 93). It is upon this truth that Paul's argument turns in 2 Cor 1:17-18.

III. RHETORICAL STRATEGY

When Paul came to write his letter of reconciliation (2 Cor 1:1–2:13; 7:5-16; 13:11-13),[194] he found himself in a difficult position. He had defended himself effectively against attacks upon his apostolic legitimacy (in 2 Cor 10:1–13:10). But the contest of grave accusations, and the way

---

Deconstruction and Criticism, ed. H. Bloom (New York: Seabury, 1979) 85.

[194] A growing number of scholars regard 2 Cor 1:1–2:13; 7:5-16; 13:11-13 as an independent work (though some append ch. 8, others ch. 9). Johannes Weiss was the first to suggest that 2 Cor 1:1–2:13; 7:5-16 was once an independent work, in his review of Halmel in *ThLZ* 19 (1894): 513-14, then in idem, *Das Urchristentum*, ed. R. Knopf (Göttingen: Vandenhoeck & Ruprecht, 1917) 245ff. Weiss was followed by A. Loisy, "Les epitres de Paul," *Revue d'histoire et litterature religieuses* 7 (1921): 213, who referred to 2 Cor 1:1–2:13; 7:5-16 as a "lettre de concilation." See also G. Bornkamm, *Die Vorgeschichte des sogennanten Zweiten Korintherbriefes*, SAH 1961, 2. Abhandlung (Heidelberg: Winter, 1961). Characteristic is the conclusion of Dieter Georgi in the "Epilogue" to *The Opponents of Paul in Second Corinthians* (Philadelphia: Fortress, 1986) 335: "The seams in 2:13-14 and 7:4-5 are the best examples in the entire New Testament of one large fragment secondarily inserted into another text. The splits are so basic, and the connections so obvious, that the burden of proof now lies with those who defend the integrity of the canonical text."

in which they were surmounted, disclosed a new horizon of suspicion, at once wider and more personal. The Corinthians now had reason to doubt that their apostle had been sincere (1:12). Paul had promised, indeed he had threatened, to come to Corinth (12:14; 13:1ff.). He had not come (1:23-24); he sent a letter instead, a letter which caused the Corinthians grief (2:3-4). He had accomplished by an ironical epistle what he could not have achieved in person (10:10; 12:21). By postponing his visit and sending a harsh epistle, Paul seemed to have manipulated their response; they felt that Paul had dealt with them in a capricious manner (1:17). At the heart of Paul's conciliatory epistle lies a question about the constancy of his character.

Paul must endeavor to demonstrate that he had dealt with the Corinthians in a sincere manner, that in this, as in all previous instances, he had been guided by a single principle—the promotion of the Corinthians' joy (1:24). Paul knew that he had always been sincere: had the Corinthians understood him completely, had their knowledge corresponded to his desire (1:15-16), they would have seen that he was motivated by love, even when he refused to come to Corinth (1:23), even when he composed an epistle which by its nature occasioned grief (2:4; 7:8). Paul's motives were pure, but the evidence stood against him. Paul could not rely upon himself alone. He knew that he would have to call God to witness.

Paul's reluctance to take an oath in this case was well founded. An oath was a weak, inartificial proof,[195] by definition an unprovable statement.[196] It carried weight only on the assumption that one would not run the risk of swearing falsely for fear of incurring divine displeasure.[197] To offer to take an oath unconditionally, without demanding that one's opponent take an oath as well, was regarded as a sign of bad faith (Quintilian 5.6.1). One who took this course was obliged to defend his action by appealing to the blamelessness of his life as rendering perjury incredible (Quintilian 5.6.2). An oath was easily countered: one need only point out that many persons have not been hindered in the least from swearing falsely by fear of divine intervention in their affairs (Quintilian

---

[195]*Rhet ad Alex* 17, 1428a23f.; Aristotle *Rhet* 1.2, 1355b37; Quintilian 5.1.2.

[196]*Rhet ad Alex* 17, 1432a; cf. J. Martin, *Antike Rhetorik* (München: Beck, 1974) 100.

[197]*Rhet ad Alex* 17, 1432a34ff.; Martin, *Rhetorik*, 100.

5.6.3); "and further that one who is ready to take an oath without being asked to do so, is really proposing to pass sentence on his own case" (Quintilian 5.6.3).[198]

A second reason for Paul's reluctance lay in what an oath revealed about his relationship with the Corinthians. The Greeks held Oath ("Ορκος) to be the child of Strife ("Ερις); the Furies assisted at its birth (Hesiod *Opera et Dies* 804); its task was to trouble men on earth when anyone knowingly swore falsely (Hesiod *Theogonia* 231).[199] It had its place in the court of law between parties to a dispute.[200] The author of the *Rhetorica ad Alexandrum* (17-18, 1432a33-b40) describes it as a legal expedient. That Paul felt obliged to take an oath belied the intent of his epistle;[201] it revealed that his relationship with the Corinthians was still troubled by suspicion.

---

[198]Text and translation of Quintilian in *The Institutio Oratoria of Quintilian*, vol. 2, ed. H. E. Butler, LCL (Cambridge MA: Harvard University Press, 1977) 166-67; cf. *Rhet ad Alex* 17, 1432b40.

[199]Cf. Hesiod, *Opera et Dies* 282; see the discussion in Hirzel, *Der Eid*, 2-3, 176-77.

[200]G. Gilbert, *Beiträge zur Entwicklungsgeschichte des griechischen Gerichts-verfahren, Jahrbuch für classischen Philologie*, suppl. 23 (Leipzig: Teubner, 1896) 467; M. Kaser, *Das römische Zivilprozessrecht* (München: Beck, 1966) 197ff.

[201]The aim of the ἐπιστολή θεραπευτική, according to Ps.-Libanius, Ἐπιστολιμαῖοι χαρακτῆρες 15, was to conciliate someone who had been caused grief; thus one avoided insofar as possible mention of the cause of strife; see esp. the example of a conciliatory letter given by Ps-Libanius: "But if you were vexed at what was said or done, be assured, most excellent sir, that I shall most certainly no longer speak of what was said. For it is my aim always to heal my friends rather than to cause them sorrow" (εἰ δ' ἐπὶ τοῖς λεχθεῖσιν ἢ πραχθεῖσιν ἠχθέσθης, ἴσθι, κράτιστε ἀνδρῶν, ὡς οὐκέτι τῶν ῥηθέντων λόγον ὅλως ποτὲ ποιήσομαι. σκοπὸς γάρ μοι θεραπεύειν ἀεὶ τοὺς φίλους ἐστὶν ἥπερ λυπεῖν). Text and translation of Ps-Libanius in A. Malherbe, "Ancient Epistolary Theorists," *Ohio Journal of Religious Studies* 5 (1977) 64-65, 72-73; repr. in idem, *Ancient Epistolary Theorists* (Atlanta: Scholars Press, 1988). It was Windisch, *Der zweite Korintherbrief*, 8, who first observed that 2 Cor 1:1–2:13; 7:5-16 fits the description of the ἐπιστολή θερατευτική in Ps-Libanius.

Paul found the solution to his dilemma within the ancient concept of oath. For there was a second, and broader, understanding of oath as a gift of the gods, as a means among men whereby faith and trust might be engendered.[202] The wise Cheiron was praised by the author of the *Titanomachia* (fr. 6) because he led mortals to righteousness through the introduction of oath (Εἴς τε δικαιοσύνην θνητῶν γένος ἤγαγε δείξας ὅρκους καὶ θυσίας ἱερὰς καὶ σχήματ' Ὀλύμπου).[203] The author of the *Kore Kosmou* (*Corp Herm* fr. 23.67) credits Isis and Osiris with the introduction of "the great god Ὅρκος" into human life, along with the other gifts of culture—order (εὐνομία) and justice (δικαιοσύνη).[204] By such authors, oath was understood in a promissory sense.[205] This understanding of oath predominated in antiquity, outside the confines of the judicial situation, owing to its usefulness in everyday life, and to the influence of the philosophers, who repudiated the asseverative oath, but made a place for the promissory oath among the proper ὁμολογίαι.[206]

With this understanding of oath in mind, Paul set about the difficult task of redefining his situation. Paul includes his word to the Corinthians among the promises of God (1:18f.). God's word to the Corinthians was an unequivocal "Yes" (1:19). The divine "yes" is a promissory oath (1:20) which cannot fail, because God is faithful.[207] Philo, similarly,

---

[202]See the discussion of the promissory oath in Hirzel, *Der Eid*, 2ff., 176-77.

[203]Text in G. Kinkel, *Epicorum Graecorum Fragmenta* I (Leipzig: Teubner, 1877) 8. The *Titanomachia* was ascribed to Eumelus of Corinth.

[204]Text and translation in *Hermès Trismégiste, Corpus Hermeticum IV: Fragments Extraits de Stobée* (XXIII-XXIX), ed. A. J. Festugière and A. D. Nock (Paris: Societe d' Edition "Les Belles Lettres," 1980) 21.

[205]Cicero conceives of oath as a promise related to a future action, e.g., *De off.* 3.104: *Est enim jusjurandum adfirmatio religiosa: quod autem adfirmate quasi deo teste promiseris, id tenendum est.* Further on oath in Roman law, see K.-H. Ziegler, *Das private Schiedsgericht im antiken römischen Recht* (München: Beck, 1971) 22-23, 104-105. See also Clement of Alexandria *Strom* 7.8: ὅρκος μὲν γάρ ἐστιν ὁμολογία καθοριστικὴ μετὰ προσπαραλήψεως θείας. Augustine *Enar In Psalm* 131.4: *jurare est firme promittere.*

[206]E.g., Plato *Rep* 443A: ἢ κατὰ ὅρκους ἢ κατὰ τὰς ἄλλας ὁμολογίας. Cf. Hirzel, *Der Eid*, 4-5.

[207]Halmel, *Der zweite Korintherbrief*, 56: "Die ἐπαγγελία des griech-

regards the divine "yes" as an agreement, or affirmative proposition (*Quaes in Gen* 3.58). Philo explains God's "Yes" to Abraham in Gen. 17:19 (LXX):

> Why is the divine oracle an agreement, for He says to Abraham, "Yes, behold (ναί, ἰδού), Sarah thy wife shall bear thee a son"? What is indicated is somewhat as follows. "My agreement," He says, "is an affirmative proposition to be kept inviolate" (ἡ ὁμολογία, φησίν, ἡ ἐμὴ κατάφασίς ἐστιν ἀκραιφνής). "And thy faith (πίστις) is not ambiguous but is unhesitating and partakes of modesty and reverence (αἰδοῦς καὶ ἐντροπῆς μετέχουσα). Wherefore that which thou didst formerly receive as destined to come about because of thy faith in Me, shall wholly be." For this is shown by the "Yes" (τοῦτο γὰρ μηνύει τὸ ναί).[208]

Paul could count on the Corinthians to accept the proposition that Christ's coming demonstrates the faithfulness of God (1:18ff.). Jesus Christ is God's "Yes" to the world (1:19). In Jesus' death on the cross for the sins of the world, God confirmed the promise given to Abraham, "In you shall all the nations be blessed" (Gal. 3:6-14). Thus Paul can say: ὅσαι γὰρ ἐπαγγελίαι θεοῦ, ἐν αὐτῷ τὸ ναί (1:20). Paul argues that, as the herold of God's Son (1:19), his promises have a "yes" character.[209] By a massive transumption, everything that pertains to the gospel proclamation is predicated of Paul's speech as well.[210] Paul

---

ischen Rechts (vgl. die *pollicitatio* des römischen Rechts) ist eine streng einseitige bindende Zusage." See also Windisch, *Der zweite Korintherbrief*, 68.

[208]The text of the Greek fragment (*apud* Procopius, Cod. Aug. f.98ᵛ) is cited according to *Philo, Supplement II: Questions and Answers on Exodus*, ed. R. Marcus, LCL (Cambridge MA: Harvard University Press, 1953) 212-13. The Armenian version follows the original Greek closely, so that the translation modifies slightly that of Marcus, *Philo, Supplement I: Questions and Answers on Genesis*, LCL (Cambridge MA: Harvard University Press, 1971) 260-61.

[209]Halmel, *Der zweite Korintherbrief*, 56; Windisch, *Der zweite Korintherbrief*, 67.

[210]This is the effect of Paul's decision to speak first of his λόγος to the Corinthians in general (vs. 18), and only subsequently of the proclamation of God's Son (vs. 19). On the direction of inference thereby established, see Windisch, *Der zweite Korintherbrief*, 66-67.

presents the gospel proclamation as a paradigmatic instance of a univocacy that characterizes his speech in general. His trustworthiness is guaranteed thereby; his sincerity is placed beyond doubt.[211]

When Paul finally calls God to witness (1:23), it is after he has successfully included his oath among the promises of God. The transformation of an asseverative into a promissory oath is a rhetorical sleight of hand. Paul's situation remains forensic, the issue juridical.[212] That which Paul calls God to witness is a motive which operated in a past decision. Nevertheless, it is rhetorically effective; it contributes to the defense of Paul's character, so crucial to the letter of reconciliation (cf. 1:12).[213] What Paul achieves is the effect of an ὅρκος ἠθικός, just as the rhetorical theorists recommended.[214] Hermogenes (*Meth* 20, Rabe 435)

---

[211]It is not possible to enter here into a discussion of τὸ ἀμήν (vs. 20), or βεβαιῶν (vs. 21). But the investigation has shown that both terms belong to the topic of oaths, even if they also allude to the liturgical practise of the community.

[212]The issue (στάσις) of the letter of reconciliation is juridical. There is no question here of the facts of the case, of what did or did not happen: Paul failed to pay a visit to Corinth; he wrote a letter which caused the Corinthians grief. Nor is the issue one of definition; there is no question about the meaning of terms. When the accused cannot deny the deed, and cannot argue from definition, it remains for him to represent the act as just and lawful and to the public advantage (*Rhet ad Alex* 17, 1425a; Aristotle *Rhet* 3.17, 1417b25f.). It is a question, then, of the nature of the deed, so that the issue is called one of quality (ποιότης, *Stat.* 2.37.14ff, Rabe). The auctor *ad Herennium* (1.14.24) calls it a juridical issue (*iuridicalis constitutio*) because "the right or wrong of the act is in question." This is the issue of the letter of reconciliation: whether Paul's conduct (ἀναστροφή) towards the Corinthians has been right or wrong, helpful or hurtful (1:12).

[213]The proposition (1:12-14) forcefully illustrates how completely the point to be adjudicated (κρινόμενον) involves the matter of Paul's character. In evidence of his sincerity, Paul appeals to τὸ μαρτύριον τῆς συνειδήσεως. Among Paul's contemporaries, Greek and Roman, conscience was believed to play an important role in the development of character: it permitted scrutiny of one's life; the wise man must attend to its voice, e.g., Polybius 18.43.13. The terms ἁπλότης and εἰλικρίνεια describe the inner disposition of the ethical; cf. *Test Reuben* 4:1; *Test Benj* 6:5; Philo *Ques in Gen* 30.

[214]See the discussion of the ὅρκος ἠθικός in Hirzel, *Der Eid*, 7, 63, 87,

advises: "Never swear upon the facts, . . . but upon the confirmation of character" (οὐδέποτε ἐπὶ πράγματος ὀμεῖται, . . . ἀλλ' ἐπὶ ἤθους βεβαιώσει).[215] For, as Hermogenes (*Id* 8, Rabe 326) observes: "Simple and character-revealing in thought is the appeal to an oath rather than to facts" (Ἔτι ἀφελές τε καὶ ἠθικὸν κατ' ἔννοιαν καὶ τὸ δι' ὅρκων πιστοῦσθαι ὁτιοῦν ἀλλὰ μὴ διὰ τῶν πραγμάτων).[216]

How much it cost Paul to achieve this effect is indicated not only by the beauty of his description of the gospel as God's "Yes" to the world, but also by the gracelessness of his portrait of himself—as a man locked in combat with his own character, parrying doubts and suspicions, countering charges of vacillation and self-interestedness, stumbling over his own words as over cobblestones, colliding with his own promises, forced to repeat, to recite, to reiterate, to establish the truth of his every statement by employing what amounts to an oath.

115.

[215]Text in *Hermogenes Opera*, ed. H. Rabe (Stuttgart: Teubner, 1969) 435; among his examples, he cites Plato *Grg* 489E; Demosthenes *De Corona* 208. Hermogenes' distinction between the πραγματικός and the ἠθικὸς ὅρκος is reminiscent of Aristotle *Rhet* 1.15, 1376a24f.

[216]Hermogenes continues (*Id* 8, Rabe 327): "There are countless such examples in Demosthenes and all these oaths are in character (ἠθικά) and simple (ἀφελῆ)."

BIBLIOGRAPHY

REFERENCE WORKS

Balz, H., and G. Schneider, eds. *Exegetisches Wörterbuch zum Neuen Testament.* 3 vols. Stuttgart: Kohlhammer, 1980–1983.

Bauer, W. *A Greek English Lexicon of the New Testament and Other Early Christian Literature.* Trans. and rev. W. F. Arndt, F. W. Gingrich, and F. W. Danker. 2nd edition. Chicago: University of Chicago Press, 1979.

Blass, F., and A. Debrunner. *A Greek Grammar of the New Testament and Other Early Christian Literature.* Trans. and rev. R. W. Funk. Chicago: University of Chicago Press, 1961.

Burton, E. *Syntax of the Moods and Tenses in New Testament Greek,* 3rd ed. Edinburgh: T.&T. Clark, 1898; repr. 1973.

Galling, K. von, ed. *Die Religion in Geschichte und Gegenwart.* 6 vols. Tübingen: Mohr/Siebeck, 1957–1962.

Glare, P. G. W. *Oxford Latin Dictionary.* Oxford: Clarendon, 1982.

Hammond, N. G. L., and H. H. Scullard. *The Oxford Classical Dictionary.* Oxford: Clarendon, 1970.

Kittel, G., and G. Friedrich, eds. *Theological Dictionary of the New Testament.* 10 vols. Trans. and ed. G. W. Bromiley. Grand Rapids MI: Eerdmans, 1964–1976.

Klauser, T., E. Dassman, et al., eds. *Reallexikon für Antike und Christentum.* 14 vols. Stuttgart: Hiersemann, 1950– .

Lampe, G. W. H. *A Patristic Greek Lexicon.* Oxford: Clarendon, 1961.

Liddell, H. G., and R. Scott. *A Greek-English Lexicon.* Rev. H. S. Jones and R. McKenzie. 9th ed. Oxford: Clarendon, 1940.

Moulton, J. H. *A Grammar of the New Testament Greek.* 3 vols. Edinburgh: T.&T. Clark, 1908.

Moulton, J. H., and G. Milligan. *The Vocabulary of the Greek New Testament Illustrated from the Papyri and Other Non-Literary Sources.* London: Hodder & Stoughton, [2]1930; repr.: Grand Rapids MI: Eerdmans, 1976.

Passow's Wörterbuch der griechischen Sprache völlig neu bearbeitet von W. Crönert. Göttingen: Vandenhoeck & Ruprecht, 1912.

Robertson, A. T. *A Grammar of the Greek New Testament in Light of Historical Research.* New York and London: Hodder & Stoughton, [1]1914; Nashville: Broadman Press, [4]1923, [5]1931.

Smyth, H. W. *Greek Grammar.* Cambridge MA: Harvard University Press, 1920; repr. 1980.

Wissowa, G., W. Kroll, et al., eds. *Paulys Realencyclopädie der classischen Altertumswissenschaft.* Vols. I-XXIV, IA.1-X.A, Suppl I-XV. Stuttgart: Metzler; Munich: Druckenmüller, 1894–1978.

TEXTS, EDITIONS, TRANSLATIONS

Acta Apostolorum Apocrypha. Pars II. Vol. II. *Acta Philippi et Acta Thomae accedunt Acta Barnabae.* Ed. M. Bonnett. Lipsiae: Teubner, 1903.

Aelian: On the Characteristics of Animals. 3 vols. Trans. A. F. Scholfield. LCL. Cambridge MA: Harvard University Press, 1958.

Aeschines. Trans. C. D. Adams. LCL. Cambridge MA: Harvard University Press, 1919.

Aeschinis quae feruntur epistolae. Ed. E. Drerup. Leipzig: Weicher, 1904.

Aeschylus. 2 vols. Trans. H. W. Smyth. LCL. Cambridge MA: Harvard University Press, 1922–1926.

Alciphron. *The Letters of Alciphron, Aelian and Philostratus.* Ed. and trans. F. Fobes. LCL. Cambridge MA: Harvard University Press, 1979.

Andocides. *Minor Attic Orators.* Vol. 1. Trans. K. J. Maidment. LCL. Cambridge MA: Harvard University Press, 1941.

Antiphon. *Minor Attic Orators.* Vol. 1. Trans. K. J. Maidment. LCL. Cambridge MA: Harvard University Press, 1941.

The Apocrypha and Pseudepigrapha of the Old Testament. Vol. 2. *Pseudepigrapha.* Ed. R. H. Charles. Oxford: Clarendon, 1964.

The Letters of Apollonius of Tyana. A Critical Text with Prolegomena, Translation and Commentary. Ed. R. J. Penella. Leiden: Brill, 1979.

The Apostolic Fathers. 2 vols. Trans. K. Lake. LCL. New York: Putnam's Sons/Macmillan, 1912–1913.

The Apostolic Fathers. Ed. J. B. Lightfoot and J. R. Harmer. Repr.: Grand Rapids MI: Baker Book House, 1984.

Die apostolischen Väter. Ed. F. X. Funk and K. Bihlmeyer. SAQ n.s. 1. Tübingen: Mohr/Siebeck, 1970.

Appian: Roman History. 4 vols. Trans. H. White. LCL. New York: Macmillan, 1912–1928.

Aelii Aristidis Smyrnaei quae supersunt omnia. 2 vols. Ed. B. Keil. Berlin: Weidmann, 1898; repr. 1958.

Aristides: Orations. Vol. 1. Trans. C. A. Behr. LCL. Cambridge MA: Harvard University Press, 1973.

P. Aelius Aristides. The Complete Works. 2 vols. Trans. and ed. C. A. Behr. Leiden: Brill, 1981–1986.

Aristophanes. 3 vols. Trans. B. B. Rogers. LCL. Cambridge MA: Harvard University Press, 1924.

Aristophanis Comoediae. Vol. 1. Ed. F. W. Hall and W. M. Geldart. Oxford: Clarendon, 1976.

Aristophanes Wasps. Ed. D. M. MacDowell. Oxford: Clarendon, 1971.

Aristotle. Trans. H. P. Cooke, H. Tredennick, et al. 23 vols. LCL. Cambridge MA: Harvard University Press, 1938–1960.

[Aristotle]. *De Mundo.* Trans. D. J. Furley. LCL. In *Aristotle. On Sophistical Refutations, On Coming-to-Be and Passing Away.* Cambridge MA: Harvard University Press, 1955.

[Aristotle]. *Rhetorica ad Alexandrum.* Trans. H. Rackham. LCL. In *Aristotle. Problems II.* Cambridge MA: Harvard University Press, 1937.

Athenaeus: Deipnosophistae. Ed. C. Gulick. LCL. Cambridge MA: Harvard University Press, 1978.

Caesar: The Civil Wars. Trans. A. G. Peskett. LCL. Cambridge MA: Harvard University Press, 1914.

Calimachus: Hymns and Epigrams. Ed. A. W. Mair. LCL. Cambridge MA: Harvard University Press, 1977.

Callimachus. *Fragmenta nuper reperta.* Ed. R. Pfeiffer. Bonn: Hanstein, 1923.

Catalogus Codicum Astrologorum Graecorum. Vol. 3, pt. 2. Ed. C. O. Zuretti. Brussels: Lamertin, 1934.

John Chrysostom. *Hom. I-XLIV in I Cor.* Migne, *PG* 61.9-382.

S. Joannis Chrysostomi Interpretatio omnium Epistolarum Paulinarum per Homilias facta. Tom. 3. Ed. F. Field. Oxford: Bibliotheca Patrum, 1845.

Cicero. 28 vols. Trans. G. L. Hendrickson, H. M. Hubbell, et al. Cambridge MA: Harvard University Press, 1912–1972.

Cicero: Epistulae ad Familiares. Vol. 1. Ed. D. R. Shackleton Bailey. Cambridge: Cambridge University Press, 1977.

[Cicero]. *Ad C. Herennium De Ratione Dicendi (Rhetorica ad Herennium).* Trans. H. Caplan. LCL. Cambridge MA: Harvard University Press, 1954.

Cicero's Letters to His Friends. Atlanta: Scholars Press, 1988.

Clement of Alexandria. Trans. G. W. Butterworth. LCL. New York: Putnam's Sons, 1919.

Clement of Alexandria. *Stromateis.* Migne, *PG* 8.685-1382.

Comicorum Atticorum Fragmenta. Vol. 1. Ed. T. Kock. Leipzig: Teubner, 1880.

Comicorum Graecorum Fragmenta. Ed. G. Kaibel. Berlin: Weidmann, 1899.

Corinth: The Inscriptions, 1926-1950. Vol. 8, pt. 3. Ed. J. H. Kent. Princeton: American School of Classical Studies at Athens, 1966.

Corpus Papyrorum Judaicarum. 3 vols. Ed. V. Tcherikover and A. Fuks. Cambridge MA: Harvard University Press, 1960.

Corpus Scriptorum Historiae Byzantinae. Ed. W. Dindorff. Bonn, 1829.

Cramer, J. A., ed. *Catenae in Sancti Pauli Epistolas ad Corinthios*. Oxford: Oxford University Press, 1841.

The Cynic Epistles. Ed. A. J. Malherbe. SBLSBS 12. Missoula MT: Scholars Press, 1977.

Demetrius. On Style. Trans. W. R. Roberst. LCL. In *Aristotle* vol. 23, *The Poetics*. Cambridge MA: Harvard University Press, 1927.

Demosthenes. 7 vols. Trans. J. H. Vince, C. A. Vince, et al. LCL. Cambridge MA: Harvard University Press, 1930–1949.

Demosthenis orationes. Vol. 3. Ed. F. Blass. Leipzig: Teubner, 1907.

Demosthenis orationes. Vol. 4. Ed. S. Butcher and W. Rennie. Oxford: Clarendon, 1931.

Dio Cassius: Roman History. 9 vols. Trans. E. Cary. LCL. Cambridge MA: Harvard University Press, 1914–1927.

Dio Chrysostom. 5 vols. Trans. J. W. Cohoon and H. L. Crosby. LCL. Cambridge MA: Harvard University Press, 1932–1951.

Diodorus Siculus. 12 vols. Trans. C. H. Oldfather, L. L. Sherman, *et al*. LCL. Cambridge MA: Harvard University Press, 1933–1967.

Diogenes Laertius: Lives of Eminent Philosophers. 2 vols. Trans. R. P. Hicks. LCL. Cambridge MA: Harvard University Press, 1925.

Dionysius of Halicarnassus: Critical Essays. 2 vols. Trans. S. Usher. LCL. Cambridge MA: Harvard University Press, 1974–1985.

Dionysius of Halicarnassus: Roman Antiquities. 7 vols. Trans. E. Cary. LCL. Cambridge MA: Harvard University Press, 1937–1950.

Elegy and Iambus. Vol. 2. Ed. J. M. Edmonds. New York: Putnam's Sons, 1931.

Epicorum Graecorum Fragmenta. Ed. G. Kinkel. Leipzig: Teubner, 1877.

Epictetus. 2 vols. Trans. W. A. Oldfather. Cambridge MA: Harvard University Press, 1925–1928.

Epistolographi Graeci. Ed. R. Hercher. Paris: Didot, 1871.

Euripides. 4 vols. Trans. A. S. Way. LCL. New York: Macmillan/Putnam's Sons, 1912.

Eubebii Pamphili praeparatio evangelica. 4 vols. Trans. E. H. Gifford. Oxford: Academy, 1903.

Eusebius. Ecclesiastical History. 2 vols. Trans. K. Lake and J. E. L. Oulton. LCL. Cambridge MA: Harvard University Press, 1926–1932.

Eusebius Werke. Achter Band. Praeparatio Evangelica. Ed. K. Mras. GCS. Berlin: Akademie-Verlag, 1956.

Eustathius. *Commentarii ad Homeri Iliadem et Odysseam*. Leipzig: Teubner, 1825.

Fragmenta Historicorum Graecorum. 5 vols. Ed. C. Müller. Paris: Didot, 1841–1970.

Die Fragmente der griechischen Historiker. 3 vols. Ed. F. Jacoby. Berlin: Weidmann; Leiden: Brill, 1923–1950.

Die Fragmente der Vorsokratiker. 3 vols. Ed. H. Diels and W. Kranz. Berlin: Weidmann, 1974–1975.

Gnostische Schriften in koptischer Sprache aus dem Codex Brucianus. TU 8, 1-2. Leipzig: Hinrichs, 1892.

The Greek Anthology. 5 vols. Trans. W. R. Paton. LCL. Cambridge MA: Harvard University Press, 1979.

The Greek Bucolic Poets. Trans. J. M. Edmonds. LCL. London: Macmillan, 1912.

The Greek Magical Papyri in Translation, Including the Demotic Spells. Ed. H. D. Betz, R. Kotansky, et al. Chicago: University of Chicago, 1986.

Greek Papyri in the British Museum. Ed. F. G. Kenyon. London: British Museum, 1893– .

The Hebrew-English Edition of the Babylonian Talmud: Ta'anith. Ed. J. Rabbinowitz. London: Soncino, 1984.

Hellenica Oxyrhynchia. Ed. P. B. Grenfell and A. S. Hunt. Oxford: Clarendon, 1090.

Hellenica Oxyrhynchia. Ed. V. Bartoletti. Leipzig: Teubner, 1959.

Hennecke, E. *New Testament Apocrypha.* 2 vols. Ed. W. Schneemelcher. Trans. R. McL. Wilson. Philadelphia: Fortress Press, 1963.

Hermes Trismegiste, Corpus Hermeticum. 4 vols. Ed. A. D. Nock and A. J. Festugiere. Paris: Société d'Edition "Les Belles Lettres," 1980.

Hermogenes Opera. Ed. H. Rabe. Stuttgart: Teubner, 1969.

[Herodes Atticus]. ΠΕΡΙ ΠΟΛΙΤΕΙΑΣ. *Ein politisches Pamphlet aus Athen 404 vor Chr.* Ed. Drerup. *Studien zur Geschichte und Kultur des Altertums,* vol. 2, pt. 1. Paderborn: Schöningh, 1908.

Herodotus. 4 vols. Trans. A. D. Godley. LCL. Cambridge MA: Harvard University Press, 1921–1925.

Hesiod, The Homeric Hymns and Homerica. H. G. Evelyn-White. LCL. Cambridge MA: Harvard University Press, 1977.

Hippocrates and the Fragments of Heracleitus. 4 vols. Trans. W. H. S. Jones and E. T. Withington. LCL. Cambridge MA: Harvard University Press, 1930–1934.

Horace: Satires, Epistles, Ars Poetica. Trans. H. R. Fairclough. LCL. Cambridge MA: Harvard University Press, 1979.

Inscriptiones Graecae. Ed. F. Hiller von Gaertringen. Vol. 12, fasc. 1. Berlin: Reimer, 1895.

Inscriptiones graecae ad res romanas pertinentes. 4 vols. Ed. R. Cagnat. Chicago: Ares, 1975.

Iscrizioni pompeiane: La Vita pubblica. Ed. G. O. Onorato. Florence, 1957.

Isocrates. 3 vols. Trans. G. Norlin and L. Van Hook. LCL. Cambridge MA: Harvard University Press, 1928–1945.

Jebb, R. C. *Selections from the Attic Orators.* London: Macmillan, 1957.

Josephus. 9 vols. Trans. S. St. J. Thackeray, R. Marcus and L. H. Feldman. LCL. Cambridge MA: Harvard University Press, 1956–1965.

The Works of the Emperor Julian. 3 vols. Trans. W. C. Wright. LCL. Cambridge MA: Harvard University Press, 1913.

Imp. Caesaris Flavii Claudii Iuliani epistulae leges poemata. Ed. J. Bidaz and F. Cumont. Paris: Didot, 1922.

Justinus' des Philosophen und Märtyrers Apologien. Ed. J. Pfättisch. Münster: Aschendorff, 1933.

Livy. 14 vols. Trans. B. O. Foster, F. G. Moore, et al. LCL. Cambridge MA: Harvard University Press, 1919–1959.

Lucian. 8 vols. Trans. A. M. Harmon, K. Kilburn and M. D. Macleod. LCL. Cambridge MA: Harvard University Press, 1913–1967.

Lyrica Graeca Selecta Ed. D. L. Page. Oxford: Oxford University Press, 1968.

Lysias. Trans. W. R. M. Lamb. LCL. Cambridge MA: Harvard University Press, 1930.

The Third and Fourth Books of Maccabees. Ed. and trans. M. Hadas. New York: KTAV, 1976.

Manilius. *Astronomica.* Trans. G. P. Goold. LCL. Cambridge MA: Harvard University Press, 1977.

Marcus Aurelius. Trans. C. R. Haines. LCL. Cambridge MA: Harvard University Press, 1916, rev. ed. 1930.

Mekilta de-Rabbi Ishmael. 3 vols. Ed. J. Lauterbach. Philadelphia: Jewish Publication Society of America, 1933.

Menander Rhetor. Ed. and trans. D. A. Russell and N. G. Wilson. Oxford: Clarendon Press, 1981.

"Musonius Rufus. 'The Roman Socrates.' " Ed. and trans. C. E. Lutz. *YCIS* 10 (1947): 1-147.

Novum Testamentum Graece. 26th ed. Ed. E. Nestle. Rev. and ed. K. Aland, et al. Stuttgart: Deutsche Bibelgesellschaft, 1979; 7th ptg. 1983.

Novum Testamentum Graece. Ed. C. Tischendorf. 2 vols. Leipzig: Giesecke & Devrient, 1872.

Orientis Graeci Inscriptiones Selectae. 2 vols. Ed. W. Dittenberger. Leipzig: Hirzel, 1903-1905.

The Oxyrhynchus Papyri. Ed. B. P. Grenfell and A. S. Hunt, et al. London: Egypt Exploration Fund, 1898–   .

Papyri Graecae Magicae: Die Griechischen Zauberpapyri. Ed. K. Preisendanz. Stuttgart: Teubner, 1973.

Petronius. Trans. M. Heseltine. LCL. Cambridge MA: Harvard University Press, 1969.

Philo. 12 vols. Trans. F. H. Colson, G. H. Whitaker, et al. LCL. Cambridge MA: Harvard University Press, 1929–1953.

Philo, Supplement I: Questions and Answers on Genesis. Trans. R. Marcus. LCL. Cambridge MA: Harvard University Press, 1971.

Philo, Supplement II: Questions and Answers on Exodus. Trans. R. Marcus. LCL. Cambridge MA: Harvard University Press, 1949.

Philostratus: The Life of Apollonius of Tyana. 2 vols. Trans. F. C. Conybeare. LCL. Cambridge MA: Harvard University Press, 1912.

Philostratus and Eunapius: The Lives of the Sophists. Trans. W. C. Wright. LCL. New York: Putnam's Sons, 1922.

Pindar. Sir J. E. Sandys. LCL. Cambridge MA: Harvard University Press, 1919.

Plato. 12 vols. Trans. H. N. Fowler, W. R. M. Lamb, et al. LCL. Cambridge MA: Harvard University Press, 1914–1935.

Plato. Epistulae. Ed. J. Moore-Blunt. BT. Leipzig: Teubner, 1985.

Plato, Gorgias. Ed. E. R. Dodds. Oxford: Clarendon, 1959.

Pliny: Letters and Panegyricus. 2 vols. Trans. B. Radice. LCL. Cambridge MA: Harvard University Press, 1969.

Plotinus. 7 vols. Trans. A. H. Armstrong. LCL. Cambridge MA: Harvard University Press, 1985.

Plutarch's Lives. 11 vols. Trans. B. Perrin. LCL. Cambridge MA: Harvard University Press, 1914–1926.

Plutarch's Moralia. 15 vols. Trans. F. C. Babbitt, W. Helmbold, et al. LCL. Cambridge MA: Harvard University Press, 1927–1969.

Polybius. 6 vols. Trans. W. R. Paton. LCL. Cambridge MA: Harvard University Press, 1922–1927.

Quintilian. 4 vols. Trans. H. E. Butler. LCL. New York: Putnam's Sons, 1921–1922.

Res Gestae Divi Augusti: The Achievements of the Divine Augustus. Ed. P. A. Brunt and J. M. Moore. Oxford: Oxford University Press, 1967.

Rhetores Graeci. 3 vols. Ed. L. Spengel. Leipzig: Teubner, 1854–1956.

Sallust. Trans. J. C. Rolfe. LCL. Cambridge MA: Harvard University Press, 1921; rev. ed. 1931.

Sallust: Invective und Episteln. Ed. and trans. K. Vretska. Heidelberg: Winter, 1961.

Sammelbuch griechischer Urkunden aus Ägypten. Ed. F. Preisigke. Wiesbaden: Harrasowitz, 1950.

Seneca: Ad Lucilium Epistulae Morales. 3 vols. Trans. R. M. Gummere. LCL. Cambridge MA: Harvard University Press, 1918–1925; rev. ed. 1943, 1953.

Seneca: Moral Essays. Trans. J. W. Basore. 3 vols. LCL. Cambridge MA: Harvard University Press, 1928–1935.

Septuaginta. Ed. A. Rahlfs. Stuttgart: Deutsche Bibelgesellschaft, 1935.

Sifra, Commentar zu Leviticus aus dem Anfange des III. Jahrhunderts. Ed. R. ben David with Masoret ha-Talmud by J. H. Weiss. Vienna: Schlossberg, 1862.

Sophocles. 2 vols. Trans. F. Storr. LCL. Cambridge MA: Harvard University Press, 1912–1923.

Spengel, L., ed. *Rhetores Graeci.* 3 vols. BT. Leipzig: Teubner, 1853–1956.

Staab, K. *Pauluskommentare aus der griechischen Kirche.* NTAbh 15. Munster: Aschendorff, 1933.

Stoicorum Veterum Fragmenta. 4 vols. Ed. Arnim. Leipzig: Teubner, 1905–1924.

Strabo: Geography. 8 vols. Trans. H. L. Jones. LCL. Cambridge MA: Harvard University Press, 1917–1932.

Suetonius. 2 vols. Trans. J. C. Rolfe. LCL. Cambridge MA: Harvard University Press, 1914.

Sylloge Inscriptionum Graecarum. 4 vols. Ed. W. Dittenberger. Leipzig: Hirzel, 1915–1924³.

Tacitus: Histories and Annals. 4 vols. Trans. C. H. Moore and J. Jackson. LCL. Cambridge MA: Harvard University Press, 1925–1937.

The Talmud of Babylonia: An American Translation. Vol. 27b: *Tractate Shevuot.* Ed. J. Neusner. Atlanta: Scholars Press, 1992.

Terence. 2 vols. Trans. J. Sargeaunt. LCL. Cambridge MA: Harvard University Press, 1970.

The Testaments of the Twelve Patriarchs. Ed. M. de Jonge. Leiden: Brill, 1978.

Theodoret. *Interpretationes in Pauli epistulas. I Cor.* Migne, *PG* 82.225-376.

Theophylactus. *Epistola catholica Sancti Jacobi apostoli.* Migne. *PG* 125.1188-89.

Thucydides. 4 vols. Trans. C. F. Smith. LCL. Cambridge MA: Harvard University Press, 1919–1923.

Virgil. 2 vols. Trans. H. R. Fairclough. LCL. Cambridge MA: Harvard University Press, 1918; rev. ed. 1934.

Walz, C., ed. *Rhetores Graeci.* 9 vols. Stuttgart: Cotta 1832–1936.

Weichert, V., ed. *Demetrii et Libanii qui feruntur* ΤΥΠΟΙ ΕΠΙΣΤΟΛΙΚΟΙ *et* ΕΠΙΣΤΟΛΙΜΑΙΟΙ ΧΑΡΑΚΤΗΡΕΣ. BT. Leipzig: Teubner, 1910.

Xenophon. 7 vols. Trans. C. L. Brownson, O. J. Todd, et al. LCL. Cambridge MA: Harvard University Press, 1918–1925.

SECONDARY LITERATURE

Aalders, G. J. D. *Plutarch's Political Thought*. Verhandelingen der Koninklijke Nederlandse Akademie van Wetenschappen, afd. Letterkunde 116. Amsterdam/Oxford/New York: North-Holland Publishing Company, 1982.

Abbott, F. "The Theater as a Factor in Roman Politics." *Transactions of the American Philological Association* 38 (1907) 49-56.

_____. "Municipal Politics in Pompeii." *Society and Politics in Ancient Rome*. New York: Scribner's, 1916.

_____. and A. C. Johnson. *Municipal Administration in the Roman Empire*. Princeton: Princeton University Press, 1926.

Adkins, A. *Poetic Craft in the Early Greek Elegists*. Chicago: University of Chicago, 1985.

Alewell, K. *Über das rhetorische PARADEIGMA*. Leipzig: Hoffmann, 1913.

Alföldi, A. "Die Ausgestaltung des monarchischen Zeremoniells am römischen Kaiserhofe." *Mitteilungen des deutschen archäologischen Instituts*, Römische Abteilung 49 (1934): 79-83.

Allo, E.-B. *Saint Paul. Première Epître aux Corinthiens*. Ebib. Paris: LeCoffre, ²1956.

_____. *Saint Paul. Seconde Epître aux Corinthiens*. Ebib. Paris: Gabalda, 1956.

Altaner, B. *Kleine patristische Schriften*. Berlin: Akademie Verlag, 1967.

_____. and A. Stuiber. *Patrologie. Leben, Schriften und Lehre der Kirchenväter*. Freiburg: Herder, 1966.

Amit, M. "Concordia, idéal politique et instrument de propagande," *Iura* 13 (1962): 133-69.

Asheri, D. *Distribuzioni di terre nell' anitca Grecia*. Memorie dell' Accademia delle Scienze di Torino. Ser. 4. No. 10. Turin: Accademia delle Scienze, 1966.

_____. "Leggi greche sul problema dei debiti." *Studi classici e orientali* 18 (1969) 5-122.

Aurenche, O. *Les Groupes d'Alcibiade, de Leogoras et de Teucros*. Paris: Société d'Edition les Belles Lettres, 1974.

Avenarius, G. *Lukians Schrift zur Geschichtsschreibung*. Meisenheim: Glan, 1956.

Bachmann, P. *Der erste Brief des Paulus an die Korinther* KNT 7. Leipzig: Deichert, 1905.

_____. *Der zweite Brief des Paulus an die Korinther*. KNT 8. Leipzig: Deichert, ³1918.

Badian, E. *Foreign Clientelae*. Oxford: Oxford University Press, 1958.

_____. "Tiberius Gracchus and the Beginning of the Roman Revolution." *ANRW* 1/1. Ed. H. Temporini. Berlin: de Gruyter, 1972.

Baird, W. *1 Corinthians*. Atlanta: John Knox Press, 1980.

Baldry, H. C. *The Unity of Mankind in Greek Thought*. Cambridge MA: Harvard University Press, 1965.

Baljon, J. M. S. *De Tekst der Brieven van Paulus aan de Romeinen, de Corinthiërs en de Galatiers als voorwerp van de conjecturalkritiek beschowd*. Utrecht: J. van Boekhoven, 1884.

Bardenhewer, O. *Geschichte der altkirchlichen Literatur*. 2 vols. Freiburg: Herder, 1913.

Barker, A. "The Digression in the Theatetus." *Journal of the History of Philosophy* 14 (1976): 457-62.

Barnett. A. E. *Paul Becomes a Literary Influence*. Chicago: University of Chicago Press, 1941.

Barrett, C. K. *Essays on Paul*. Philadelphia: Westminster, 1982.

_____. *The First Epsitle to the Corinthians*. HNTC. New York: Harper & Row, 1968.

_____. *The Second Epistle to the Corinthians*. HNTC. New York: Harper & Row, 1973.

Bartchy, S. *Mallon Chresai: First-Century Slavery and the Interpretation of 1 Corinthians 7:21*. SBLDS 11. Missoula, MT: Scholars Press, 1973.

Bauer, W. *Orthodoxy and Heresy in Earliest Christianity*. Trans. Philadelphia Seminar on Christian Origins. Philadelphia: Fortress Press, 1971.

Bauernfeind, O. "Wachsen in allen Stücken," *ZST* 14 (1937): 480-89.

_____. *Eid und Frieden*. Stuttgart: Kohlhammer, 1956.

Baur, F. C. "Die Christuspartei in ker korinthischen Gemeinde, der Gegensatz des paulinsichen und petrinischen Christentums in der ältesten Kirche, der Apostel Patrus in Rom." *Tübinger Zeitschrift fur Theologie* 4 (1831): 61-206. Repr.: *Paul*. London: Williams & Norgate, 1875.

Beck, I. "Untersuchungen zur Theorie des Genos Symbuleutikon." Diss. Hamburg, 1970.

Bell, H. I. *Jews and Christians in Egypt: The Jewish Troubles in Alexandria and the Athanaslan Controversy, Illustrated by Texts from the Greek Papyri*. London: British Museum, 1924.

Belleville, L. "A Letter of Apologetic Self-Commendation: 2 Cor. 1:8-7:16." *NovT* 31/2 (1989): 142-63.

Belser, J. E. *Die Epistel des heiligen Jakobus*. Freiburg: Herder, 1909.

Bengel, J. A. *Gnomon of the New Testament*. 3 vols. Trans. A. Fausset. Edinburgh: T.&T. Clark, 1877.

Béranger, J. "Remarques sur la 'concordia' dans la propagande monétaire impériale et la nature du principat." In *Beiträge zur Alten Geschichte und deren Nachleben. Festschrift F. Altheim*, 477-91. Berlin: DeGruyter, 1969.

_____. *Recherches sur l'aspect idéologique du principat*. Bâle, 1953.

Berger, K. *Die Amen-Worte Jesu: Eine Untersuchung zum Problem der Legitimation in apokalyptischer Rede.* Berlin: de Gruyter, 1970.

Berlinger, L. "Beiträge zur inoffiziellen Titulatur der romischen Kaiser." Diss., Breslau, 1935.

Betz, H. D. *Nachfolge und Nachahmung Jesu Christi im Neuen Testament.* BHTh 37. Tübingen: Mohr-Siebeck, 1967.

_____. "The Problem of Rhetoric and Theology according to the Apostle Paul." *L'Apôtre Paul: Personnalité, Style et conception du ministère.* Ed. A. Vanhoye. BETL 73. Leuven: Peeters, 1986.

_____. *Der Apostel Paulus und die sokratische Tradition: Eine exegetische Untersuchung qu seiner "Apologie" 2 Kor 10-13.* BHTh 45. Tübingen: Mohr/Siebeck, 1972.

_____. *2 Corinthians 8 and 9, A Commentary on Two Administrative Letters of the Apostle Paul.* Hermeneia. Philadelphia: Fortress, 1985.

Beyschlag, W. *Kritisch-exegetisches Handbuch über den Brief des Jacobus.* KEK 15. Göttingen: Vandenhoeck & Ruprecht, 1897.

Bitzer, L. F. "The Rhetorical Situation." *Philosophy and Rhetoric* 1 (1968): 168-71.

Bjerkelund, C. *Parakalo: Form, Funktion und Sinn der parakalo Sätze in den paulinischen Briefen.* Bibliotheca theologlca Norvegica 1. Oslo: Universitetsforlaget, 1967.

Blank, S. "The Curse, the Blaspheny, the Spell, the Oath." *HUCA* 23/1 (1950–1951): 73-96.

Bleek, F. "Erorterungen in Beziehung auf die Briefe Pauli an die Korinther." *ThStKr* 3 (1830): 614-32.

Blum, G. G. *Tradition und Sukzession. Studien zum Normbegriff des Apostolischen von Paulus bis Irenäus.* AGTL 9. Berlin: Lutherisches, 1963.

Boer, W. P. de. *The Imitation of Paul.* Kampen: Kok, 1962.

Bohatec, J. "Inhalt und Reihenfolge der 'Schlagwörter der Erlösungsreligion,' 1 Kor. 1:26-31." *TZ* 4 (1948): 252-71.

Bonniec, H. Le. "Aspects religieux de la guerre à Rome." *Problèmes de la querre à Rome.* Ed. J.-P. Brisson. Paris: Sueil, 1969.

Bornkamm, G. *Early Christian Experience.* New York: Harper & Row, 1969.

_____. *Die Vorgeschichte des sogenannten Zweiten Korintherbriefes.* SHAW.PH 1961. 2. Abhandlung. Heidelberg: Winter, 1961.

Böttrich, C. *Weltweisheit, Menschheitsethik, Urkult: Studien zum slavischen Henochbuch.* Tübingen: Mohr/Siebeck, 1992.

Bousset, W. *Der erste Brief an die Korinther. Die Schriften des Neuen Testaments.* Vol. 2. Ed. W. Bousset and H. Heitmuller. Göttingen: Vandenhoeck & Ruprecht, [3]1917.

_____. *Der zweite Brief an die Korinther*. Göttingen: Vandenhoeck & Ruprecht, ²1908.

_____. *Die Evangeliencitate Justins des Märtyrers in ihrem Wert für die Evangelienkritik von neuem untersucht*. Göttingen: Huth, 1891.

Bowersock, G. W. *Greek Sophists in the Roman Empire*. Oxford: Clarendon Press, 1969.

Bowyer, W. *Critical Conjectures and Observations on the New Testament, collected from various Authors*. London, ³1782.

Brink, C. O. *Horace on Poetry, II: The Ars Poetica*. Cambridge: Cambridge University Press, 1971.

Bruce, F. F. *1 and 2 Corinthians*. NCBC. Grand Rapids MI: Eerdmans, 1971.

Brun, L. "Noch einmal die Schriftnorm I Kor. 4:6." *TSK* 103 (1931): 453-56.

Brunt, P. A. "'Amicitia' in the Late Roman Republic." *Proceedings of the Cambridge Philological Society* 191 (1965): 1-20.

_____. *Social Conflicts in the Roman Republic*. London: Chatto & Windus, 1971.

Bünker, M. *Briefformular und rhetorische Disposition im 1. Korintherbrief*. GTA 28. Göttingen: Vandenhoeck & Ruprecht, 1984.

Bultmann, R. *Faith and Understanding*. New York: Harper & Row, 1969.

_____. *The Gospel of John: A Commentary*. Philadelphia: Westminster, 1971.

_____. *Der Stil der paulinischen Predigt und die kynisch-stoische Diatribe*. Göttingen: Vandenhoeck & Ruprecht, 1910; repr. 1984.

_____. *Theology of the New Testament*. 2 vols. Trans. Kendrick Grobel. New York: Scribner's, 1951 and 1955.

_____. *Der zweite Brief an die Korinther*. KEK 6. Ed. E. Dinkler. Göttingen: Vandenhoeck & Ruprecht, 1976.

Cadbury, H. J. "Erastus of Corinth." *JBL* 50 (1931): 42-58.

Cairns, F. "Concord in the *Aeneid* of Virgil," *Klio* 67 (1985): 210-15.

_____. *Generic Composition in Greek and Latin Poetry*. Edinburgh: University of Edinburgh Press, 1972.

_____. *Virgil's Augustan Epic*. Cambridge: Cambridge University Press, 1989.

Calhoun, G. M. *Athenian Clubs in Politics and Legislation*. Austin: University of Texas Press, 1913.

Calvin, J. *The First Epistle of Paul the Apostle to the Corinthians*. Trans. J. W. Fraser. Calvin's Commentaries. Grand Rapids MI: Eerdmans, 1960.

Case, S. J. *Studies in Early Christianity*. New York: Century, 1928.

Castrén, P. *Ordo Populusque Pompeianus. Polity and Society in Roman Pompeii*. Rome: Bardi, 1975.

Chadwick, H. "'All Things to All Men' (1 Cor. IX.22)." *NTS* 1 (1955): 261-75.

Clarke, A. *Secular and Christian Leadership in Corinth: A Socio-Historical and Exegetical Study of 1 Corinthians 1-6*. AGAJU 18. Leiden: Brill, 1993.

Clemen, C. *Die Einheitlichkeit der paulinischen Briefe, an Hand der bisher mit bezug auf sie aufgestellten Interpolations- und Compilations-hypothesen geprüft.* Göttingen: Vandenhoeck & Ruprecht, 1894.

Cohen, D. *Law, Violence, and Community in Classical Athens.* KTAH. Cambridge: Cambridge University Press, 1995.

Cole, T. "The Sources and Composition of Polybius VI." *Historia* 13 (1964): 440-47.

Collange, J.-F. *Enigmes de la deuxieme épître de Paul aux Corinthiens: Etude exegetique de 2 Cor 2.14-7.4.* SNTSMS 18. Cambridge: Cambridge University Press, 1972.

Colson, F. H. "Μετεσχημάτισα in 1 Cor. iv.6." *JTS* 17 (1915–1916): 379-84.

Conzelmann, H. *1 Corinthians.* Trans. J. W. Leitch. Hermeneia. Philadelphia: Fortress Press, 1975.

_____. *Heiden-Juden-Christen.* BHTh 62. Tübingen: Mohr-Siebeck, 1981.

Couchoud, P.-L. "Reconstitution et classement des lettres de saint Paul." *Revue d'histoire et de litterature religieuses* 87 (1923): 8-34.

Coulanges, Fustel de. "Le Patronat et la 'commendatio' dans la société romaine." *Les Origenes du systeme feodal.* Paris, 1890.

Dahl, N. A. "Paul and the Church at Corinth according to 1 Cor. 1:10-4:21." In *Christian History and Interpretation: Studies Presented to John Knox*, ed. W. R. Farmer, C. F. D. Moule, and R. R. Niebuhr. Cambridge: Cambridge University Press, 1967. Repr.: in *Studies in Paul.* Minneapolis: Augsburg, 1977.

Dalman, G. *The Words of Jesus.* Edinburgh: T.&T. Clark, 1902.

Dautzenberg, E. "Eid IV: Neues Testament." *TRE* 9 (1982): 379-82.

_____. "Ist das Schwurverbot Mt. 5, 33-37; Jak. 5,12 ein Beispiel für die Torakritik Jesu?" *BZ* 25 (1981): 47-66.

Delling, G. στάσις. *TDNT* 7:568-71.

_____. τέλειος. *TDNT* 8:69-72.

Denniston, J. D. *The Greek Particles.* Oxford: Clarendon, 1950.

_____. *Greek Prose Style.* Oxford: Clarendon, 1952.

Desideri, P. *Dione di Prusa: un intellecttuale greco nell' Impero romano.* Biblioteca di Cultura Contemporanea 135. Firenze, 1978.

Dibelius, M. "Rom und die Christen im ersten Jahrhundert." In *Botschaft und Geschichte. Gesammelte Aufsätze II. Zum Urchristentum und zur hellenistischen Religlonsgeschichte*, ed. H. Kraft, 177-228. Tübingen: Mohr-Siebeck, 1956.

_____. *James: A Commentary on the Epistle of James.* Hermeneia. Philadelphia: Fortress, 1976.

Dietzfelbinger, C. "Die Antithesen der Bergpredigt im Verständnis des Matthäus." *ZNW* 70 (1979): 1-15.

Dinkler, E. *Eirene. Der urchristlicher Friedensgedanke.* SHAW 1973/1. Heidelberg: Winter, 1973.

Dobschutz, E. von. *Die urchristlichen Gemeinden.* Leipzig: Hinrichs, 1902.

Dodd, C. H. *New Testament Studies.* Manchester: Manchester University Press, 1933.

Dover, K. J. *Greek Word Order.* Cambridge: Cambridge University Press, 1960.

Downing, E. οἷον ψυχή: An Essay on Aristotle's *muthos.*" *Classical Antiquity* 3 (1984): 164-78.

Drescher, R. "Der zweite Korintherbrief und die Vorgänge in Korinth seit Abfassung des ersten Korintherbriefes." *ThStKr* 70 (1897): 43-111.

Edelstein, L. *Plato's Seventh Letter.* Leiden: Brill, 1966.

Eggenberger, C. *Die Quellen des politischen Ethik des 1. Klemensbriefes.* Zurich: Zwingli, 1951.

Ehrhardt, A. A. T. *Politische Metaphysik von Solon bis Augustin.* 2 vols. Tübingen: Mohr-Siebeck, 1959.

Ellis, E. E. "Exegetical Patterns in 1 Corinthians and Romans." *Prophecy and Hermeneutic in Early Christianity.* Tübingen: Mohr-Siebeck, 1978.

Engels, D. *Roman Corinth: An Alternative Model for the Classical City.* Chicago: University of Chicago, 1990.

Epstein, D. F. *Personal Enmity in Roman Politics 218–43 B.C.* London: Croom Helm, 1987.

Erasmus, D. *In Novum Testamentum Annotationes, ab ipso autore iam postremum recognitae.* Basel: Apud Io. Frobenium, 1542.

_____. *Paraphrasis in duas epistolas Pauli ad Corinthios.* Lovanii, 1519. Repr.: Opera Omnia, vol. 7. Lugduni Batavorum: Petrus van der Aa, 1706.

Estius, W. *In omnes Divi Pauli Apostoli Epistolas commentariorum.* Moguntiae: Sumptibus F. Kirchhemii, 1859.

Ewald, G. H. *Die Sendschreiben des Apostels Paulus überstezt und erklärt.* Göttingen: Dieterich, 1857.

Feine, P. *Jesus Christus und Paulus.* Leipzig: Hinrichs, 1902.

Ferguson, J. *Moral Values in the Ancient World.* London: Methuen, 1958.

Feuillet, A. *Le Christ Sagesse de Dieu d'apres les epitres pauliniennes.* EB. Paris: Gabalda, 1966.

Filson, F. V. "The Significance of the Early House Churches." *JBL* 58 (1939): 105-12.

Finley, M. I. *Politics in the Ancient World.* Cambridge: Cambridge University Press, 1983.

Fiore, B. "'Covert Allusion' in 1 Corinthians 1-4." *CBQ* 45 (1985): 85-102.

_____. *The Function of Personal Example in the Socratic and Pastoral Epistles.* AnBib 105. Rome: Biblical Institute, 1986.

Fiorenza, E. S. *In Memory of Her. A Feminist Theological Reconstruction of Christian Origins.* New York: Crossroad, 1983.

Franke, P. R. *Kleinasien zur Römerzeit. Griechisches Leben im Spiegel der Münzen.* Munich: Beck, 1968.

Franklin, James L. *Pompeii: The Electoral Programmata, Campaigns and Politics 71-79.* University Park: Pennsylvania State University Press, 1980.

Freese, W. L. *Der Parteikampf der Reichen und der Armen in Athen zur Zeit der Demokratie.* Stralsund: C. Löffler, 1848.

Fritz, K. von. *The Theory of the Mixed Constitution. A Critical Analysis of Polybius' Political Ideas.* New York: Columbia University Press, 1954.

Fritzsche, K. F. A. *De nonnullis posterioris Pauli ad Corinthios epistolae locis dissertationes duae.* Leipzig: Reclam, 1824.

Fuchs, H. *Augustin und der antike Friedensgendanke.* Neue Philologische Untersuchungen 3. Ed. W. Jaeger. Berlin: Weidmann, 1926.

Fuks, A. *The Ancestral Constitution.* London: Routledge & Kegan Paul, 1953.

––––––. "Plato and the Social Question: The Problem of Poverty and Riches in the *Republic.*" *Ancient Society* 8 (1977): 49-83.

––––––. "The Jewish Revolt in Egypt (A.D. 115–17) in the Light of the Papyri." In *Social Conflict in Ancient Greece*, 322-49. Leiden: Brill, 1984.

––––––. "Social Revolution in Dyme in 116–114 B.C.E." In *Studies in History*, ed. D. Asheri. Scripta Hierosolymitana 23. Jerusalem: Magnes, 1972.

Funk, R. W. "The Apostolic Parousia: Form and Significance." In *Christian History and Interpretation: Studies Presented to John Knox*, ed. W. R. Farmer, C. F. D. Moule, and R. R. Niebuhr, 249-69. Cambridge: Cambridge University Press, 1967.

Funke, P. *Homonoia und Arche: Athen und die griechische Staatenwelt vom Ende des peloponnesischen Krieges bis zum Königsfrieden (404/3-387/6 v. Chr.).* Wiesbaden: Franz Steiner, 1980.

Furnish, V. *II Corinthians.* AB 32A. Garden City NY: Doubleday, 1984.

Galsterer, H. "Politik im römischen Städten: Die 'Seditio' des Jahres 59 N. Chr. In Pompeii." In *Studien zur antiken Sozialgeschichte. Festschrift F. Vittinghoff*, ed. W. Eck, H. Galsterer, and H. Wolff, 322-38. Köln: Böhlau, 1980.

Gehrke, H.-J. *Stasis. Untersuchungen zu den inneren Kriegen in den griechischen Staaten des 5. und 4. Jahrhunderts v. Chr.* Vestigia 35. Munich: Beck, 1985.

Gelzer, M. *Die Nobilität der Römischen Republik.* Leipzig: Teubner, 1912.

Georgi, D. *Theocracy in Paul's Praxis and Theology.* Minneapolis: Fortress Press, 1991.

––––––. *Die Gegner des Paulus im 2. Korintherbrief: Studien zur religiösen Propaganda in der Spätantike.* WMANT 11. Neukirchen-Vluyn: Neukirchener, 1964.

_____. *The Opponents of Paul in Second Corinthians.* Philadelphia: Fortress, 1986.

_____. "Second Letter to the Corinthians." *IDBSup.* 183-86.

Gilbert, G. *Beiträge zur Entwicklungsgeschichte des griechischen Gerichtsverfahren.* Jahrbuch für classischen Philologie. Suppl. 23. Leipzig: Teubner, 1896.

Godet, F. *Commentary on St. Paul's First Epistle to the Corinthians.* 2 vols. Trans. A. Cusin. Edinburgh: T.&T. Clark, 1889.

Goldstein, J. A. *The Letters of Demosthenes.* New York: Columbia University Press, 1968.

Goodenough, E. R. "The Political Philosophy of Hellenistic Kingship," *Yale Classical Studies* 1 (1928): 55-102.

_____. *The Jurisprudence of the Jewish Courts in Egypt: Legal Administration by the Jews under the Early Roman Empire as described by Philo Judaeus.* New Haven: Yale University Press, 1929.

Goodman, M. *The Ruling Class of Judaea: The Origins of the Jewish Revolt against Rome A.D. 66-70.* Cambridge: Cambridge University Press, 1987.

Goodspeed, E. J. "Pseudonymity and Pseudepigraphy in Early Christian Literature." In *New Chapters in New Testament Study,* 169-88. New York: Macmillan, 1937.

_____. *Die ältesten Apologeten.* Göttingen: Vandenhoeck & Ruprecht, 1914.

Goudge, H. L. *The Second Epistle to the Corinthians.* London: Hodder & Stoughton, 1927.

Grant, R. M. *Augustus to Constantine.* New York: Harper & Row, 1970.

_____. "Hellenistic Elements in 1 Corinthians." In *Early Christian Origins. Studies in Honor of Harold R. Willoughby,* ed. A. Wikgren, 60-66. Chicago: Quandrangle Books, 1961.

_____. "The Wisdom of the Corinthians." In *The Joy of Study: Papers on the New Testament and Related Subjects Presented to Honor F. C. Grant,* ed. S. E. Johnson, 51-55. New York: Macmillan, 1951.

Grant, R. M. and H. Graham. *The Apostolic Fathers.* Vol. 2. *First and Second Clement.* New York: Thomas Nelson, 1965.

Grosheide F. W. *Commentary on the First Epistle to the Corinthians.* NICNT. Grand Rapids MI: Eerdmans, 1953.

Grossmann, G. *Politische Schlagworter aus der Zeit des Peloponnesischen Krieges.* Zurich: Leemann, 1950.

Grotius, H. *Annotationes in Novum Testamentum.* Vol. 2. Paris: Sumptibus autoris, 1646.

Grube, G. M. A. *The Greek and Roman Critics.* Toronto: University of Toronto, 1968.

Gruen, E. S. *Roman Politics and the Criminal Courts, 149-70 B.C.* Cambridge MA: Harvard University Press, 1968.

Hahn, F. "Das Ja Paulus und das Ja Gottes. Bemerkungen zu 2 Kor 1,12-2." In *Neues Testament und christliche Existenz, Festschrift für Herbert Braun*, 229-39. Tübingen: Mohr/Siebeck, 1973.

_____. "Ist das textkritische Problem von 2 Kor 1,17 lösbar?" In *Studien zum Text und zur Ethik des Neuen Testaments. Festschrift zum 80. Geburtstag von Heinrich Greeven*, ed. W. Schrage, 158-65. Berlin: de Gruyter, 1986.

Halliwell, S. *Aristotle's Poetics*. Chapel Hill: University of North Carolina Press, 1986.

Halmel, A. *Der zweite Korintherbrief des Apostels Paulus*. Halle: Niemeyer, 1904.

Harnack, A. von. *Die Briefsammlung des Apostel Paulus*. Leipzig: Hinrichs, 1926.

_____. *Marcion: Das Evangelium vom Fremden Gott*. TU 45. Leipzig: Hinrichs, [2]1924.

Hausrath, A. von. *Der Vier-Capitel-Brief des Paulus an die Korinther*. Heidelberg: Bassermann, 1870.

Heath, M. *Unity in Greek Poetics*. Oxford: Clarendon, 1989.

_____. *The Poetics of Greek Tragedy*. London, 1987.

Heinimann, F. φύσις und νόμος. *Herkunft und Bedeutung einer Antithese im griechischen Denken*. Schweizer Beiträge zur Altertumswissenschaft 1. Zürich, 1945.

Heinrici, C. F. G. *Der erste Brief an die Korinther*. KEK 5. Göttingen: Vandenhoeck & Ruprecht, [8]1896.

_____. *Das erste Sendschreiben des Apostel Paulus an clie Korinther*. Berlin: Hertz, 1880.

_____. *Der zweite Brief an die Korinther*. KEK 6. Göttingen: Vandenhoeck & Ruprecht, 1900.

_____. *Das zweite Sendschreiben des Apostel Paulus an die Korinther*. Berlin: Hertz, 1887.

_____. "Zur Geschichte der Anfänge paulinischer Gemeinden." 1 (1877) 119-32.

Hellegouarc'h, J. *Le vocabulaire Latin des relations et des partis politiques sous la Republique*. Paris: Société d'Edition les Belles Lettres, 1963.

Hengel, M. *Eigentum und Reichtum in der frühen Kirche: Aspekte einer frühchristlichen Sozialgeschichte*. Stuttgart: Calwer, 1973.

Héring, J. *The First Epistle of Saint Paul to the Corinthians*. Trans. A. W. Heathcote and P. J. Allcock. London: Epworth, 1962.

_____. *La Seconde Epître aux Corinthiens*. Neuchatel: Delachaux, 1958.

Hirzel, R. *Der Eid: Ein Beitrag zu seiner Geschichte*. Leipzig: Hirzel, 1902.

Hofmann, J. C. K. Von. *Die heilige Schrift neuen Testaments zusammenhängend untersucht II/3: Der zweite Brief Paul; an die Korinther.* Nördlingen: Beck, ²1877.

Höistad, R. *Cynic Hero and Cynic King.* Lund: Carl Bloms, 1948.

Hölscher, T. "Concordia." In *Lexicon Iconographicum Mythologiae Classicae* *5.1,* 479-98. Zürich/München: Artemis, 1990.

Holmes, S. T. "Aristippus in and out of Athens," *The American Political Science Review* 73 (1979): 113-28.

Holsten, C. *Das Evangelium des Paulus.* Vol. 1. *Der Brief an die Gemeinden Galatiens und der erste Brief an die Gemeinde in Korinth.* Berlin: Reimer, 1880.

Holtzmann, H. *Die Synoptiker.* HCNT 1/1. Tübingen: Mohr/Siebeck, ³1901.

Hooker, M. D. "Beyond the Things Which Are Written: An Examination of 1 Cor. IV.6." *NTS* 10 (1964): 127-32.

Horrell, David A. *The Social Ethos of the Corinthian Correspondence. Interests and Ideology from 1 Corinthians to 1 Clement.* Edinburgh: T.&T. Clark, 1996.

Horsley, R. A. "The Wisdom of Word and Words of Wisdom in Corinth." *CBQ* 39 (1977): 224-39.

Hosek, R. "Die Auffassung der Concordia bei den Dichtern des Prinzipats," *Sbornik Praci Filosoficke Fakulty Brnenske University* 12 (1967): 153-62.

Hughes, P. *Paul's Second Epistle to the Corinthians.* NICNT. Grand Rapids MI: Eerdmans, 1962.

Hurd, J. C. *The Origin of 1 Corinthians.* London: S.P.C.K., 1965. New ed. (corr. and new preface): Macon GA: Mercer University Press, 1983.

Hutter, H. *Politics as Friendship: The Origins of Classical Notions of Politics in the Theory and Practise of Friendship.* Waterloo, Ont.: Wilfrid Laurier University Press, 1978.

Hyldahl, N. "Die Frage nach der literarischen Einheit des Zweiten Korintherbrief." *ZNW* 64 (1973): 289-306.

Ingenkamp, H. G. *Untersuchungen zu den pseudoplatonischen Definitionen.* Wiesbaden: Harrasowitz, 1967.

Jacoby, E. "De Antiphontis Sophistae περὶ ὁμονοίας libro." Diss., Berlin, 1908.

Jaeger, W. *Early Christianity and Greek Paideia.* Cambridge MA: Harvard University Press, 1961.

_____. "Echo eines unerkannten Tragikerfragments in Clemens' Brief an die Korinther." *RhMus* 102 (1959): 330-40.

_____. *Paideia: The Ideals of Greek Culture.* 3 vols. Trans. G. Highet. New York: Oxford University Press, 1939–1944.

_____. "Tyrtaeus on True Arete." *Werner Jaeger. Five Essays.* Trans. A. M. Fiske. Montreal: Casilini, 1966, 103-42.

Jal, P. "Pax civilis-concordia." *Rev. Et. Lat.* 39 (1961): 210-31.

Jannaris, A. N. *An Historical Greek Grammar* (London, 1897).

Jeremias, J. *Unbekannte Jesusworte.* Göttingen: Vandenhoeck & Ruprecht, 1948.

Jewett, R. *Paul's Anthropological Terms. A Study of their Use in Conflict Settings.* Leiden: Brill, 1971.

Jocelyn, H. D. "The Roman Nobility and the Religion of the Republican State." *JRH* 4 (1966/1967): 89-104.

Johanson, B. *To All the Brethren. A Test-Linguistic and Rhetorical Approach to 1 Thessalonians.* CBNTS 16. Stockholm: Almqvist & Wiksell, 1987.

Jones, A. H. M. "The Election of the Metropolitan Magistrates in Egypt." *JEA* 24 (1938): 62-74.

_____. *The Greek City from Alexander to Justinian.* Oxford: Clarendon Press, 1940.

Jones, C. P. *Plutarch and Rome.* Oxford: Clarendon Press: 1971.

_____. *The Roman World of Dio Chrysostom.* Cambridge MA: Harvard University Press, 1978.

_____. "A New Letter of Marcus Aurelius to the Athenians." *ZPE* 8 (1971): 161-83.

Jones, F. S. *"Freiheit" in den Briefen des Apostels Paulus. Eine historische, exegetische und religionsgeschichtliche Studie.* GTA 34. Göttingen: Vandenhoeck & Ruprecht, 1987.

Jost, K. *Das Beispiel und Vorbild der Vorfahren bei den attischen Rednern und Geschichtsschreibern bis Demosthenes.* Rhetorische Studien 19. Paderborn: Schöningh, 1936.

Judge, E. A. "The Early Christians as a Scholastic Community." *JRH* 1 (1960): 129-41.

_____. *The Social Pattern of Christian Groups in the First Century.* London: Tyndale, 1960.

Jülicher, A. *Einleitung in das Neue Testament.* Tübingen: Mohr/Siebeck, 1906.

Käsemann, E. *New Testament Questions of Today.* Philadelphia: Fortress Press, 1969.

_____. "Die Legitimität des Apostels. Eine Untersuchung zu II Korinther 10-13." *ZNW* 41 (1942): 42-64.

Kagan, D. G. *The Great Dialogue. History of Greek Political Thought from Homer to Polybius.* New York: Free Press, 1965.

Kaser, M. *Das römische Zivilprozessrecht.* Munich: Beck, 1966.

Keil, B. "Ein Logos Systatikos." In *Nachrichten der Göttingen Akademie der Wissenschaften,* 1-41. Phil.-hist. Klasse. Göttingen: Vandenhoeck & Ruprecht, 1913.

Kennedy, J. H. "Are There Two Epistles in 2 Corinthians?" *The Expositor* 6 (1897): 232-94.

_____. *The Second and Third Epistles of St. Paul to the Corinthians*. London: Methuen, 1900.

Kienast, D. "Die Homonoiaverträge in der Kaiserzeit." *JNG* 14 (1964): 51-64.

Kilpatrick, G. D. "Conjectural Emendation in the New Testament." In *New Testament Textual Criticism. Essays in Honor of Bruce M. Metzger*. Oxford: Clarendon Press, 1981.

Klaiber, W. *Rechtfertigung und Gemeinde. Eine Untersuchung zum paulinischen Kirchenverständnis*. FRLANT 127. Göttingen: Vandenhoeck & Ruprecht, 1982.

Klauck, H.-J. *Hausgemeinde und Hauskirche lm frühen Christentum*. SBS 103. Stuttgart: Katholisches Bibelwerk, 1981.

_____. *Herrenmahl und hellenistischer Kult. Eine religionsgeschichtliche Untersuchung zum ersten Korintherbrief*. NTAbh n.s. 15. Munster: Aschendorff, 1982.

_____. *2. Korintherbrief*. Würzburg: Echter, 1986.

Klek, J. *Symbuleutici qui dicitur sermonis historia critica*. Rhetorische Studien 8. Paderborn: Schöningh, 1919.

Klöpper, A. *Commentar über das zweite Sendschreiben des Apostel Paulus an die Gemeinde zu Korinth*. Berlin: Reimer, 1874.

Klostermann, E. *Das Matthäusevangelium*. HNT 4. Tübingen: Mohr/Siebeck, ²1927.

Koch, L. J. *Fortolkning til Paulus' Andet Brev til Korinthierne* (Niva, ²1927).

Koester, H. *Introduction to the New Testament*. 2 vols. Philadelphia: Fortress Press, 1982.

Kramer, H. "Quid valeat ὁμόνοια in litteris Graecis." Diss., Göttingen, 1915.

Krenkel, M. "Der persönliche und briefliche Verkehr des Apostels mit der Gemeinde zu Korinth." *Beiträge zur Aufhellung der Geschichte und der Briefe des Apostels Paulus*. Braunschweig: Schwetschke, 1895.

Kümmel, W. G. *Introduction to the New Testament*. Nashville: Abingdon, ²1975.

Kutsch, E. "Eure Rede aber sei ja ja, nein nein." *EvT* 20 (1960): 206-18.

Lake, K. *The Earlier Epistles of St. Paul*. London: Rivingtons, 1911.

Lampe, P. *Die stadtrömischen Christen in den ersten beiden Jahrhunderten. Untersuchungen zur Sozialgeschichte*. WUNT II/18. Tübingen: Mohr-Siebeck, 1987.

Landvogt, P. "Epigraphische Untersuchungen über den οἰκονόμος: Ein Beitrag zum hellenistischen Beamtenwesen." Diss. Strasbourg, 1908.

Larsen, J. A. O. "Freedom and Its Obstacles in Ancient Greece." *CPhil* 57 (1962): 230-34.

_____. *Greek Federal States*. Oxford: Oxford University Press, 1968.

_____. *Representative Government in Greek and Roman History*. Berkeley/Los Angeles: University of California Press, 1966.

Lausberg, H. *Handbuch der literarischen Rhetorik*. Munich: Hueber, [2]1973.

Levick, B. "Concordia at Rome." In *Scripta Nummaria Romana to H. Sutherland*, 217-33. London: Spink and Son, 1978.

Lieberman, S. *Greek in Jewish Palestine*. New York: Jewish Theological Seminary, 1942.

Lietzmann, J. *An die Korinther I, II*. Rev. W. G. Kummel. HNT 9. Tübingen: Mohr-Siebeck, 1949.

_____. *Geschichte der Alten Kirche I*. Tübingen: Mohr-Siebeck, 1932.

Lightfoot, J. B. *Notes on the Epistles of St. Paul from Unpublished Commentaries*. London/New York: Macmillan, 1895.

Linton, O. "'Nicht über das hinaus was geschrieben steht' (1 Kor 4,6)." *TSK* 102 (1930): 425-37.

Lintott, A. *Violence, Civil Strife and Revolution in the Classical City*. Baltimore: Johns Hopkins University Press, 1982.

Lisco, H. *Die Entstehung des zweiten Korintherbriefes*. Berlin: Schneider, 1896.

Loenen, D. *Stasis. Enige aspecten van de begrippen partijen klassenstrijd in oud-Griekenland*. Amsterdam: Noord-Hollandsche Uitgevers Maatschappij, 1953.

Loening, T. C. *The Reconciliation Agreement of 403/402 B.C. in Athens. Its Context and Application*. Hermes 53. Stuttgart: Franz Steiner, 1987.

Loisy, A. "Les épîtres de S. Paul." *Revue d'histoire et de litterature religieuses* 7 (1921): 213-50.

Lüdemann, G. *Paul, Apostle to the Gentiles. Studies in Chronology*. Trans. F. S. Jones. Philadelphia: Fortress Press, 1984.

_____. *Paulus, der Heidenapostel. Bd. II. Antipaulinismus im frühen Christentum*. FRLANT 130. Göttingen: Vandenhoeck & Ruprecht, 1983.

Lührmann, D. *Das Offenbarungsverständnis bei Paulus und in den paulinischen Gemeinden*. WMANT 16. NeukirchenVluyn: Neukirchener Verlag, 1965.

Lütgert, W. *Amt und Geist im Kampf*. Gütersloh: Bertelsmann, 1911.

_____. *Freiheitspredigt und Schwarmgeister in Korinth*. BFCT 12/3. Gütersloh: Bertelsmann, 1908.

Lumpe, A. "Exemplum." *RAC* 6 (1966): 1229-57.

Luz, U. *Das Evangelium nach Matthäus (Mt 1-7)*. EKK 1/1. Zürich: Benziger, 1985.

MacDermot, V. *The Books of Jeu and the Untitled Text in the Bruce Codex*. Leiden: Brill, 1978.

MacMullen. R. *Enemies of the Roman Order*. Cambridge MA: Harvard University Press, 1966.

_____. *Roman Social Relations 50 B.C. to A.D. 284*. New Haven: Yale University Press, 1974.

Machelet, C. "Paulus und seine Gegner. Eine Untersuchung zu den Korintherbriefen." *Theokratia*. Ed. W. Dieterich. Leiden: Brill, 1973.

Maiuri, A. "Pompei e Nocera." *Rendiconti della Accademia di archeologia, Napoli* 33 (1958) 35-40.

Malherbe, A. J. *Ancient Epistolary Theorists.* SBLSBS 19. Atlanta: Scholars Press, 1988.

_____. *Paul and the Popular Philosophers.* Minneapolis: Fortress, 1989.

Mann, J. "Oaths and Vows in the Synoptic Gospels." *AJT* 21 (1917): 260-74.

Manson, T. W. *Studies in the Gospels and Epistles.* Ed. M. Black. Manchester: Manchester University Press, 1962.

Maricq, A. "Factions du cirque et partis populaires." *Bulletin de l'Académie royale de Belgique* 36 (1950): 396-421.

Marshall, P. *Enmity in Corinth: Social Conventions in Paul's Relations with the Corinthians.* WUNT 2/23. Tübingen: Mohr-Siebeck, 1987.

Martin, D. *Slavery as Salvation: The Metaphor of Slavery in Pauline Christianity.* New Haven: Yale University Press, 1990.

Martin, J. *Antike Rhetorik: Technik und Methode.* HAW 2/3. Munich: Beck, 1974.

Marxsen, W. *Einleitung in das Neue Testament.* Gütersloh: Mohn, 1963.

Maurer, C. σχίζω. *TDNT* 8:959-65.

May, J. H. "The *Ethica Digressio* and Cicero's *Pro Milone.*" *CJ* 74 (1979): 240-47.

Meeks, W. A. *The First Urban Christians. The Social World of the Apostle Paul.* New Haven/London: Yale University Press, 1983.

Meier, C. *Die Entstehung des politischen bei den Griechen.* Frankfurt: Suhrkamp, 1984.

_____. *Res publica amissa: Eine Studie zu Verfassung und Geschichte der späten römischen Republik.* Wiesbaden: Steiner, 1966.

Meier, M. H. E. "Die Privatschiedsrichter und die öffentlichen Diateten Athens." Diss., Halle, 1846.

Meinertz, M. "Σχίσμα und αἵρεσις im Neuen Testament." *BZ* n.s. 1 (1957): 114-18.

Meinhardt, P. *De forma et usu iuramentorum.* Frommani: Pohle, 1892.

Menzies, A. *The Second Epistle of the Apostle Paul to the Corinthians.* London: Macmillan, 1912.

Merkelbach, R. "Der Rangstreit der Städte Asiens und die Rede des Aelius Aristides über Eintracht." *ZPE* 32 (1978): 287-96.

Merklein, H. "Die Einheitlichkeit des ersten Korintherbriefes." *ZNW* 75 (1984): 153-83.

Merrill, E. T. *Essays in Early Christian History.* London: Macmillan, 1924.

Metzger, B. M. *A Textual Commentary on the Greek New Testament.* London/New York: United Bible Societies, 1971.

Meyer, A. *Das Rätsel des Jacobusbriefes.* Giessen: Töpelmann, 1930.

Meyer, H. A. W. *Der erste Brief an die Korinther.* KEK 1. Göttingen: Vanden-hoeck & Ruprecht, 1839.

Michel, C. *Recueil d'inscriptions greques.* Paris, 1900.

Michel, O. οἶκος. *TDNT* 5:119-59.

Minear, P. "Yes or No: The Demand for Honesty in the Early Church." *NovT* 13 (1971) 1-13.

Mitchell, M. *Paul and the Rhetoric of Reconciliation: An Exegetical Investigation of the Language and Composition of 1 Corinthians.* HUNT 28. Tübingen: Mohr-Siebeck, 1991.

Moffat, J. *The First Epistle of Paul to the Corinthians.* London: Hodder & Stoughton, 1938.

―――. *The Historical New Testament.* New York: Scribner's, 1901.

―――. *An Introduction to the Literature of the New Testament.* New York: Scribner's, ³1918.

Mohrmann, C. "Les origines de la latinite chretienne à Rome." *VC* 3 (1949): 67-106.

Momigliano, A. "Biblical Studies and Classical Studies: Simple Reflections about Historical Method." *Biblical Archaeologist* 42 (1982): 220-27.

―――. *On Pagans, Jews, and Christians.* Middletown CT: Wesleyan University Press, 1987.

―――. "Camillus and Concord." *Classical Quarterly* 46 (1942): 111-120.

Mommsen, T. *History of Rome.* New York: Scribner's, 1900.

Morrow, G. R. *Plato's Epistles.* New York: Harper & Row, 1962.

Moulakis, A. *Homonoia: Eintracht und die Entwicklung eines politischen Bewusstseins.* Munich: List, 1973.

Moule, C. F. D. *An Idiom Book of New Testament Greek.* Cambridge: Cambridge University Press, ²1959.

Mouritsen, H. *Elections, Magistrates and Municipal Elite. Studies in Pompeian Epigraphy.* Rome: Bretschneider, 1988.

Munck, J. "The Church Without Factions. Studies in I Corinthians 1–4." In *Paul and the Salvation of Mankind,* trans. F. Clarke, 135-67. Richmond: John Knox Press, 1959.

Münzer, F. *Römische Adelsparteien und Adelfamilien.* Stuttgart: Metzler, 1920.

Murphy-O'Connor, J. *St. Paul's Corinth. Texts and Archaeology.* GNS 6. Wilmington DE: Glazier, 1983.

―――. *The Theology of the Second Letter to the Corinthians,* Cambridge: Cambridge University Press, 1991.

Mussner, F. *Der Jakobusbrief.* HTKNT 13/1. Freiburg: Herder & Herder, ²1967.

Neil, R. A. *Aristophanes' Knights.* Cambridge: Cambridge University Press, 1901.

Nestle, W. "Die Fabel des Menenius Agrippa." *Klio* 21 (1927): 350-60.

Newman, W. L. *The Politics of Aristotle.* 4 vols. Oxford: Clarendon Press, 1887–1902.

Nippel, W. "Die *plebs urbana* und die Rolle der Gewalt in der späten römischen Republik." In *Vom Elend der Handarbeit,* ed. H. Mommsen and W. Schulz, 70-92. Stuttgart: Klett-Cotta, 1981.

_____. *Mischverfassungstheorie und Verfassungsrealität in Antike und früher Neuzeit.* Stuttgart, 1980.

Nissen, T. "Philologisches zum Text des Hebraeer-und 2. Korintherbriefes." *Philologus* 92 (1937): 247-52.

Nock, A. D. *St. Paul.* New York/London: Harper & Brothers, 1938.

Ober J. *Mass and Elite in Democratic Athens: Rhetoric Ideology, and the Power of the People.* Princeton: Princeton University Press, 1989.

_____. "Aristotle's Political Sociology: Class, Status, and Order in the *Politics.*" In *Essays on the Foundations of Aristotelian Political Science,* ed. C. Lord and D. O'Connor, 87-103. Berkeley: University of California Press, 1991.

Oliver, J. H. "The Ruling Power." *TAPA* 43 (1953): 87-103.

_____. *Marcus Aurelius, Aspects of Civic and Cultural Policy in the East.* Hesperia Suppl. 13. Princeton: Princeton University Press, 1970.

Orr, W. F. and J. A. Walther. *I Corinthians.* AB 32. Garden City, NJ: Doubleday, 1976.

Pagels, E. "The Demiurge and his Archons." *HTR* 69 (1976): 302-12.

Patte, D. *Paul's Faith and the Power of the Gospel.* Philadelphia: Fortress Press, 1983.

Pekáry, T. "Tiberius und der Tempel der Concordia in Rom," *Mitteilungen der deutschen archäologischen Instituts, Römische Abteilung* 74 (1966–1967): 105-20.

Penella, R. *The Letters of Apollonius of Tyana. A Critical Text with Prolegomena, Translation and Commentary.* Leiden: Brill, 1979.

Pera, R. *Homonoia sulle monete da Augusto agli Antonini.* Geneva, 1984.

Peterson E. "1 Korinther 1,18f. und die Thematik des jüdischen Busstages." *Bib* 32 (1951): 47-103.

_____. ΕΙΣ ΘΕΟΣ. *Epigraphische, formgeschichtliche und religionsgeschichtliche Untersuchungen.* Göttingen: Vandenhoeck & Ruprecht, 1926.

Pflaum, H.-G. "Das römische Kaiserreich." *PWG* 4 (1963): 317-36.

Piccirilli, L. *Gli Arbitrati Interstali Greci.* Pisa, 1973.

Plessis, P. J. du. *TELEIOS: The Idea of Perfection in the New Testament.* Kampen: Kok, 1959.

Plümacher, E. *Identitätsverlust und Identitätsgewinn: Studien zum Verhältnis von kaiserzeitlicher Stadt und frühern Christentum.* BTS 11. Neukirchen-Vluyn: Neukirchener, 1987.

———. *Lukas als hellenistischer Schriftsteller: Studien zur Apostelgeschichte.* Göttingen: Vandenhoeck & Ruprecht, 1972.

Plummer, A. *A Critical and Exegetical Commentary on the Second Epistle of St. Paul to the Corinthians.* ICC. Edinburgh: T.&T. Clark, 1915.

Pogoloff, S. *Logos and Sophia: The Rhetorical Situation of 1 Corinthians.* SBLDS 134. Atlanta: Scholars Press, 1992.

Pöhlmann R. von. *Geschichte der sozialen Frage und der Sozialismus in der antiken Welt.* 2 vols. Munich, 1925.

Pöschl, V. *Römischer Staat und griechisches Staatsdenken bei Cicero.* Berlin, 1926.

Preisker, H. "Zur Komposition des zweiten Korintherbriefes." *Theologische Blätter* 5 (1926): 154-57.

Price, S. *Rituals and Power.* Cambridge: Cambridge University Press, 1984.

Procksch, O. "Das Eidesverbot Jesu Christi." *Thüringer Kirchliches Jahrbuch* 12 (1907): 14-25.

Prümm, K. *Diakonia Pneumatos.* Vienna: Herder, 1967.

Quasten, J. *Patrology.* 2 vols. (Utrecht, 1950).

Quell, G. ἀλήθεια. *TDNT* 1:232-37.

Race, W. H. "*Panathenaicus* 74-90: The Rhetoric of Isocrates' Digression on Agamemnon." *TAPA* 108 (1978): 175-85.

———. "Some Digressions and Returns in Greek Authors." *CJ* 76 (1980): 1-8.

Rajak, T. *Josephus the Historian and his Society.* Philadelphia: Fortress Press, 1984.

Rathke, H. *Ignatius von Antiochien und die Paulusbriefen.* TU 99. Berlin: Akademie-Verlag, 1967.

Reiche, J. G. *Commentarius criticus in Novum Testamentum.* Göttingen: Vandenhoeck & Ruprecht, 1853.

Reitzenstein, R. *Hellenistic Mystery-Religions.* Pittsburgh: Pickwick, 1978.

Rendall, G. *The Epistles of St. Paul to the Corinthians.* London: Macmillan, 1909.

Resch, A. "Miscellen zur neutestamentlichen Schriftforschung." *ZWL* 9 (1888): 283-90.

Rhodes, P. J. *A Commentary on the Aristotelian 'Athenaion Politeia'.* Oxford: Oxford University Press, 1981.

Richard, J.-C. "Pax, Concordia et la religion officielle de Janus à la fin de la République romaine." *MEFR* 75 (1963): 303-86.

Rissi, M. *Studien zum zweiten Korintherbrief.* ATANT 56. Zürich: Zwingli, 1969.

Robbins, V. "By Land and by Sea: The We-Passages and Ancient Sea Voyages." In *Perspectives on Luke-Acts*, ed. C. Talbert, 215-42. Danville VA: Association of Baptist Professors of Religion; Edinburgh: T.&T. Clark, 1978.

Robert, L. *Les Gladiateurs dans l'Orient grec.* Bibliethèque de l'Ecole des hautes études 278. Paris: Gabalda, 1940.

Roberts, C., T. C. Skeat, and A. D. Nock. "The Guild of Zeus Hypsistos." *HTR* 29 (1936): 38-88.

Robertson, A. and A. Plummer. *A Critical and Exegetical Commentary on the First Epistle of St. Paul to the Corinthians.* ICC. New York: Scribner's, 1925.

Rohde, J. "Häresie und Schisma im ersten Clemensbrief und in den Ignatius-Briefen." *NovT* 10 (1968): 217-33.

Romilly, J. de. "Vocabulaire et propaganda, ou les premier emplois du mot ὁμόνοια." In *Melanges de Linguistique et de Philologie Greques offerts a Pierre Chantraine,* 199-209. Études et commentaires 79. Paris: Klincksieck, 1972.

Russell, D. A., and M. Winterbottom, *Ancient Literary Criticism.* New York: Oxford University Press, 1972.

Sacks, K. S. "Historiography in the Rhetorical Works of Dionysius of Halicarnassus." *Athenaeum* 60 (1983): 65-87.

Sagnard, F. *Irénée de Lyon: Contre les hérésies Livre III.* Paris: Editions du Cerf, 1952.

Sanders, L. *L'Hellénisme de Saint Clément de Rome et le Paulinisme.* Studia Hellenistica 2. Louvain: Universitas Catholica Louvainiensis, 1943.

Sänger, D. "Die δυνατοί in 1 Kor 1,26." *ZNW* 76 (1985): 285-91.

Sartori, F. *Le eterie nella vita politica ateniese del VI e V secolo a.c.* Rome: Bretschneider, 1957.

Schauf, W. *Sarx.* Münster: Aschendorff, 1924.

Scheller, P. *De Hellenistica Historia Conscribendae Arte.* Leipzig: Noske, 1911.

Schenk, W. "Der 1. Korintherbrief als Briefsammlung." *ZNW* 60 (1969): 219-43.

Schenke, H.-M., and K. M. Fischer. *Einleitung in die Schriften des Neuen Testaments I. Die Briefe des Paulus und die Schriften des Paulinismus.* Gütersloh: Mohn, 1978.

Schlatter, A. *Die korinthische Theologie.* BFCT 18/2. Gütersloh: Bertelsmann, 1914.

_____. *Der zweite Brief an die Korinther.* Stuttgart: Calwer, 1909.

_____. *Paulus, der Bote Jesu, Eine Auslegung seiner Briefe an die Korinther.* Stuttgart: Calwer, ²1956.

Schlechter, S. "Rabbinic Parallels to the New Testament." *JQR* 12 (1900): 415-33.

Schlier, H. ἀμήν. *TDNT* 1:337.

Schmiedel, P. *Die Briefe an die Thessalonicher und an die Korinther.* HCNT 2.1. Tübingen: Mohr-Siebeck, ²1892.

Schmithals, W. "Die Korintherbriefe als Briefsammlung." *ZNW* 64 (1973): 263-88.

_____. *Die Gnosis in Korinth.* FRLANT 66. Göttingen: Vandenhoeck & Ruprecht, ³1969.

_____. Gnosticism in Corinth. Trans. J. E. Steely. Nashville: Abingdon, 1971.

Schneider, J. μερός. *TDNT* 4:594-98.

_____. ὀμνύω. *TDNT* 5:176-80.

_____. ὅρκος. *TDNT* 5:458-60.

_____. συζητέω. *TDNT* 7:747-48.

Schniewind, J. "Die Archonten dieses Äons, 1 Kor. 2,6-8." In *Nachgelassene Reden und Aufsätze*, ed. E. Kähler, 104-109. Berlin: Töpelmann, 1952.

_____. *Das Evangelium nach Matthäus.* Göttingen: Vandenhoeck & Ruprecht, 1968.

Schreiber, A. *Die Gemeinde in Korinth. Versuch einer gruppendynamischen Betrachtung der Entwicklung der Gemeinde von Korinth auf der Basis des ersten Korintherbriefes.* NTAbh n.s. 12. Münster: Aschendorff, 1977.

Schütz, J. H. *Paul and the Anatomy of Apostolic Authority.* SNTSMS 26. Cambridge: Cambridge University Press, 1975.

Schweizer, E. "Die hellenistische Komponente im neutestamentlichen σάρξ-Begriff." *ZNW* 48 (1957): 237-53.

_____. πνεῦμα. *TDNT* 6:396-455.

_____. σάρξ. *TDNT* 7:124-51.

Scott, J. C. "Patronage or Exploitation?" In *Patrons and Clients in Mediterranean Societies*, ed. E. Gellner and J. Waterbury. London: Duckworth, 1977.

Scott, K. *The Imperial Cult under the Flavians.* New York: Arno, 1975.

Seibert, J. *Metropolis und Apoikie.* Würzburg, 1963.

Sellin, G. "Das 'Geheimnis' der Weisheit und das Rätsel der 'Christuspartei' (zu 1 Kor 1-4)." *ZNW* 73 (1982): 69-96.

Senft, C. *La première Epître de Saint Paul aux Corinthiens.* CNT n.s. 7. Neuchatel/Paris: Delachaux & Niestle, 1979.

Shapiro, H. "Homonoia." In *Lexicon Iconographicum Mythologiae et Classicae* 5/1, 476-79. Zürich/München: Artemis, 1990.

Sheppard, A. R. R. "HOMONOIA in the Greek Cities of the Roman Empire." *Ancient Society* 15-17 (1984–1986): 229-52.

Sherk, R. K. *Roman Documents from the Greek East. Senatus Consulta and Epistulae to the Age of Augustus.* Baltimore: Johns Hopkins University Press, 1969.

Sherwin-White, A. N. *Roman Society and Roman Law in the New Testament.* Oxford: Oxford University Press, 1969.

Sicking, C. M. J. "Organische Komposition und Verwandtes." *Mnemosyne* 16 (1963): 225-42.

Simon, M. "From Greek Hairesis to Christian Heresy." In *Early Christian Literature and the Classical Intellectual Tradition: In honorem R. M. Grant,* ed. W. R. Schoedel and R. L. Wilken, 101-16. Theologie Historique 54. Paris: Editions Beauchesne, 1979.

Skard, E. *Zwei religiös-politische Begriffe: euergetes/concordia*. Avhandlinger utgitt av Det Norske Videnskaps-Akademi i Oslo, II. Hist.-Filo. Klasse 1931 no. 2. Oslo: Dybwad, 1932.

_____. "Sallust als Politiker," *Symbolae Osloenses* 9 (1930): 69-91.

Skydsgaard, J. *Non-slave Labor in Graeco-Roman Antiquity*. Cambridge: Cambridge University Press, 1980.

Slings, S. R. *A Commentary on the Platonic Clitophon*. Amsterdam: Academische Pers, 1981.

Stählin, G. "Zum Gebrauch von Beteuerungsformeln im Neuen Testament." *NovT* 5 (1962): 115-43.

Ste. Croix, G. E. M. de. *The Origins of the Peloponnesian War*. Ithaca: Cornell University Press, 1972.

_____. *The Class Struggle In the Ancient Greek World*. Ithaca: Cornell University Press, 1981.

_____. "Suffragium: from vote to patronage." *British Journal of Sociology* 5 (1954): 33-48.

Steinwenter, A. *Streitbeendigung durch Urteil, Schiedspruch und Vergleich nach griechischen Recht*. Berlin, 1925.

Stowers, S. *Letter Writing in Greco-Roman Antiquity*. LEC 5. Philadelphia: Westminster, 1986.

Strachan, R. H. *The Second Epistle of Paul to the Corinthians*. MNTC. London: Hodder & Stoughton, 1935.

Strack, H. L., and P. Billerbeck. *Kommentar zum Neuen Testament aus Talmud und Midrasch*. München: Beck, 1922.

Strasburger, H. "Concordia ordinum. Eine Untersuchung zur Politik Ciceros." Diss., Leipzig, 1931.

_____. "Der 'Scipionenkreis'." *Hermes* 94 (1966): 60-72.

Strauss, B. S. *Athens after the Peloponnesian War: Class, Faction, and Policy, 403-386 B.C.* Ithaca: Cornell University Press, 1986.

Strecker, G. *Die Bergpredigt: Ein exegetischer Kommentar*. Göttingen: Vandenhoeck & Ruprecht, 1985.

Strobel, A. *Der erste Brief an die Korinther*. Züricher Bibelkommentare NT 6, pt. 1. Zürich: Theologischer Verlag, 1989.

_____. "Der Begriff des Hauses im griechischen und römischen Privatrecht." *ZNW* 56 (1965): 91-100.

Strugnell, J. "A Plea for Conjectural Emendation in the New Testament, with a Coda on 1 Cor. 4:6." *CBQ* 36 (1974): 543-58.

Sykutris, J. "Epistolographie." *PWSup* 5 (1931): 185-220.

_____. *Die Briefe des Socrates und die Sokratiker.* GKA 18. Paderborn: Schöningh, 1933.

_____. "Proclus Περὶ Ἐπιστολιμαίου. *Byzantinisch Neugriechische Jahrbücher* 7 (1928–1929): 108-18.

Syme, R. "Seianus on the Aventine," *Hermes* 84 (1956): 527-40.

_____. *The Roman Revolution.* Oxford: Clarendon Press, 1939.

_____. *Roman Papers.* Oxford: Clarendon Press, 1979.

_____. "Seianus on the Aventine." *Hermes* 84 (1956): 527-40.

Tarn, W. W. *Alexander the Great.* 2 vols. Cambridge: Cambridge University Press, 1948.

_____. *Alexander the Great and the Unity of Mankind.* Proc. Brit. Acad. 19. London: Amen, 1933.

Tasker, R. V. G. *The Second Epistle of Paul to the Corinthians.* London: Tyndale, 1958.

Taylor, L. R. "Nobles, Clients and Personal Armies." In *Friends, Followers, and Factions. A Reader in Political Clientelism*, ed. S. Schmidt, 179-91. Berkeley: University of California, 1977.

_____. *Party Politics in the Age of Caesar.* Berkeley/Los Angeles: University of California Press, 1949.

Theissen, G. *The Social Setting of Pauline Christianity. Essays on Corinth.* Ed. and trans. J. H. Schutz. Philadelphia: Fortress Press, 1982.

Thraede, K. *Grundzüge griechisch-römischer Brieftopik.* Zetemata 48. Munich: Beck, 1970.

Thrall, M. E. *The Second Epistle to the Corinthians.* Vol. 1. ICC. Edinburgh: T.&T. Clark, 1994.

_____. "A Second Thanksgiving Period in II Corinthians." *JSNT* 16 (1982): 102-17.

Tierney, H. M. "Corinthian Power Politics." Diss., University of Chicago, 1968.

Tod, M. N. *International Arbitration amongst the Greeks.* Oxford: Clarendon Press, 1913.

Touloumakos, J. "Der Einfluss Roms auf die Staatform der griechischen Stadtstaaten des Festlandes und der Inseln lm ersten und zweiten Jhdt. v. Chr." Diss., Göttingen, 1967.

Unnik, W. C. van. "'Tiefer Friede' (1. Klemens 2,2)." *VC* 24 (1970): 261-79.

_____. "Reisepläne und Amen-Sagen, Zusammenhang und Gedankenfolge in 2. Korinther 1:15-24." In *Studia Paulina in honorem Johannis de Zwaan.* Haarlem: Bohn, 1953.

_____. *Studies over de zogenaamde eerste brief van Clemens I. Het Litteraire Genre.* Medelingen der koninklijke Nederlandse akademie van wetenschappen, afd. letterkunde 33. Amsterdam: N.V. Noord-Hollandsche Uitgevers Maatschappij, 1970.

_____. "De la regle Μήτε ποσθεῖναι μήτε ἀφελεῖν dans l'histoire du canon." *VC* 3 (1949): 1-36. Repr.: *Sparsa collecta II*. NovTSup 30. Leiden: Brill, 1980.

Veyne, P. *Le pain et le cirque: Sociologie historique d'un pluralisme politique.* Paris: Seuil, 1976.

Vielhauer, P. *Geschichte der urchristlichen Literatur.* Berlin/New York: de Gruyter, 1975.

_____. *Oikodome. Das Bild vom Bau in der christlichen Literatur vom Neuen Testament bis Clemens Alexandrinus.* Karlsruhe-Durlach: Tron, 1940. Repr.: in *Aufsätze zum Neuen Testament*, ed. G. Klein, 2:1-168. TB 65. Munich: Kaiser, 1979.

_____. "Paulus und die Kephaspartei in Korinth." *NTS* 21 (1975): 341-52.

Volkmar, G. *Die Religion Jesu.* Leipzig: Hinrichs, 1857.

Vollenweider, S. *Freiheit als neue Schöpfung. Eine Untersuchung zur Eleutheria bei Paulus und in seiner Umwelt.* FRLANT 147. Göttingen: Vandenhoeck & Ruprecht, 1989.

Walbank, F. W. *A Historical Commentary on Polybius.* 3 vols. Oxford: Clarendon Press, 1957–1979.

_____. *Polybius.* Berkeley/Los Angeles: University of California Press, 1972.

Wallis, P. "Ein neuer Auslegungsversuch der Stelle 1. Kor. 4:6." *TLZ* 75 (1950): 506-508.

Wardman, A. *Plutarch's Lives.* Berkeley/Los Angeles: University of California Press, 1974.

Watson, F. "2 Cor. x-xiii and Paul's Painful Letter to the Corinthians." *JTS* 35/2 (1984): 324-46.

Wehnert, J. *Die Wir-Passagen der Apostelgeschichte.* Göttingen: Vandenhoeck & Ruprecht, 1989.

Weische, A. *Studien zur politischen Sprache der römischen Republik.* Münster: Aschendorff, 1966.

Weiss, B. *Der Jakobusbrief und die neuere Kritik.* Leipzig: Deichert, 1904.

Weiss, J. "Beiträge zur paulinischen Rhetorik." In *Theologische Studien: B. Weiss zu seinem 70. Geburtstag dargebracht*, 165-247. Göttingen: Vandenhoeck & Ruprecht, 1897.

_____. *Der erste Korintherbrief.* KEK 7. Göttingen: Vandenhoeck & Ruprecht, 1910.

_____. *The History of Primitive Christianity.* 2 vols. Ed. and trans. F. C. Grant, et al. New York: Scribners, 1937.

_____. Review of Halmel. *ThLZ* 19 (1894): 513-14.

_____. *Das Urchristentum.* Ed. R. Knopf. Göttingen: Vandenhoeck & Ruprecht, 1917.

Wendland, H. D. *Die Briefe an die Korinther.* NTD 7. Göttingen: Vandenhoeck & Ruprecht, 1968.

Wengst, K. *Pax Romana and the Peace of Jesus Christ.* Trans. J. Bowden. London: SCM, 1987.

Wenham, D. "2 Corinthians 1:17,18: Echo of a Dominical Logion." *NovT* 28/3 (1986): 271-79.

Werres, J. "Die Beteuerungsformeln in der attischen Komödie." Diss. Bonn, 1936.

Westlake, H. D. *Essays on the Greek Historians and Greek History.* Manchester: Manchester University Press, 1969.

Wettstein, J. J. *Novum Testamentum Graecum.* 2 vols. Amsterdam: Ex officina Dommeriana, 1752.

Wheeler, M. "Aristotle's Analysis of the Nature of Political Struggle." *AJP* 72 (1951): 145-61.

Whibley, L. *Political Parties in Athens.* Cambridge: Cambridge University Press, 1889.

Widman, M. "1 Kor. 2,6-16: Ein Einspruch gegen Paulus." *ZNW* 70 (1979): 44-53.

Wilckens, U. *Weisheit und Torheit.* BHT 26. Tübingen: Mohr-Siebeck, 1959.

Williams, S. K. *Jesus' Death as Saving Event. The Background and Origin of a Concept.* HDR. Missoula, MT: Scholars Press, 1975.

Windisch, H. *Der zweite Korintherbrief.* KEK 6. Göttingen: Vandenhoeck & Ruprecht, 1924; repr. 1970.

_____. *Die katholischen Briefe.* HNT 15. Ed. H. Preisker. Tübingen: Mohr/Siebeck, ³1951.

Winer, G. *A Treatise on the Grammar of New Testament Greek.* Edinburgh: T.&T. Clark, 1882.

Winter, M. *Pneumatiker und Psychiker in Korinth: Zum religionsgeschichtlichen Hintergrund von 1. Kor. 2,6-3,4.* Marburger theologische Studien 12. Marburg: Elwert, 1975.

Wire, A. *The Corinthian Women Prophets: A Reconstruction through Paul's Rhetoric.* Minneapolis: Fortress/ Augsburg, 1990.

Wiseman, J. "Corinth and Rome I: 228 B.C.-A.D 267." *ANRW* 7/1. Ed. H. Temporini. Berlin: de Gruyter, 1979.

Wolfson, H. A. *Philo.* Cambridge MA: Harvard University Press, 1947.

Wood, N. *Cicero's Social and Political Thought.* Berkeley/Los Angeles: University of California Press, 1988.

Wrege, W. *Die Überlieferungsgeschichte der Bergpredigt.* WUNT 9. Tübingen: Mohr/Siebeck, 1968.

Wuellner, W. "Haggadic Homily Genre in 1 Corinthians 1-3." *JBL* 89 (1970): 199-204.

Wünsch, A. *Neue Beiträge zur Erläuterung der Evangelien aus Talmud und Midrasch.* Göttingen: Vandenhoeck & Ruprecht, 1878.

Yavetz, Z. *Plebs and Princeps.* Oxford: Clarendon, 1969.

_____. "Plebs sordida." *Athenaeum* 43 (1965): 295-311.

Young, F. "Note on 2 Corinthians 1:17b." *JTS* 37 (1986): 404-15.

Zahn, T. *Forschungen zur Geschichte des neutestamentlichen Kanons und der altkirchlichen Literatur. VI. 2. Bruder und Vettern Jesu.* Leipzig: Hinrichs, 1900.

_____. *Introduction to the New Testament.* New York: Scribner's Sons, 1917.

Zeilinger, F. *Krieg und Friede in Korinth. Kommentar zum 2. Korintherbrief des Paulus.* Vienna: Bohlau, 1992.

Ziegler, K. H. *Das Private Schiedsgericht im antiken römischen Recht.* MBPAR 58. Munich: Beck, 1971.

Zillig, P. "Die Theorie von der gemischten Verfassung." Diss., Wurzburg, 1916.

Zwicker, H. "Homonoia." *PW* 8, pt. 2 (1913) 2265-69.

INDEXES

Modern Authors

Politics and Rhetoric in the Corinthian Epistles.
  by L. L. Welborn.

Mercer University Press, 6316 Peake Road, Macon, Georgia 31210-3960.
Isbn 0-86554-463-8. Catalog and warehouse pick number: MUP/H437.
Interior (text) design and composition by Edmon L. Rowell, Jr.
Camera-ready pages composed by Mercer University Press
  on a Gateway 2000, via WordPerfect dos 5.1, WP/Win 5.1/5.2,
    and Corel WordPerfect 8, and printed on a LaserMaster 1000.
Text font: TimesNewRomanPS, plus ATECH Hebrew and Greek.
Titles font: TimesNewRomanPS (csc).
Jacket and cover designed by Burt&Burt Studios.
Printed and bound by McNaughton & Gunn Inc., Saline MI 48176.
Printed via offset lithography on 55# Writers Natural, 360ppi.
Smyth sewn in 32s with 80# natural endsheets, with headbands
  and footbands, and cased into A grade cloth over .080 binders board,
    with one-hit foil on spine and c. 4.
Dust jacket on 80# enamel printed four-color process
  and with matte film lamination.
                                                    [October 1997]

                                                    093097elr